Mr. Justice Brennan and Freedom of Expression

Mr. Justice Brennan and Freedom of Expression

W. WAT HOPKINS

New York
Westport, Connecticut
London

Library of Congress Cataloging-in-Publication Data

Hopkins, W. Wat.
 Mr. Justice Brennan and freedom of expression / W. Wat Hopkins.
  p. cm.
 Includes bibliographical references and index.
 ISBN 0-275-93363-6 (alk. paper)
 1. Judicial opinions—United States. 2. Brennan, William J.
(William Joseph), 1906– . 3. Freedom of speech—United States.
4. Freedom of the press—United States. I. Title.
KF213.B73H66 1991
342.73′0853—dc20
[347.302853]   91-8753

British Library Cataloguing in Publication Data is available.

Library of Congress Catalog Card Number: 91-8753
ISBN: 0-275-93363-6

First published in 1991

Praeger Publishers, One Madison Avenue, New York, NY 10010
An imprint of Greenwood Publishing Group, Inc.

Printed in the United States of America

The paper used in this book complies with the
Permanent Paper Standard issued by the National
Information Standards Organization (Z39.48-1984).

10 9 8 7 6 5 4 3 2 1

For another of my heroes,
Bill Hopkins,
my father

Contents

Preface

Early one sunny Saturday morning in July I stumbled out the front door, still in my robe and clinging to a mug of coffee. I had been up late Friday night working on this book. Groggy, but satisfied that the work was going reasonably well, I pulled my newspaper from the box and opened it to the disheartening banner headline: "Brennan Quits Supreme Court."

My initial shock soon gave way to gloom. It was a minor inconvenience that I had only three months to retool a manuscript so that it referred to Justice Brennan in the past tense rather than in the present tense. What was more significant was that William J. Brennan, Jr., was not going to be at One First Street, NE, Washington, D.C. on the first Monday in October.

Long before I began this project, Justice Brennan had been a hero. From the time I first read *New York Times Co. v. Sullivan* several years after it was delivered until two years ago, when I decided to examine the body of Justice Brennan's free expression jurisprudence, the justice had been, for me, the prime protector of the sacred rights of free speech and free press. So long had I looked through new First Amendment opinions to find what he had written that I could not conceive of a term of Court passing without seeing the slogan, "Mr. Justice Brennan delivered the opinion of the Court."

My opinion of Justice Brennan as the Court's premier protector of expression did not change as my work continued. Admittedly, the resignation made it more difficult for me to carry out my responsibility as a scholar and look at the justice's work with a critical eye. I found little of which to be critical, however. Brennan's theory of free expression, which is built on the marketplace of ideas metaphor, has some workability problems, but is philosophically sound. Its major failing may be that it needs a strong advocate for it to be applied as Justice Brennan would have it applied.

Thus my gloom when I opened my newspaper on July 21, 1990.

★   ★   ★

This project is based primarily on an examination of the opinions and voting record of Justice Brennan. I attempted, through a WESTLAW search, to locate every free expression case the Court delivered from 1957 through 1990. I eliminated a number of cases that dealt with some aspects of communications law but did not implicate constitutional protections. I am sure I eliminated some cases that some readers will say should have been included. I am just as sure that some scholars will complain that I miscategorized some cases and overlooked others. For those errors, I apologize. For the most part, however, I believe I have examined all the significant free expression cases during Justice Brennan's thirty-four-year term. My major finding was that Justice Brennan developed a philosophically sound First Amendment theory that has been accepted by the Court, but is not being applied with the force with which Justice Brennan applied it. It is a theory, however, that will have a long-lasting effect on First Amendment jurisprudence.

I owe thanks to a number of people for their help on this project. First and most obviously, I must thank Justice William Brennan, not only for the body of First Amendment law he helped develop, but also for granting me access to his papers in the Library of Congress. Not only were they essential for this project, they were fascinating reading.

The research staff of the Newman Library at Virginia Polytechnic Institute and State University, especially Dave Beagle and Jan Spahr, provided many favors and much assistance for which I am grateful. I also wish to thank the College of Arts and Sciences and the Department of Communication Studies at Virginia Tech for travel grants that allowed me to visit the Library of Congress to examine Justice Brennan's papers.

In addition, I must thank the students in my spring 1989 communication-law class for their probing questions and helpful legwork, and for keeping me on my toes. Special thanks go to John Autry, Robin Cheers, Diana Cioffi, Judy Earley, Michael Fritz, Charlie Fulp, Shani Galvin, Kevin McDowell, Kristin Ruestow, Richell Slepetz, Kimberly Taylor, Diego Vaccarezza, Kat Van Wey, Deidre Yoast, Biniam Yohannes, Mark O'Connor, Suzanne Pahl, and Helen Rock.

Finally, thanks to my sons, Lincoln, Jonathan, and Sam, for their constant inspiration, and to my wife, Roselynn, for her everlasting love and patient understanding.

Mr. Justice Brennan and Freedom of Expression

1

Mr. Justice Brennan . . .

In February of 1957, Supreme Court nominee William J. Brennan, Jr., was asked about his method of interpreting the U.S. Constitution. Does the Constitution have "a fixed and definite meaning . . . that . . . does not change at a later time?" asked Senator James O. Eastland of Mississippi, chairman of the Senate Judiciary Committee. Brennan said he could not answer the question because his opinion in each case depends upon the facts in that particular case and the precedent applying to those facts.[1]

"I am not asking as to any particular case," Eastland said. Brennan again equivocated. Only when a case is before him, he said, could he examine the applicable precedents and know how to apply the Constitution.[2] Eastland continued to press. Could a book written by some college professor become a precedent and change the Constitution?

Brennan: Well, of course it doesn't change the Constitution of the United States, Senator, but . . .

Eastland: It couldn't change the meaning of the Constitution?

Brennan: But what I am trying to make clear is that in the search in any case for the right decision, . . . it is part of the judicial process to consult a lot of things which may bear upon the particular case. . . . I think that is the judicial process.

Eastland: Do you think the Constitution of the United States could have one meaning this week and another meaning next week?

Brennan: I think that puts it in rather a narrow compass, Senator. The application of the Constitution is a problem of applying to living matter, cases that come before us. Where the differences often arise is, . . . like fingerprints, it is hard to say that any two cases are always alike. Rarely does that ever happen. All I can say for myself, Senator, is that as I have tried . . . ever since I have been a judge . . . with an approach of disinterestedness if I may phrase it that way, conscientiously to the best of my ability to apply the law whether the applicable law is constitutional, legislative, or common law or otherwise to the facts of the given case that is before us. I don't think it is possible for a judge otherwise to discharge his function.[3]

Nearly thirty years later, Brennan was again asked to justify his method of interpreting the U.S. Constitution. Attorney General Edwin Meese, advocating interpretation based on the original intent of the framers, criticized Brennan as being a constitutional activist.[4] Meese's banner was picked up by others in his office. In 1986 Assistant Attorney General William Bradford Reynolds, in a speech at the University of Missouri Law School, said that Brennan "has allowed his liberal orthodoxy to shape his jurisprudence." Reynolds described Brennan's "radical egalitarianism" as a "major threat to individual liberty."[5]

Brennan was not nearly so compromising with his modern-day critics as he was with Eastland and other members of the Senate Judiciary Committee in 1956. Speaking at Georgetown University October 12, 1985, Brennan said the doctrine of following the original intent of the framers was "little more than arrogance cloaked as humility."[6] He continued:

It is arrogant to pretend that from our vantage we can gauge accurately the intent of the Framers on application of principle to specific, contemporary questions. . . . Typically, all that can be gleaned is that the Framers themselves did not agree about the application or meaning of particular constitutional provisions, and hid their differences in cloaks of generality. Indeed it is far from clear whose intention is relevant—that of the drafters, the congressional disputants, or the ratifiers in the states?—or even whether the idea of an original intention is a coherent way of thinking about a jointly drafted document drawing its authority from a general assent of the states.[7]

Indeed, Brennan has sometimes seemed baffled at criticism that he is liberal in either his constitutional philosophy or in his writings. In time, he says, he might be thought of as a right-winger.[8]

For thirty-four years—from October 1956, when he joined the Court as an interim appointee, until July 20, 1990, when he retired at age eighty-four—William Brennan attacked with a serious passion the task of interpreting the Constitution. During that time he has established a remarkable legacy. He has served with one-fifth of all Supreme Court Justices. Only two justices served until they were of a more advanced age—Oliver Wendall Holmes served until he was ninety-one; Hugo L. Black served until he was eighty-five. Only one justice was on the court longer: William O. Douglas served for thirty-six years.[9]

It is not merely his years of service that established Brennan as one of America's leading jurists, however; it is what he has done on the Court. Judge Abner J. Mikva of the Court of Appeals for the District of Columbia noted that Brennan's "footprints are everywhere; his influence can be felt in nearly every area of the law."[10] Nina Totenberg, law correspondent for National Public Radio, echoed those sentiments: "You cannot name an area of the law in which there is not a landmark opinion written by William Brennan."[11] Norman Dorsen, president of the American Civil Liberties Union, has observed that Brennan's landmark opinions have greatly strengthened freedom of expression and the concept of equal protection under the law, writing that "we would be living under a very different Constitution if Justice Brennan were not on the Supreme Court."[12] Former congresswoman Barbara Jordan called Brennan "an institution within an institution. He was the lightning rod for individual rights and individual freedom and individual autonomy," she said.[13] And, New York University law professor Burt Neuborne has written that Brennan is the most influential justice since Chief Justice John Marshall. Brennan's success on the Court and his influence, Neuborne said, are largely due to his ability to develop a theory of the Constitution that will endure beyond his tenure and the tenure of most justices.[14]

Even Brennan's critics recognized his influence on the law. Former federal appellate judge Robert Bork, whose nomination to the Supreme Court by Ronald Reagan failed, charged that Brennan made up law, but also called Brennan "the most powerful justice of this century on the Supreme Court."[15]

Brennan joined the Court in 1956, filling a recess appointment caused by the ill health of Justice Sherman Minton. He joined a liberal coalition made up of Earl Warren, Hugo L. Black, and William O. Douglas, but the personality of the Court was yet to be determined. In 1956, one scholar wrote, the Court "had no clear direction or identity."[16] Another wrote that the Court was "groping for a means of reconciling judicial protection of First Amendment freedoms with the deep respect for majoritarian decision making that was the legacy of the Court's confrontation with President Franklin D. Roosevelt's New Deal."[17] Brennan, "through a blend of pragmatism and principle, with an ebullient, gregarious and easy personal manner, . . . helped change all that."[18]

He became a bridge-builder,[19] although he bristles at the characterization. "I am not a playmaker," he says. "I don't go around cajoling and importuning my colleagues to go along with my point of view."[20] Despite the denials, however, Brennan was clearly able to build coalitions between the Court's liberal and conservative factions. Stephen J. Friedman, who was one of Brennan's law clerks in 1963, wrote that during his early years on the Court "time and again, Mr. Justice Brennan wrote opinions relying upon relatively narrow, sometimes technical grounds, gathering a majority for the disposition of cases when, in the words of Dean Erwin Griswold, 'The Court seemed hopelessly split into minor fragments.' "[21] Totenberg said Brennan was able to build coalitions because he had "an instinct for what was important to other judges" and included those important points in his opinions.[22]

In the 1960s Brennan's leadership role became more pronounced. He became Chief Justice Earl Warren's "most capable lieutenant"[23]—a "judicial technician,"[24] to whom the chief justice assigned majority opinions in some of the Court's most important areas.[25] Former justice Arthur J. Goldberg wrote, for example, that Brennan was the principal architect of the Court's freedom-of-expression doctrines.[26] By the 1980s, the Court had gone from solidly liberal to solidly conservative. Brennan found himself writing in dissent more often than for the Court.[27]

Brennan eschews all labels that attribute to him any role other than simply that of a justice. He was not a play-maker, judicial technician, chief lieutenant, or chief dissenter. He did nothing other than his duty as a justice. He attempted to win other justices to his opinions, he says, because that is what justices do:

> When I have been able to draw a consensus, I have done it by the drafts I circulated among my colleagues. Rather than try to talk something out with another Justice, I sit down and write concrete suggestions as to what I don't like about what he has done or what I do like about it. . . . It's quite important to get these differences out by written exchanges.[28]

He continued to state his opinions, even when he was in dissent, because, he says, an opinion of the Court is neither infallible nor final, and a justice is duty-bound to continue stating the constitutional principles that have governed his decisions.[29] And, he says, a new Court may adopt what was once a dissenting view. Said Brennan: "One dissents and has to dissent and is expected to dissent when he disagrees with the constitutional interpretation of the majority because the day may well come when what he says in dissent, when greater wisdom prevails, may become the law of the land."[30]

As Brennan tells it, his career in law was planned by his father who, as a politician in Newark, New Jersey, had a number of prominent lawyers as friends. "He watched them and decided he was going to make a lawyer of me," the junior Brennan said. "Everything I am, I am because of my father."[31]

William J. Brennan, Jr., was born April 25, 1906, in Newark, to Irish immigrants. He was the second of eight children. His father, who had come to the United States in 1893, became active in the New Jersey labor movement when he believed his employer, Ballentine Brewery, was mistreating workers. The police department was helping break labor strikes, however, so the elder Brennan decided the only way to succeed was to infiltrate local government. He sponsored a movement to change Newark city government to make it more responsive, then ran for office, finishing third among eighty-six candidates and assuring his appointment as director of public safety. The strike-breaking stopped.

Brennan attended public high school in Newark, then entered the Wharton School of Finance at the University of Pennsylvania. He received his law degree from Harvard University. While in law school he married Marjorie Leonard. They would have three children. A year after her death in 1982, Brennan married Mary Fowler, his secretary for more than twenty-six years. He announced the marriage to his colleagues on the Court with a simple "Memorandum to the Conference" in March of 1982.[32]

Also in law school, Brennan had one of his first confrontations with his father over the law. At Harvard, Brennan had studied the case of *Public Welfare Pictures v. Brennan.* The Brennan in the case was William J. Brennan, Sr., the director of public safety for Newark. The senior Brennan had lost in his attempts to keep the theater from showing a film he believed to be obscene, and was outraged when Brennan junior commented that he believed the case had been properly settled. "Brennan has written a lot of opinions that would have appalled his father on the obscenity question," said Nina Totenberg.[33]

After law school Brennan took a position with the Newark firm of Pitney, Hardin & Skinner, working primarily on labor cases. He became a partner in the firm in 1937. Five years later he resigned to accept a commission in the Army, where he worked on industrial and labor cases involving unions and companies working on war contracts. He won the Legion of Merit for his contributions to military procurement programs. For part of his Army career he was legal aide to a personnel officer, James P. Mitchell, who later became President Eisenhower's secretary of labor.

Following the war Brennan returned to his law firm, which became Pitney, Hardin, Ward & Brennan. He was quickly overloaded with work from large companies wanting his expertise in solving labor-management problems. In 1949 he left the firm to accept an appointment by Governor Alfred Driscoll to the New Jersey Superior Court. The appointment meant a significant decrease in income and removed Brennan from the sphere of politics, a move that surprised many since it had seemed that the bright, young lawyer was a sure candidate for political office. In less than two years he was appointed to the Appellate Division of the Superior Court where he became involved in devising ways to relieve the congestion in the New Jersey courts. He was so successful and his proposals so impressed state chief justice Arthur Vanderbilt that Vanderbilt suggested that Driscoll appoint Brennan to the state's highest court, which Driscoll did in 1952.

Brennan continued to work to improve the justice system and, possibly because of his success, was asked by Vanderbilt to speak at a conference in Washington, D.C., in 1956. Vanderbilt was scheduled as the keynote speaker to the assembly of judges, scholars, and others interested in improving the administration of justice, but was taken ill. Brennan greatly impressed U.S. Attorney General Herbert Brownell, who was responsible for the conference, and four months later when Justice Sherman Minton announced he was retiring for health reasons, Brownell suggested to Eisenhower that Brennan might be a good replacement. Brennan was also recommended by Secretary of Labor Mitchell and by Vanderbilt.[34]

Presidential Press Secretary James C. Hagerty reported that the appointment was made after an examination of Brennan's record on the New Jersey court, but there are indications that Brennan's record was never a factor. The *Washington Post,* for example, reported that Brennan was known on the state court as a moderate liberal with a record of defending civil rights,[35] and Brennan reported that he was never asked about his record, although he was asked if he had voted for Eisenhower. When he told Hagerty that shortly before election day he had changed residences and was ineligible to vote, Hagerty asked whether Brennan would have voted for the president. "I really can't answer that—I don't know," Brennan reported telling the press secretary.[36]

What may have been more important to Eisenhower than Brennan's record was the judge's background. The Eisenhower campaign apparently believed that a Roman Catholic Democrat from the Northeast would help win some extra support for the president's reelection bid.

Brennan was "absolutely flabbergasted" by the appointment. He said he believed he was being called to the White House to be appointed to a judicial reform commission. Indeed, Brennan's first response to Brownell at 5 P.M. September 28, 1956, was that he did not have time to visit the president to discuss the appointment. Brownell insisted, however, and Brennan learned the next morning that he was being asked to join the Supreme Court.[37] Brennan's reaction was duly noted by the *New York Times:* "The New Jersey jurist looked surprised and immensely pleased about his appointment."[38]

Brennan's appointment was made and received with little fanfare. Eisenhower did not introduce Brennan to the press, but left that chore to Press Secretary Hagerty. The *Washington Post* praised the appointment,[39] but the *New York Times* mentioned it almost as an afterthought in an editorial on the opening of the Court's term. The main point of the editorial was that the opinions of the Supreme Court "are enforced by the common sense and patriotism of the citizens."[40] The *Times* predicted that Brennan would be confirmed without controversy because of his "comparative obscurity."[41]

The *Times* also ran a brief profile of Brennan, under the headline "The

Jaunty Judge." The lead of that story was a quote from an unidentified man who had served with Brennan in World War II. He said:

> Bill Brennan is a hell of a nice guy. A real personality kind of a guy. I hear he's made a great judge but it's hard to imagine him on the bench. There's nothing austere about him as you'd look for in a judge. He's the kind of guy you'd expect to find sitting at the next desk in a newspaper office or carrying a briefcase in a Madison Avenue advertising agency.[42]

The same man referred to Brennan as "Very convivial, easy-going. A great story-teller" and "Dapper and jaunty."[43]

Brennan, himself, much later, would also remark on the lack of fanfare he received that fall of 1956. He told Nina Totenberg this story for National Public Radio:

> Chief Justice Warren invited me to his chambers and then from his chambers we went up to the third floor of the Supreme Court Building, and in a small room the seven new colleagues were sitting around the table having sandwiches. The room was dark, and we put on the light, and there they were watching the opening game of the 1956 World Series. And I was introduced to each one of them, and someone said, "Put out the light." They put out the light, and they went on watching the game.[44]

Thus, William J. Brennan, Jr., fifty, joined the U.S. Supreme Court. For about four months he retreated into the "comparative obscurity" about which the *Times* had written. He joined the Court October 15, 1956, but the hearing on his nomination could not be held until the Eighty-Fifth Congress convened in January 1957. During the interim, little notice was taken of Brennan, the junior justice in both age and service.

There was little of which to take note.

During that time, Brennan wrote only four majority opinions.[45] Three of those came down the day before the Senate Judiciary Committee opened hearings on his appointment. All three grew from cases brought against railroad companies by injured employees under the Employer's Liability Act and were so obscure that they were not even mentioned during the nomination hearings of February 26 and 27, 1957.

Members of the Senate Judiciary Committee focused on two areas during the hearings. One, as previously indicated, was whether Brennan believed the Constitution to be fixed or flexible. The second was whether he would allow his religious beliefs to affect his decisions on the Court.

The issue of constitutional interpretation was defused when Arthur J. Watkins of Utah agreed with Brennan that the document is flexible rather than fixed. The exchange, in part, went this way:

Watkins: Actually, the meaning of the Constitution doesn't change but different men at different times have divergent ideas as to what it meant?

Brennan: That is true. But I think always you must remember that the different situations that arise in which the meaning has to be applied.

· · ·

Watkins: I have a strong feeling that the Constitution . . . does not change and should not change. But human beings are likely to err . . . and as we try to interpret that Constitution, we may get different points of view.

Brennan: That's right and it has happened.

Watkins: If I were on a court and my responsibility was to interpret a constitutional issue, I would have to try to interpret it in the best light I had and the best intelligence according to my conscience.

Brennan: That is what I attempted to say.

Watkins: The idea that simply because some judge, shortly after the Constitution was framed, rendered an opinion, that it has to be binding precedent for all time, I don't think that is correct.[46]

Brennan agreed again, and Watkins concluded, "I like the way you have met these questions and I believe you can render great service to the country."[47]

The Senate Judiciary Committee entered its second area of interest—that of Brennan's religious beliefs—almost apologetically. Senator Joseph C. O'Mahoney of Wyoming, although he said that "there is no doubt about what the answer of the Justice will be," found himself duty-bound, "in the interest of fairness," to read a question posed by the National Liberal League. The organization was concerned that Brennan, as a Roman Catholic required to "follow the pronouncements of the Pope," might not be able to decide "matters of faith and morals" on constitutional rather than religious grounds.[48] Brennan answered that

categorically . . . in everything I have ever done, in every office I have held in my life or that I shall ever do in the future, what shall control me is the oath that I took to support the Constitution and laws of the United States and so . . . upon cases that come before me for decision that it is that oath and that alone which governs.[49]

Brennan has often repeated this pronouncement. When constitutional issues conflict with a principle of his faith, Brennan notes, it is his responsibility to apply the Constitution rather than personal beliefs. And, he says, "I don't see any inconsistency whatever between that responsibility . . . and my going to church and receiving the sacraments as I do every week."[50] He has admitted, however, that he has at times had difficulty resolving issues of religion. He still lists the school-prayer cases, for example, as the most difficult to resolve during his term on the Court.[51]

Most of the questioning at the hearings, however, was not by members of the Senate Judiciary Committee but by a senator who sought and received permission to attend and question the nominee. Senator Joseph McCarthy monopolized the first day of the hearings. He appeared because of Brennan's apparent hostility toward McCarthy's efforts to expose the communist conspiracy.[52] "He knew about me," Brennan would later say.[53]

In a speech to the Charitable Irish Society in Boston on March 17, 1954, Brennan decried communism and said, "Americans of all races and creeds have closed ranks against the godless foe," but warned against methods that sacrificed the guarantees of justice, fair play, and human dignity. He said some practices were "reminiscent of the Salem witch hunts."[54] And, on February 25, 1955, Brennan, in a speech to the Monmouth Rotary Club in New Jersey, attacked the notion that persons invoking the constitutional protection against self-incrimination should be condemned. After a review of the historical underpinnings of the guarantee, he noted that efforts to undermine it bordered on "destroying liberty in liberty's name."[55]

McCarthy read the two speeches into the record as evidence of Brennan's "underlying hostility" to McCarthy's efforts to expose "the Communist conspiracy."[56] McCarthy began his questioning of Brennan, therefore, by asking whether the justice approved of congressional investigations and exposure of the Communist conspiracy:

> *Brennan:* Not only do I approve, Senator, but personally I cannot think of a more vital function of the Congress than the investigatory function of its committees, and I can't think of a more important or vital objective of any committee investigation than that of rooting out subversives in Government.
>
> *McCarthy:* You, of course, I assume, will agree with me—and a number of the members of the committee—that communism is not merely a political way of life, it is a conspiracy designed to overthrow the United States government.
>
> *Brennan:* Will you forgive me an embarrassment, Senator. You appreciate that I am a sitting Justice of the Court. There are presently pending before the Court some cases in which I believe will have to be decided the question what is communism, at least in the frame of reference in which those particular cases have come to the Court. I know, too, that you appreciate that having taken an oath of office it is my obligation not to discuss any of those pending matters. With that qualification, whether under the label communism or any other label, any conspiracy to overthrow the Government of the United States is a conspiracy that I not only would do anything appropriate to aid suppressing, but a conspiracy which, of course, like every American, I abhor.

. . .

McCarthy: Mr. Brennan, we are asked to either vote to confirm or reject you. One of the things I have maintained is that you have adopted the gobbledegook that communism is merely a political party, is not a conspiracy. The Supreme Court has held that it is a conspiracy to overthrow the Government of this country. I am merely asking you a very simple question. It doesn't relate to any lawsuit pending before the Supreme Court. Let me repeat it. Do you consider communism merely as a political party or do you consider it as a conspiracy to overthrow this country?

Brennan: I can only answer, Senator, that believe me there are cases now pending in which the contention is made, at least in the frame of reference in which the case comes to the Court, that the definitions which have been given by the Congress to communism do not fit the particular circumstances.

McCarthy: Will you repeat that?

Brennan: I say the contention is being made in those cases that the congressional definition does not fit the particular circumstances presented by the cases.

McCarthy: I don't want to interrupt you, but would you tell us where and when?

Brennan: Where and when?

McCarthy: Yes.

Brennan: I can't say anything to you, Senator, about a pending matter.

McCarthy: You just did. You said that the Congress, that the definition of the Congress does not fit—what is the word you used?

Brennan: I said the contention made in the particular case—and for that reason the issue which is presented to the Court for decision—is whether on the particular facts in the case now before the Court that definition does or does not fit.

McCarthy: I wonder if the reporter would read that to me?
          (Answer read)
          You know that the Congress has defined communism as a conspiracy. You are aware of that aren't you?

Brennan: I know the Congress has enacted a definition, yes, sir.

McCarthy: And I think it is important before we vote on your confirmation that we know whether you agree with that?

Brennan: You see, Senator, that is my difficulty, that I can't very well say more to you than that there are contending positions taken in given cases before us.[57]

Senator O'Mahoney came to Brennan's rescue. O'Mahoney pointed out that President Eisenhower had sent the Senate a resolution asking that the president be allowed to deploy troops at the request of any nation in the Middle East that was being attacked by international communism. Based on that clarification, O'Mahoney asked Brennan if he believed "international communism is a conspiracy against the United States as well as against all other free nations?" To that question, Brennan responded, "Yes, . . . definitely and affirmatively."[58]

McCarthy turned to the two speeches Brennan had made. Brennan said he was making reference to no specific committee or ongoing congressional investigation, but was concerned with what might happen if congressional investigators lost sight of fair play.[59] McCarthy asked specifically if Brennan had seen any indications of Salem witch hunts in the congressional investigations of communism.

> *Brennan:* That is just the point, Senator. I don't make any reference to congressional committees in that comment.
>
> *McCarthy:* Could you answer that, Mr. Justice?
>
> *Brennan:* I shall, Senator.
>
> *McCarthy:* Have you seen any indication?
>
> *(Senator Alexander) Wiley:* Let him answer.
>
> *McCarthy:* I will do the questioning unless I yield to you.
>
> *The Chairman:* Proceed.
>
> *McCarthy:* The question is do you find any evidence of Salem witch hunts?
>
> *Brennan:* I couldn't say that of any congressional committee. What I was thinking of was this: There was a general atmosphere that bothered me, and I think of lot of other Americans about this time. This was in 1954 and before that. . . . It was the general notion—not congressional committees—but there was a general feeling of hysteria that I felt was very unfortunate and many things were symptoms of it.[60]

McCarthy was not satisfied. He did not return for the second day of the hearings, as he promised, but wrote a letter to the committee instead. Further questioning of the justice would be futile, he wrote, because "the written record of this committee now confirms that Justice Brennan harbors an underlying hostility to congressional attempts to investigate and expose the Communist conspiracy."[61]

Neither McCarthy's concern about Brennan's hostility to his efforts nor Brennan's argument that the Constitution was not a fixed document had an effect on the confirmation. The Senate Judiciary Committee voted 11–0 to recommend confirmation (with four senators absent),[62] and the full Senate confirmed the appointment, with only McCarthy shouting "No" when the voice vote was taken.[63]

Following his confirmation, Brennan retreated into his comparative obscurity—but only for four months. From March through late June 1957, Brennan would write only six opinions, none catching the attention of any court-watchers. They were mostly deportation cases and labor or business disputes.[64] He wrote no concurrences or dissents.

On June 24, however, the Court handed down its only major free-expression case of the term. In *Roth v. U.S.*,[65] for the first time, the Court held that obscenity lay outside First Amendment protection. The majority opinion, written by Brennan, also provided a test of obscenity.[66]

Ironically, the justice who would become a leading protector of free expression, in his first major opinion for the Court, would uphold the conviction of a man for publishing some rather tame sexual material. In fact, one writer has noted that, had he wanted to, before he served out his sentence, Samuel Roth would have been able to receive, through the mails into his jail cell, the very material he was convicted of disseminating.[67] One justice called Brennan's opinion "a grand job,"[68] and over the next sixteen years the definition of obscenity was refined primarily through the writings of William Brennan. That changed in 1973 with *Miller v. California*.[69]

In his dissents to *Miller* and its companion case, *Paris Adult Theatre v. Slaton*,[70] Brennan wrote that obscenity could not be sufficiently defined to give notice to publishers that some sexually explicit material was proscribed; those publishers, therefore, could not be punished under the Constitution for what they produced.

"I put sixteen years into that damn obscenity thing," Brennan would later say. "I tried and I tried, and I waffled back and forth, and I finally gave up. If you can't define it, you can't prosecute against it."[71]

While Brennan's first opinion in free-expression jurisprudence was in the area of obscenity, his best known is probably in the area of libel. His opinion in *New York Times Co. v. Sullivan*[72] is the Court's most important statement on libel, and is one of the most important decisions ever delivered in any area of the law. Its centerpiece—actual malice—remains a sturdy protection for the expression of ideas in a free society.[73] That protection has subsequently been extended to some invasion-of-privacy[74] and intentional-infliction-of-emotional-distress[75] cases. In addition, the language of the opinion has been adapted to many other areas of the law. Dozens of times, justices have used

the general proposition that freedom of expression upon public questions is secured by the First Amendment has long been settled by our decisions.[76]

★ ★ ★

Thus we consider this case against the background of a profound national commitment to the principle that debate on public issues should be uninhibited, robust, and wide-open, and that it may well include vehement, caustic, and sometimes unpleasantly sharp attacks on government and public officials.[77]

★ ★ ★

Erroneous statement is inevitable in free debate, and . . . it must be protected if the freedoms of expression are to have the "breathing space" that they "need . . . to survive."[78]

★ ★ ★

If neither factual error nor defamatory content suffices to remove the constitutional shield from criticism of official conduct, the combination of the two elements is no less inadequate. This is the lesson to be drawn from the great controversy over the Sedition Act of 1798 . . . which first crystallized a national awareness of the central meaning of the First Amendment.[79]

But Brennan's contributions to the jurisprudence of free expression extend beyond the areas of obscenity and libel. For example:

- Brennan, in what became an oft-quoted passage, established that any system of prior restraint, "comes to this Court bearing a heavy presumption against its constitutional validity."[80] For that reason, an informal system of regulating objectionable material is as obnoxious as a formal system of prior restraint, film censorship boards must take on the burden of proving material is objectionable,[81] and school systems may not remove books from a school library on the basis of content.[82]
- Brennan wrote a series of opinions ruling loyalty oaths unconstitutional and upholding the rights of individuals to refuse to respond to invalid questions by investigating agencies.[83] When oaths proscribed certain types of speech, he wrote, methods for identifying those types of speech "must be subjected to close analysis and critical judgment."[84]
- After some squabbling among the justices over the years, Brennan wrote the opinion establishing that the burning of the U.S. flag is protected speech.[85] He also hammered away at the Court's more restrictive attitudes toward expressive conduct, arguing for more permissiveness in the areas of picketing, demonstrating, and verbal abuse.
- Brennan wrote the opinion striking down a federal statute prohibiting editorializing on public broadcast stations,[86] and the opinion establishing that businesses could advertise contraceptives.[87]

As a matter of fact, during the course of his thirty-four years on the Supreme Court, Brennan has amassed a record favoring free expression that is unmatched by any justice. During the period, nearly 300 free-expression cases were resolved by the Court. In those cases:

- Brennan wrote forty-two majority or plurality opinions—more than any justice. Only three other justices wrote as many as twenty: Warren Burger wrote twenty-six; Byron R. White wrote twenty-nine; William H. Rehnquist wrote twenty-four.
- Brennan wrote nine of the sixty-nine unanimous opinions on free-speech or free-press cases issued during the period. Only two other justices wrote as many: Rehnquist wrote ten, Burger wrote nine.

• In thirteen other cases, Brennan, by virtue of being the senior associate justice, appointed the writers of majority opinions. Only two chief justices, Warren and Burger, appointed more majority-opinion writers.

• Thirty-six of Brennan's majority opinions (eighty-six percent) were pro-speech or pro-press. Three opinions (seven percent) neither favored nor hindered speech causes, and three opinions (seven percent) might be considered anti-speech or anti-press opinions. Those figures include some of Brennan's early obscenity opinions. No justice had a better record of opinions supporting free expression.[88]

• In addition, Brennan voted a pro-free speech or press stance 227 times in the 273 cases in which he participated, or about 83 percent of the time. Justices Black, Douglas, and Warren had slightly better voting records in free-expression cases.[89]

• Brennan wrote seventy-five concurring or dissenting opinions in free speech or free press cases. Only Douglas came close to writing as many—he wrote seventy-four. No justice, however, drew as many associates to his opinions. In three-fourths of the concurring or dissenting opinions he wrote, Brennan was joined by at least one justice. Douglas was joined by other justices in 36 percent of his concurrences and dissents. Only four justices were joined in as many as half of their concurring and dissenting opinions during the period, and three of those justices wrote fewer than ten opinions each.[90]

The true test of a justice's contributions to free-expression jurisprudence, however, is whether the justice has developed a theory of free expression that is philosophically sound, workable, and lasting. A search for such a theory developed by Brennan can best take place by examining the major areas of free expression in which the justice was active.

NOTES

1. Nomination of William Joseph Brennan, Jr., to the United States Supreme Court, Hearings before the Senate Judiciary Committee, 85th Congress, 1st Session, February 26, & 27, 1957, at 36. Hereafter cited as Hearings.

2. *Id.* at 37.

3. *Id.* at 38.

4. *See, generally,* Taylor, The Court and The Constitution, The New Republic, Jan. 6 & 13, 1986, at 45.

5. Quoted in J. Leeds, A Life on the Court, New York Times Magazine, October 5, 1986, at 25.

6. Brennan, My Encounters with the Constitution, 26 The Judge's Journal, 6, 8 (Summer 1987).

7. *Id.*

8. Leeds, *supra* note 5, at 25.

9. Justice Douglas served from 1939 until 1975. Four justices in addition to

Brennan have served thirty-four years: John Marshall (1801–35), Stephen J. Field (1863–97), John M. Harlan (1877–1911), and Hugo L. Black, (1937–91).

10. Leeds, *supra* note 5, at 26.

11. MacNeil-Lehrer Newshour, PBS, July 23, 1990.

12. Quoted in N. Hentoff, The Constitutionalist, The New Yorker, March 12, 1990, at 45.

13. MacNeil-Lehrer, *supra* note 11.

14. Hentoff, *supra* note 12, at 45.

15. MacNeil-Lehrer, *supra* note 11.

16. Gora, Justice William J. Brennan, Jr.: A Justice for All Seasons, 72 A.B.A.J. 18 (June 15, 1986).

17. Anastaplo, Justice Brennan, Due Process and the Freedom of Speech: A Celebration of Speiser v. Randall. 20 J. Marshall L. Rev. 7 (Fall 1986).

18. Gora, *supra* note 16.

19. *See, generally,* Gora, *id.*

20. Hentoff, *supra* note 12, at 59.

21. S. J. Friedman, William J. Brennan, Jr.—An Affair With Freedom 11 (1967).

22. MacNeil-Lehrer, *supra* note 11.

23. B. Schwartz, Super Chief: Earl Warren and His Supreme Court—A Judicial Biography 204 (1983).

24. E. White, Earl Warren: A Public Life 185 (1982).

25. Schwartz, *supra* note 23, at 204.

26. Goldberg, Mr. Justice Brennan and the First Amendment, 4 Rut.-Cam. L.J. 8 (1972).

27. *See, e.g.,* Ray, Justice Brennan and the Jurisprudence of Dissent, 61 Temp. L.R. 307 (Summer 1988); D. O. Stewart, Justice Brennan at 80, 73 A.B.A.J. 61 (January 1987); Wermeil, Four Justices Seem Prepared to Assent to a Full-Time Role Focusing on Dissent, Wall Street Journal, Oct. 18, 1989, p 8.

28. Hentoff, *supra* note 12, at 59.

29. Leeds, *supra* note 5, at 77.

30. W. J. Brennan, Interview with Nina Totenberg, All Things Considered, National Public Radio, 1987.

31. Leeds, *supra* note 5, at 26. Additional biographical information on Justice Brennan may be found in Hentoff, *supra* note 12; Friedman, *supra* note 21; L. Friedman and F. L. Israel, The Justices of the United States Supreme Court, vol. 5 (1969).

32. "Conference" is a term used to identify the members of the Court as a body, particularly when they are not sitting on the bench.

33. Totenberg interview, *supra* note 30.

34. President Names Jersey Democrat to Supreme Court, New York Times, Sept. 30, 1956, at 1, 76.

35. M. Weiner, Brennan, Son of Irish Immigrants, Is Known as Moderate Liberal, Washington Post, Sept. 30, 1956.

36. Leeds, *supra* note 5, at 77.

37. Totenberg interview, *supra* note 30.

38. President Names, New York Times, *supra* note 34, at 1.

39. Brennan for the Court, Washington Post, Oct. 1, 1956, at 24.

40. The Supreme Court, New York Times, Oct 1, 1956, at 26.

41. *Id.*

42. The Jaunty Judge, New York Times, Sept. 30, 1956, at 76.

43. *Id.*

44. Totenberg interview, *supra* note 30.

45. The opinions were Putnam v. Commissioner of Internal Revenue, 352, U.S. 82 (1956); Rogers v. Missouri Pacific Railroad Co., 352 U.S. 500 (1957); Webb v. Illinois Central Railroad Co., 352 U.S. 512 (1957); and Herdman v. Pennsylvania Railroad Co., 352 U.S. 518 (1957).

46. Hearings, *supra* note 1, at 39.

47. *Id.*

48. *Id.* at 32.

49. *Id.* at 34.

50. Totenberg interview, *supra* note 30.

51. Leeds, *supra* note 5, at 79.

52. Hearings, *supra* note 1, at 35.

53. Hentoff, *supra* note 12, at 48.

54. The speeches are included in the transcript of the hearings on the nomination of Justice Brennan, *supra* note 1, at 12.

55. *Id.* at 16.

56. *Id.* at 5.

57. *Id.* at 17–19.

58. *Id.* at 20.

59. *Id.* at 22–23.

60. *Id.* at 23.

61. *Id.* at 74.

62. Senate Unit Votes 11 to 0 for Brennan, New York Times, March 20, 1957, at 23.

63. Huston, Senate Confirms 2 for High Court, New York Times, March 20, 1957, at 38.

64. The six cases were, Ceballow v. Shaughnessy, 352 U.S. 599 (1957); National Labor Relations Board v. Truck Drivers, 353 U.S. 87 (1957); Automobile Club v. Commissioner of Internal Revenue, 353 U.S. 180 (1957); Rabang v. Boyd, 353 U.S. 427 (1957); Jencks v. United States, 353 U.S. 657 (1957); and U.S. v. E. I. DuPont de Nemours & Co., 353 U.S. 586 (1957).

65. 354 U.S. 476 (1957).

66. *Id.* at 489.

67. G. Talese, His Neighbor's Wife 131 (1980).

68. William J. Brennan Jr., Papers, Manuscript Division, Library of Congress, Washington, D.C., Box 6, Roth v. U.S., memorandum of Justice Charles Evans Whittaker, June 6, 1957. Cited hereafter as Brennan Papers. The papers consist primarily of Brennan's case files from 1956 through 1986. The name of the case file in which the cited material is located is named only when the case is not otherwise identified.

69. 413 U.S. 15 (1973).

70. 413 U.S. 49, 103 (1973), Justice Brennan dissenting.

71. Hentoff, *supra* note 12, at 56.

72. 376 U.S. 254 (1964).

73. *See, generally,* W. W. Hopkins, Actual Malice: Twenty Years after Times v. Sullivan, (1989).

74. Time, Inc. v. Hill, 385 U.S. 374 (1967).

75. Hustler Magazine v. Falwell, 108 S.Ct. 867 (1988).

76. 376 U.S. at 269 (1964).

77. *Id.* at 270.

78. *Id.* at 271.

79. *Id.* at 273.

80. Bantam Books v. Sullivan, 372 U.S. 58, 70 (1963).

81. Freedman v. Maryland, 380 U.S. 51 (1965).

82. Board of Education, Island Trees v. Pico, 457 U.S. 853 (1982).

83. *See, for example,* Communist Party of Indiana v. Whitcomb, 414 U.S. 441 (1974); First Unitarian Church v. Los Angeles, 357 U.S. 545 (1958); Keyishian v. Board of Regents, 385 U.S. 589 (1967); and Speiser v. Randall, 357 U.S. 513 (1958).

84. *Speiser,* 357 U.S. at 520.

85. Johnson v. Texas, 109 S.Ct. 2933 (1989); U.S. v. Eichman, 110 S.Ct. 2404 (1990).

86. FCC v. League of Women Voters, 468 U.S. 364 (1984).

87. Carey v. Population Services International, 431 U.S. 678 (1977).

88. The majority opinions of Justices William O. Douglas, Abe Fortas, Arthur J. Goldberg, and Charles E. Whittaker supported freedom of expression 100 percent of the time, but the justices wrote, five, three, two, and one opinion, respectively. The opinions of Chief Justice Warren supported freedom of expression 86 percent of the time; he wrote six opinions.

89. The voting records were: Justice Black, 86 percent; Justice Douglas, 88 percent; Chief Justice Warren, 86 percent.

90. Justice Fortas was joined in five of eight opinions, 63 percent; Justice Goldberg was joined in two of four opinions, 50 percent; Justice O'Connor was joined in three of six opinions, 50 percent; Justice Rehnquist was joined in 18 of 36 opinions, 50 percent.

2

"Utterly Without Redeeming
Social Value"

There is probably no area of free-expression jurisprudence with which the Court has struggled so mightily as that of pornography.[1] From its 1957 decision in *Roth v. U.S.*,[2] when the Court ruled for the first time that obscene material was not protected by the Constitution, through 1990, when the Court ruled that a person could be convicted of mere possession of child pornography,[3] thousands of words on obscenity have been published by the justices. The Court has decided more than 50 cases, issuing some 165 opinions, including 55 dissenting opinions, 25 concurrences, and 41 other opinions. In one case—*Jacobellis v. Ohio*—members of the Court produced seven different opinions.[4] In two cases, the Court produced six opinions,[5] and, in eight cases, five opinions were written.[6] These numbers do not include the dozens of *per curiam* cases and the multiple opinions in those cases.[7]

The writings of the justices extend beyond these published opinions, however. Memoranda, notes, letters, and unpublished opinions of all sorts have been circulated on the issue. In the midst of the Court's thrashings, Justice Brennan wrote a memorandum of more than 140 pages addressing a variety of issues related to obscenity, concluding that the Court should help ensure that distinctions not be based on "the supposed superior value of certain media of communication" and that "no *bona fide* work of art or information may be suppressed in the name of obscenity, even if it is deeply repulsive to the dominant current thought of the community."[8]

Brennan, of course, was a central figure in much of the Court's work in the area of pornography. He wrote opinions that established, then refined, the test for obscenity—then he figuratively threw up his hands at the whole mess, writing that, since obscenity could not be defined, a per-

son could not be punished under the Constitution for creating or disseminating sexually explicit material. And, while it was 1973 before Brennan
reached that conclusion publicly, more than ten years earlier he had begun
to recognize the problems of developing a constitutionally sound test for
obscenity. As early as 1962 Brennan was backing off attempts to refine
the test of obscenity established in *Roth v. U.S.* because of the divisiveness
it caused. He wrote to Justice John Marshall Harlan:

> I lean to the idea that we ought let the widespread ferment continue a bit
> longer in legal periodicals and courts over the soundness and meaning of the
> *Roth* test before we re-examine it. I am particularly persuaded to that view,
> of course, by the fact that the Court is hopelessly divided in this area and
> there appears almost no prospect of an agreement of five of us upon any-
> thing.[9]

And, while it was Justice Potter Stewart who, in 1964, wrote in *Jacobellis* that he could not define "hard core" pornography, but he knew it
when he saw it,[10] Brennan first expressed that sentiment in his memorandum to Harlan. "I have trouble defining 'hard core,' " he wrote, "although no trouble at all recognizing it when I see it."[11]

Brennan and Stewart were not alone, of course, in venting their frustra-
tions over what Harlan called "the intractable obscenity problem."[12] After
tracing the methods used by various justices to define obscenity, Harlan
concluded:

> The upshot of all this divergence in viewpoint is that anyone who under-
> takes to examine the Court's decisions since *Roth* which have held particular
> material obscene or not obscene would find himself in utter bewilderment.
> . . . [T]he current approach has required us to spend an inordinate amount
> of time in the absurd business of perusing and viewing the miserable stuff
> that pours into the Court, mostly in state cases, all to no better end than
> second-guessing state judges.[13]

Two years earlier, Justice Tom C. Clark had expressed a similar sentiment. Dissenting with the Court's holding that *Memoirs of a Woman of
Pleasure* was not obscene, he wrote that he had "stomached" the examination of smut for ten years "without much outcry." He regretted dissenting in the case, he wrote, but was mandated to do so because "the
public should know of the continuous flow of pornographic material
reaching this Court and the increasing problem States have controlling
it."[14]

For the first fifteen years of the Court's struggles with obscenity, Brennan was the chief spokesman. His opinion in *Roth v. U.S.* established the
test of obscenity, and his later opinions refined that test. Beginning with
Roth, the Court delivered signed opinions in seventeen major obscenity

cases before it delivered *Miller v. California* and *Paris Adult Theatre I v. Slaton* in 1973. In those cases, Brennan wrote ten majority or plurality opinions, and he dissented only twice. During the sixteen years that began with *Miller,* however, Brennan only agreed with the majority in four of the twenty-seven major cases. He wrote one majority opinion, while writing twelve dissents, three opinions concurring in judgments, and three separate opinions.

It all began in 1957 with *Roth.*

PORNOGRAPHY IN THE 1960s: FROM ROTH TO MILLER

Roth was not the Court's first confrontation with obscenity; indeed, an obscenity case had been delivered four months earlier, in February. In *Butler v. Michigan,*[15] the Court overturned the conviction of a bookstore owner for selling a book that would tend to corrupt the morals of a youth. Such a test of obscenity, Justice Felix Frankfurter wrote for a unanimous Court, reduced the reading list of adults to one fit only for children.[16] And, the same day *Roth* was delivered, the Court, in a separate case, affirmed a misdemeanor obscenity conviction, even though the trial was before a judge rather than a jury, and held that an order banning the defendant from disseminating obscene material was constitutional.[17]

In *Roth,* however, the Court for the first time squarely addressed the issue of constitutional protection for sexually explicit material. Brennan was still in his first term when he was assigned the opinion. Possibly only half-joking, Brennan would later say that he was assigned the opinion—and later obscenity opinions—"Because nobody else wanted to have anything to do with them."[18] One scholar has suggested that Chief Justice Earl Warren assigned the opinion to Brennan, in part, because Brennan was Roman Catholic and much of the censorship effort in the mid-1950s was led by the Catholic National Organization for Decent Literature.[19] A more likely reason, however, might be that Brennan was capable of writing an opinion that would win a majority.

Samuel Roth had been convicted on four of twenty-six counts of mailing obscene materials.[20] The question for the Court, Brennan wrote, was whether obscenity was protected by the First Amendment. Although the Court had never addressed the question, Brennan found sufficient evidence in the *dicta* of numerous cases to indicate that obscene material is not protected. Indeed, his file on the case contains an eighteen-page list of case citations in which various courts spoke on obscenity.[21]

The historical evidence, Brennan concluded, indicated that all ideas with "even the slightest redeeming social importance," whether unorthodox, controversial, or hateful,

have the full protection of the guaranties *[sic]*, unless excludable because they
encroach upon the limited area of more important interests. But implicit in
the history of the First Amendment is the rejection of obscenity as utterly
without redeeming social importance.[22]

Obscene material, therefore, "is not within the area of constitutionally
protected speech or press."[23] But, Brennan noted, sex and obscenity are
not synonymous, and material is not automatically obscene simply because it relates to sex. Indeed, sex is a suitable topic of discussion since "it
is one of the vital problems of human interest and public concern."[24]
Therefore, he wrote, it is "vital that the standards for judging obscenity
safeguard the protection of freedom of speech and press for material which
does not treat sex in a manner appealing to prurient interests."[25]

At one time, Brennan noted, a work was determined to be obscene if
any portion of the work had a detrimental effect on a particularly susceptible person.[26] The so-called *Hicklin* test was rejected by a number of
American courts in place of a test of "whether to the average person,
applying contemporary community standards, the dominant theme of the
material taken as a whole appeals to the prurient interests."[27] That test,
Brennan wrote, does not offend the First Amendment.[28]

Brennan circulated the first draft of his opinion June 6, 1957, about a
month after *Roth* was argued. There was immediate reaction. "I am de-
lighted to concur in your excellent opinion," Justice Charles Evans Whittaker wrote Brennan on the same day. "I think you have done a grand
job."[29] Other joiners were not so quick. William O. Douglas circulated a
dissent, Harlan circulated an opinion, and Warren concurred in the result.
On June 20, therefore, there was some question as to whether Brennan's
"grand" opinion would have a Court, and Brennan penciled the word
"tie" on the third draft of his opinion.[30] Frankfurter finally joined, however, and the case was handed down June 24.

Roth was only the beginning of the Court's attempts to define and restrict obscenity without suppressing all sexually explicit material. Two
questions arose in obscenity cases that followed *Roth:* (1) How was "community" defined in the phrase "contemporary community standards"? and
(2) How was prurient interest determined? The questions were addressed
in *Manual Enterprises v. Day*[31] and *Jacobellis v. Ohio.*[32]

In *Manual Enterprises,* the Court held that magazines aimed at homosex-
ual men were "dismally unpleasant, uncouth, and tawdry" but not obscene.[33] Therefore, while a federal statute prohibiting the mailing of obscene materials was constitutional, the defendant in *Manual Enterprises* could
not be prohibited from mailing his magazines. Harlan, delivering the
judgment of the Court, found that the Court of Appeals for the District
of Columbia had mistakenly based its ruling only on the prurient-interest
test, failing to apply the patent offensiveness requirement of the federal

statute. The interpretation, Harlan wrote, contradicted "Roth's evident purpose to tighten obscenity standards."[34] Harlan also wrote that the relevant "community" was the United States, since a federal statute reaches all parts of the country.[35]

Brennan had problems with Harlan's opinion. In addition to his objection that the Court not yet attempt to refine the *Roth* test,[36] he believed Harlan's adoption of the term "patent offensiveness" from the federal statute might "only result in still further confusing an already confused subject."[37] He was also concerned that Harlan's opinion, if it gained a majority, would have the result of rejecting a "variable obscenity" standard. Under such a standard the audience to which sexually explicit material is aimed would be considered when determining whether the material is obscene. "I am not sure that I could accept this," Brennan wrote Harlan, "but I am not yet willing to put myself on record as rejecting it."[38] He therefore decided to write separately, concurring in the result.

Three years later Brennan not only accepted but espoused a variable obscenity standard. In *Mishkin v. New York*[39] a pornography distributor argued that because it depicted deviant sexual practices, the material he distributed was not obscene: The material could not satisfy Roth's prurient-appeal requirement since it did not appeal to the prurient interest of an average person.[40] Brennan rejected the argument. When material is aimed at "a clearly defined deviant sexual group, rather than the public at large," he wrote for the majority, the prurient-appeal test of *Roth* is satisfied if the dominant theme of the material appeals to the prurient interest in sex of the members of that group.[41] Brennan also applied a variable obscenity standard in *Ginzberg v. New York*.[42] Writing for the majority, he found that sexual material can be restricted for children even if the material is not obscene for adults.

By the time the Court faced *Jacobellis* in the term that followed *Manual,* Brennan was ready to reassess *Roth*.[43] Before the Court began its 1962 session, Brennan wrote a memorandum of more than 140 pages delineating the issues he believed to be pertinent in the obscenity cases and noting, "I believe that the Court should embrace this opportunity to attempt a clarification of the applicable constitutional principles; I believe the time is ripe for such an attempt."[44]

Brennan suggested that the Court address eight issues: (1) whether the constitution permits any law for the suppression of obscene material; (2) whether the *Roth* test should be modified; (3) whether there should be a national or local test of obscenity; (4) what the role of expert testimony should be; (5) whether a distributor's honest belief that his material is not obscene is a defense; (6) whether different standards should apply to books and films; (7) what in an obscenity case is law and what is fact; and (8) what the role of the Court is.

Brennan's memorandum is a detailed attempt to address the problem of suppressing obscene pornography without infringing the dissemination of art. And that was what Brennan saw as the primary issue. He wrote:

> It is not the business of the law to interfere with the dissemination of literature and art, or even to enforce the community's standards of taste and decorum against expression that seems deplorably tawdry and vulgar, but . . . it is the business of the law to suppress clandestine trafficking in pornographic filth, which has become a social problem of major dimensions.[45]

Brennan identified two sources of guidance for the Court's task of "fleshing out the constitutional concept of obscenity." Such a fleshing-out was necessary, he wrote, since the *ad hoc* adjudication of obscenity "is downright irrational."[46] One source was the Constitution itself, which, Brennan said, was instructive on the kinds of discriminations necessary to safeguard First Amendment rights while regulating obscene pornography. The second source was the body of law derived from state actions following *Roth*. Those actions provided material from which the Court could create feasible constitutional standards for obscenity proceedings.[47]

Drawing upon those two sources, Brennan then established the line of thought he would return to in his dissent to *Paris Adult Theatre I v. Slaton:* There must be some category of material that can be identified as legally obscene in order to protect First Amendment values. If obscenity is "not susceptible of clear, legal definition," he wrote, "I am prepared to say that governmental suppression of the obscene violates the First Amendment in all but the rare cases in which a private-injury, public-nuisance, or clear-and-present-danger rationale is applicable."[48] *Roth,* Brennan wrote, did not establish obscenity as a catch-all classification for outlawing expression. It focused on the violation of sexual mores or taboos, not "unduly violent, gruesome, or scatological expression."[49] Those types of speech required different theories.

Brennan rejected the argument that pornography causes sexual crimes. The consensus among those studying the issue, he argued, was that pornography does little harm. He found two arguments generally used to justify the suppression of obscenity convincing, however. First, he wrote, smut peddling is a reprehensible form of commercial endeavor, and the palpable evils of large-scale commercial exploitation of those involved must be considered. Second, the dissemination of pornography to juveniles inflicts emotional injury.[50] Therefore, Brennan wrote, "there is substantial legitimate social interest in a general criminal law forbidding the dissemination of pornography."[51]

Brennan added, however, that pragmatic problems exist with all such laws, particularly since obscenity touches on the domain of aesthetic values. The First Amendment was intended to secure aesthetics as well as political discussion and advocacy. One might argue that art "often deals directly with current social or political problems; it has a 'message.' "[52] That is not why art is protected, however, Brennan argued. The usefulness of art does not have to be proved—its creation and enjoyment are "a cherished part of the life of the mind" and, therefore, are sufficient rationales for its existence.[53] Wrote Brennan:

> The First Amendment, to me, is a compendious guarantor of the freedom of the mind, and I reject the suggestion that political expression, or the "serious" discussion of social problems, enjoys a preferred position over artistic expression.[54]

The question, then, becomes: How is obscene pornography distinguished from genuine art? Tests for obscenity generally fall into two categories, Brennan wrote, objective and subjective. Objective tests focus on the qualities of the material rather than the intent of the creator, while subjective tests go to the state of mind of the creator.[55]

Generally, if there is a preoccupation with erotic description, disassociation of the erotic from emotions, emphasis on the bizarre, complete candor, and constant use of profane language, material is judged under an objective test to be obscene. This type of test, Brennan argued, is inadequate because "hard core" pornography has no agreed-upon content, because the prurient-interest test used in such cases is vague, and because aesthetic values are being used to suppress material.[56]

The subjective test of obscenity is premised on the intent of the creator, Brennan wrote, since art is an imitation of life:

> But the notion of art as imitation does imply, I believe, that art is not just a frenzied outpouring of the soul but a purposive and rational endeavor addressed to the understanding. If so, I cannot conceive how it could be the artist's purpose to excite his audience sexually. And I suggest that where we have writings or pictures whose purpose is predominantly aphrodisiacal, we have pornography, not art.[57]

The test, Brennan wrote, has more validity than an objective test:

> To ask a writer, say, what kind of person he was writing for, or what kind of interest his book was intended to appeal to, what induced him to write, whether he considers himself a serious, professional artist or merely a writer for the pornographic market—such questions, I believe, would be probative of pornographic intent, but would not open up large issues of morality.[58]

Circumstantial evidence that would tend to show the intent of the author, Brennan noted, would be whether the work was anonymous or pseudonymous; the background, training, and education of the creator;

and circumstances of dissemination, including advertising, presentation, and publication.[59]

Brennan made several other points before concluding his memorandum. Among them:

- Patent offensiveness is a constitutionally required finding in any obscenity adjudication.[60]
- A local-community-standards test is improper. People in one community should not be prevented from reading matter allowable in another community simply because of a less tolerant population.[61]
- Expert witnesses are important to the adjudication of an obscenity case.[62]
- A trial judge should exercise an independent judgment as to the obscenity of the material in question.[63]
- A bookseller or newsstand dealer must be shown to be a willing accomplice to the dissemination of obscene material before there can be a conviction. The dealer must have known of the circumstances of distribution, advertising, and intended audience as well as content.[64]

"The basic point of this memorandum," Brennan concluded, "is that no *bona fide* work of art or information may be suppressed in the name of obscenity, even if it is deeply repulsive to the dominant current thought of the community."[65]

There is no indication in Brennan's files of the reception of his memorandum. Indeed, there is no concrete verification that he even circulated it to the conference. If he did, it seemed to have little effect on the outcome of *Jacobellis,* in which seven opinions were delivered, none gaining more than two votes, and in which the *Roth* test was refined, but only moderately. Some of the issues raised by Brennan in the memorandum, of course, were addressed in *Jacobellis* and subsequent opinions, but there is no indication that the unique subjective test based on the intent of the writer was ever considered by the Court. In *Jacobellis* Brennan attempted to make a clearer delineation of obscene material by strengthening the test of social worth and turning the focus away from a test of prurience. He also attempted to settle the issue of the "community."

Brennan announced the judgment of the Court, reversing a conviction for the showing of a movie titled "The Lovers." In his opinion, Brennan rejected the lower court's attempt to weigh the social importance of the film against the appeal to the prurient interest in sex. The film may have only slight social importance, he wrote, but the *Roth* test did not involve balancing. Obscenity is excluded from First Amendment protection because it is "utterly without redeeming social importance." *Roth* also required material to go "substantially beyond customary limits of candor in description or representation of such matters."[66] The film, therefore, because it had social importance—however slight—was protected.

Brennan also reiterated Harlan's point that "contemporary community standards" referred to a national test. The standard, he wrote, refers to a community in the sense of "the society at large," not in the sense of a local community.[67] Warren disagreed, writing that the community standard in *Roth* did not refer to a national standard. "There is no provable 'national standard,' " he wrote, "and perhaps there should be none."[68]

The "utterly without redeeming social importance" terminology used in *Jacobellis* became part of the test for obscenity in *Memoirs v. Massachusetts*.[69] Brennan, again for only a plurality, wrote that the definition of obscenity expressed in *Roth* and elaborated in subsequent cases required that three elements coalesce:

> It must be established that (a) the dominant theme of the material taken as a whole appeals to a prurient interest in sex; (b) the material is patently offensive because it affronts contemporary community standards relating to the description or representation of sexual matters; and (c) the material is utterly without redeeming social value.[70]

The Supreme Judicial Court of Massachusetts found *Memoirs of a Woman of Pleasure* to be obscene, even though there was testimony at trial that the book had literary merit and played a part in the history of the development of the English novel. The Massachusetts court, however, ruled that

> the fact that the testimony may indicate this book has some minimal literary value does not mean it is of any social importance. We do not interpret the "social importance" test as requiring that a book which appeals to prurient interest and is patently offensive must be unqualifiedly worthless before it can be deemed obscene.[71]

But that is exactly what the social-value test means, Brennan wrote. Finding that the Massachusetts court had misinterpreted the social value criterion, he held that "a book cannot be proscribed unless it is found to be *utterly* without redeeming social value." Therefore, even if the book was found to appeal to the prurient interest in sex and to be patently offensive, it was not constitutionally obscene.[72]

Clark disagreed and took Brennan to task for a unilateral adoption of the "utterly without redeeming social value" test. The test had never been suggested, much less expounded, Clark wrote. Indeed, it had been referred to by Brennan only once—in *Jacobellis*[73]

No one, not even Clark, seemed to notice the slight semantic change Brennan made between the test espoused in *Jacobellis* and that enunicated in *Memoirs*. In *Jacobellis,* Brennan's reference was to material utterly without redeeming social *importance;* in *Memoirs* the test reference was to material utterly without redeeming social *value.* Arguably, material can have value without having importance. Indeed, the Massachusetts court made just this distinction, finding that the material might have some slight value, but had no importance.

Finally, Justice Brennan was able to garner a majority for his opinion in *Ginsburg v. U.S.*[74] In that case the Court held that evidence of pandering was relevant in determining the ultimate question of obscenity. Pandering was defined as "the business of purveying textual or graphic matter openly advertised to appeal to the erotic interest,"[75] and there was ample evidence of pandering in the case.

Ginsburg was delivered the same day as *Memoirs* and *Mishkin.* In two of the three cases Brennan wrote majority opinions, and in *Memoirs* he wrote a plurality opinion. Following the announcement in the cases, Justice Abe Fortas wrote Brennan, "I think this was a masterful statement. It makes me even prouder that I joined your opinions."[76] And Warren wrote, "You have made a great contribution to the jurisprudence of our Court and your announcement was superb."[77]

One justice, however, possibly Douglas, had a different reaction. "Bill," he wrote, "Because of the quizzical expressions on the faces of some of the Sol. General's Staff I wonder how happy they are with Ginsburg, because you know it will cast quite a work burden on that office and on the U.S. Attorneys."[78]

The three opinions, handed down March 21, 1966, marked the heydey of Brennan's leadership in the area of obscenity.

The Court would not seriously address the obscenity issue again until the 1971–72 term, when it first heard arguments in *Miller v. California.* The Court established in 1967—a year after the *Memoirs-Ginsburg* block of cases—a new approach for disposing of obscenity cases. Beginning with *Redrup v. New York,*[79] the Court began the practice of *per curiam* reversals of convictions for the dissemination of materials that at least five members of the Court, applying their separate tests, deemed not to be obscene. Between 1967 and 1972, no less than thirty-one cases were disposed of using the *Redrup* approach.[80]

During the same period, however, the makeup of the Court changed significantly. Earl Warren, Hugo L. Black, and Abe Fortas were replaced by Warren Burger, Lewis F. Powell, and Harry A. Blackmun. And, by the time the obscenity cases were decided—after being held over to the 1972 term from the 1971 term—John Marshall Harlan was replaced by William H. Rehnquist. While the new members of the Court may have been more interested in addressing the obscenity issue than their predecessors had been, it is safe to say that few justices were satisfied with the *Redrup* approach.

Brennan, of course, took the opportunity in *Miller* and *Paris Adult Theatre* to espouse publicly, for the first time, the theme he had been developing for ten years, and he wrote that obscenity should be de-criminalized. The irony was that, had he written the opinion one term earlier, he might have commanded a majority, and had he written it two terms earlier, a majority of the Court would certainly have voted to change obscenity law in the United States.[81] By 1973, however, a majority—consisting primarily of the new members of the Court, Blackmun, Powell, and Rehnquist—had coalesced under the writing of Chief Justice Warren Burger.

PORNOGRAPHY IN THE 1970s AND 1980s: *MILLER V. CALIFORNIA AND ITS PROGENY*

It became apparent early in the 1971 term that the Court was divided in *Miller*. Burger and Brennan disagreed on how the case should be decided; other justices were left to pick sides.

In mid-May 1972 the Chief Justice circulated a memorandum that was apparently his first attempt to express himself in writing on the case. In it he stated that he believed the tripartite test articulated by Brennan in *Memoirs,* "notwithstanding certain infirmities inherent in any such 'test,' is adequate."[82] Burger wrote, however, that the test needed refinement in two areas. First, it should be made clear that the "contemporary community standards" alluded to in *Roth* referred to a local rather than a national community. *Roth,* Burger wrote, indicated that the jury would apply its own concept of decency as the "common conscience" of what the trial judge referred to as "our community."[83] The judge in giving those instructions, and the Court in affirming, hardly expected the jury to apply some concept of a national standard of decency.[84] Second, Burger wrote that the "utterly without redeeming social value" test was too sweeping because it allowed producers of pornography to insulate obscenity by including in it a modicum of material of some value.[85]

Burger's "refinements" were diametrically opposed to elements Brennan held essential to the *Roth-Memoirs* test—elements that helped ensure protection for nonobscene, sexually explicit material. Three days after Burger circulated his memorandum, therefore, Brennan responded and announced to the Conference his intention to advocate formally a change in the way obscenity was treated under the law:

> With all respect, the Chief Justice's proposed solution to the obscenity quagmire will, in my view, worsen an already intolerable mess. I've been thinking for some time that only a drastic change in applicable constitutional principles promises a way out. I've decided that I shall use this case as a vehicle for saying that I'm prepared to make that change. I'll write in effect that it has proved impossible to separate expression concerning sex, called obscenity, from other expression concerning sex, whether the material takes the form of words, photographs or film; that *Stanley* (as well as the Chief Justice's *12,000 Reels of Film?*) has already eroded that concept; that we should

treat obscenity not as expression concerning sex excepted from First Amendment speech but as expression, although constituting First Amendment speech, that is regulable to the extent of legislating against its offensive exposure to unwilling adults and dissemination to juveniles. I'll try in due course to circulate my views.[86]

The cases to which Brennan referred were *Stanley v. Georgia*[87] and *U.S. v. 12 200-Ft. Reels of Film*.[88] *Stanley* was a 1969 case in which the Court held that the mere possession of obscene material was not a crime; the Constitution allowed a person to receive material regardless of the social worth of that material. The opinion in *12 200-Ft. Reels of Film* was handed down the same day as *Miller* and *Paris Adult Theatre*. In it the Court upheld the power of the government to proscribe the importation of obscene material.

A month after writing his note to the Conference, Brennan circulated a thirty-one-page memorandum, using *Miller* as a springboard to discuss the broad problem of obscenity and the First Amendment. He drew on some of the themes he developed in his obscenity memorandum of 1962, but went further. He began this way:

> I think the time has come when we should admit that the standards we have fashioned to guide administration of this Nation's obscenity laws do not work and that we must change our constitutional approach if we are to bring stability to this area of the law.[89]

Brennan traced the problem the Court faced defining obscenity and applying definitions. The "core of the problem," he noted, was the Court's failure to fashion "sensitive tools" to ensure that constitutionally protected expression not be restricted.[90] All but two members of the Court—Black and Douglas—agreed that "there is something called 'obscenity' outside the ambit of the First Amendment."[91] Because of the divergent opinions, the Court retreated to the unsatisfactory compromise offered by the *Redrup* approach.[92]

"Fifteen years experience since *Roth*," Brennan wrote, "has brought me to the firm conclusion that the effort to safeguard First Amendment values . . . has failed of its objective because certain predicates of *Roth* have proved to be unsound."[93] It had become impossible to determine what obscenity is, Brennan wrote, and, possibly, "obscenity" was not a particular type of speech at all, but "may depend upon nuances of presentation and the context of dissemination," including, for example, whether genitals are depicted and whether a penis is semi-erect or fully erect.[94] As a result, developing a standard of obscenity that would meet the test of certainty and lack of overbreadth required by the due process clause and the First Amendment may be impossible:

> Although obscenity exists and we, as has been said, "know it when we see it," . . . words are evidently inadequate to describe it in advance with sufficient specificity to preclude an abridgement of the free and precious traffic in ideas.[95]

Therefore, Brennan concluded,

> the Constitution requires us not only to abandon the effort following *Redrup* to pick out obscene materials on a case-by-case basis, but also to reconsider the attempt altogether under *Roth* to define a category of all sexually oriented expression that may properly be subject to outright suppression by government.[96]

Since obscenity cannot be defined in advance, Brennan noted, it cannot be wholly suppressed, but that does not mean that obscenity is protected expression. Brennan traced the history of obscenity laws in the United States and found support for the conclusions of *Roth* that obscenity could be suppressed because it is a form of expression "utterly without redeeming social importance. . . . I depart from these views," Brennan wrote, "only insofar as is necessary to preserve constitutionally protected expression."[97]

But, Brennan wrote, the definition of obscenity is susceptible to sufficient specificity and narrowness to allow it to be restricted so that there is no offensive exposure to unwilling individuals and no dissemination to juveniles.[98]

Material restricted from display to unconsenting viewers must be precisely described. The material must be

> central to pornographic expression—that is, . . . pictorial or three-dimensional representations of fundamentally offensive sexual acts that go beyond the mere depiction of nudity, . . . and that are described with particularity (for example, human sexual intercourse, masturbation, sodomy, and so forth).[99]

Purely textual material would be wholly excluded from the definition. The same rules would apply to material restricted from view by juveniles.[100]

Under this approach, Brennan noted, the government could "prohibit pornographers from puffing fundamentally offensive pictorial or three-dimensional depictions of sexual acts beyond offering 'adult materials' and prohibit their sending samples except upon request." The government could also limit advertising of pornographic materials and could require pornography to be out of the view of bookstore customers.[101] Brennan concluded:

The approach I have outlined does not guarantee a solution to what Mr. Justice Harlan called "the intractable obscenity problem. . . ." It does, however, frankly admit that our current doctrines and practices have not worked and does seek to accommodate the various interests and values that experience has shown to pervade this area of the law. I believe that this accommodation may bring the stabililty to our law that we have sought and not achieved—and, furthermore, may do so with minimal hazards to protected expression. If experience proves the contrary, the question can again be re-examined.[102]

Chief Justice Burger responded with a three-page memorandum in which he purported to agree with much of what Brennan had written, but the agreement was not on points of controversy. He agreed, for example, that the Court had been unable to develop a suitable definition of obscenity, that many persons were uncertain of the obscenity standards, that some material was not protected by the Constitution, and that textual material should be treated differently than visual material.[103] And, Burger wrote, he was not content with his own approach to *Miller*. "But the Court has made enough false steps," he wrote. "We now need to retrace so that I feel we need to be very cautious about embarking on a new broad scale 'solution.' I fear that no solution will ever really be final—First Amendment problems do not readily 'finalize.' "[104]

In sum, Burger wrote that he had planned to "put my hand to something of the course you have laid out," but had not finished the document. He would prefer, he wrote, "to continue one step at a time, clarifying the 'national standard' concept in *Miller* and let the other problems continue to 'marinate.' I would therefore stand on *Miller* as proposed," he concluded, welcoming "suggestions that would lead any others to join *Miller* in what I consider to be a step-by-step treatment of one problem at a time."[105]

A day later Stewart and Marshall announced their agreement with Brennan,[106] but a week after that Brennan circulated a memorandum to the conference reporting that the obscenity cases would be held over to the 1972–73 term.[107]

Miller was reargued November 7, 1972, and six days later Burger wrote the Conference asking for "a division of the House" on the obscenity cases. "Bill Brennan and I have each tried to articulate a general approach on what seems to me the basic problems in *Miller v. California* and comparable cases," he wrote. "It would now help Bill and me if you would indicate that you 'generally agree' with Bill or with me."[108]

Stewart wrote that he agreed with Brennan, but would make no final commitment until he saw what was written, since he believed at least two members of the Court to be in agreement with neither.[109] Powell indicated support of Burger, but noted that he was more concerned with achieving a majority opinion and would also await written opinions before finally deciding: "Almost any such disposition would, I think, be preferable to the present intolerable confusion and uncertainty."[110]

White, Blackmun, and Rehnquist indicated that they would adhere to the *Roth* standard, without the three-point embellishment of the plurality in *Memoirs*. They all noted that there must be "a limiting national standard imposed by the First Amendment," but all recognized that, in practice, jurors would apply a local standard. Blackmun said Brennan's approach had "a distinct appeal," which he would prefer over an expansion of *Stanley v. Georgia*. But, he added, "I am not certain that the Constitution requires that commercial exploiters of pornography may rot an unwilling community."[111] White suggested that states could move to the prior licensing of films allowed by *Freedman*,[112] and Rehnquist voiced opposition to any standard that would encourage expert witnesses to dominate obscenity trials.[113]

There is no record in Brennan's papers of responses from Marshall and Douglas. Marshall joined Brennan's dissent in *Paris Adult Theatre*, and Douglas wrote a separate dissent, adhering to his long-time stance that the First Amendment does not allow suppression of material because it is deemed obscene.

Burger announced November 20 that he would pick out one "movie case" and one "picture case" and would "propose something more concrete in the way of an opinion." Since there is no national standard that can be defined, he wrote, the thrust of the opinion "will be to define what *conduct*, publicly exhibited, is not protected by the First Amendment and hence is subject to regulation under state police power. Necessarily this will also define 'public exhibition.' " The result, Burger noted, would give the justices "a choice between the Brennan solution and mine."[114]

It would be seven months before the opinions in *Miller* and *Paris Adult Theatre* were delivered, with the Court dividing much as it had in November 1972: White, Blackmun, Powell, and Rehnquist joined Burger; Stewart and Marshall joined Brennan; Douglas wrote his own dissent.[115]

Rejecting the "utterly without redeeming social value" test of *Memoirs*, Burger wrote that the test for determining obscenity consisted of three points:

> (a) whether "the average person, applying contemporary community standards" would find that the work, taken as a whole, appeals to the prurient interest; . . . (b) whether the work depicts or describes in a patently offensive way, sexual conduct specifically defined by the applicable state law; and (c) whether the work, taken as a whole, lacks serious literary, artistic, political, or scientific value.[116]

Under the test, Burger wrote, no one would be convicted unless the materials "depict or describe patently offensive 'hard core' sexual conduct

specifically defined by regulating state law."[117] The spirit, and to some
degree the language, of the section is reminiscent of Brennan's memorandum to the Conference a year earlier, in which he noted that material
restricted from display to unconsenting viewers must be "representations
of fundamentally offensive sexual acts that go beyond the mere depiction
of nudity, . . . and that are described with particularity."[118]

Burger also established the "contemporary community standards" test
as a local rather than national test. It would be unrealistic, he wrote, to
require a state proceeding to revolve around a national standard,[119] or to
require "that the people of Maine or Mississippi accept public depiction of
conduct found tolerable in Los Vegas, or New York City."[120]

In the companion case, *Paris Adult Theatre I v. Slaton,*[121] the Court held
that the state could regulate obscene material exhibited in theaters, rejecting the concept that such regulation was unconstitutional because the dissemination of material was between consenting adults.

Brennan dissented in both cases, with the thrust of his argument published in his dissent to *Paris Adult Theatre.* The opinion was a revision of
Brennan's *Miller* memorandum circulated a year earlier.[122] Indeed, using
some of the same language, Brennan made the same basic arguments:

1. The Court has failed in its efforts to define obscenity adequately and to
   apply standards to sexual material. The nuances of determining when
   material is obscene have become so great that there is little way to make
   such a determination except on a case-by-case basis. As a result, it is
   impossible to know in advance when sexually explicit material is obscene,
   and protected expression, therefore, is suppressed or chilled.

2. The Court was wrong when it presumed in *Roth* that there exists a defin-
   able class of sexually oriented expression that may be totally suppressed.
   "Obscenity" is not a class of speech, and the Court should abandon its
   attempt to make it such.

3. Sexually explicit material, however, may be restricted so that it is not
   confronted by unwilling viewers or juveniles.

The heart of Brennan's dissent in *Paris Adult Theatre* was his conclusion
that:

the concept of "obscenity" cannot be defined with sufficient specificity and
clarity to provide fair notice to persons who create and distribute sexually
oriented materials, to prevent substantial erosion of protected speech as a
byproduct of the attempt to suppress unprotected speech, and to avoid very
costly institutional harms.[123]

The formula announced in *Miller,* Brennan wrote, is only "a slightly
altered formulation of the basic *Roth* test" that, like every other available

formula, fails to distinguish sufficiently between protected and unprotected speech.[124] No one definition, Brennan wrote, "can possibly suffice for all situations, or carve out fully suppressible expression from all media without also creating a substantial risk of encroachment upon the guarantees of the Due Process Clause and the First Amendment."[125] Despite that, and despite repeated rulings that the definition of obscenity must provide adequate notice of what is prohibited, members of the Court had articulated various tests for determining obscenity and had executed various procedures for disposing of obscenity cases, so that "the resulting level of uncertainty is utterly intolerable."[126]

Brennan proposed a solution, but not before dispatching four other alternatives also available to the Court.

First, he wrote, the Court could draw a line that resolves all doubt in favor of state power and against the guarantees of the First Amendment. The Court could hold, for example, that any depiction of human sexual organs is outside the protection of the First Amendment. Such a standard would be "appallingly overbroad," but short of that extreme it would be difficult "to reduce the vagueness problem to tolerable proportions."[127]

Second, the Court could continue to claim that certain sexually oriented material is unprotected by the First Amendment and could continue various formulations, like the newly enunciated *Miller* test. The differences between the *Miller* test and the *Memoirs* test, he wrote, are academic,[128] and it "can have no ameliorative impact on the cluster of problems that grow out of the vagueness of our current standards."[129] In addition, the *Miller* test is "an invitation to widespread suppression of sexually oriented speech."[130]

Third, the Court could reduce its role in determining obscenity. The alternative fails, however, because the Constitution does not allow such a hands-off approach, and it would only aggravate the vagueness problem.[131]

Finally, the Court could adopt the Douglas–Black approach that the First Amendment bars the suppression of any sexually oriented material. The position, however, strips the states of power to an extent that cannot be justified by the Constitution, so long as there is an alternative approach that strikes a better balance.[132]

The balance, Brennan concluded, comes by allowing consenting adults unrestricted access to sexually explicit material while regulating the display of that material so unwilling adults are not confronted and regulating access to the material by juveniles.

There is no demonstrable, legitimate state interest in keeping sexually explicit materials out of the hands of consenting adults, Brennan wrote. In fact, the Court noted in *Stanley v. Georgia* that there was little empirical basis for the assertion that exposure to obscene material leads to deviant sexual behavior.[133] The Court also rejected the notion that there is a state concern in the moral content of a person's thoughts.[134] The Court, in *Paris Adult Theatre,* is allowing the state to act on the assumption that commerce in obscenity has a tendency to exert a corrupting and debasing impact leading to antisocial behavior. It is hard, therefore, Brennan wrote, "to see how state-ordered regimentation of our minds can ever be forestalled." If the state can proscribe certain material in order to create a particular moral tone, "it would seem to follow that in pursuit of that same objective a State could decree that its citizens must read certain books or must view certain films."[135]

Although the state interests in suppressing sexually explicit material may be laudable, Brennan concluded, they do not justify "the substantial damage to constitutional rights" that would occur by suppression.[136] He would hold, therefore, that although distribution may be regulated, including regulations to prevent obtrusive exposure to unconsenting adults and juveniles, neither state nor federal governments may suppress sexually oriented materials on the basis of their alleged obscenity.[137]

With *Miller* and *Paris Adult Theatre,* Brennan went from being the Court's chief spokesman in obscenity cases to being the chief dissenter.[138] As previously indicated, following *Miller,* he agreed with the majority in only four of twenty-seven major cases. He wrote one majority opinion and wrote opinions concurring in the judgment of the Court five times, while writing twelve dissents and three separate opinions. Indeed, he began the practice of dissenting even in cases that were to be held over to a new term, an exception to his general practice.[139] And, usually with Stewart and Marshall concurring, Brennan began dissenting when *writs of certiorari* were denied to cases involving allegedly obscene material.[140]

In most cases Brennan made the same points: that the suppression of sexual material was unconstitutional and that obscenity laws were overbroad.[141] He agreed, however, with the majority in *New York v. Ferber*[142] that child pornography can be restricted, and noted that the restriction was based on protection of children rather than protection of adult consumers.[143] But even child-pornography laws must be narrowly drawn, Brennan argued. When the Court upheld child-pornography laws in *Massachusetts v. Oakes*[144] and *Osborne v. Ohio,*[145] Brennan dissented on grounds that the laws were overbroad. He also argued in *Osborne* that private possession of child pornography could not be punished:

> When speech is eloquent and the ideas expressed lofty, it is easy to find restrictions on them invalid. But were the First Amendment limited to such discourse, our freedom would be sterile indeed. Mr. Osborne's pictures may be distasteful, but the Constitution guarantees both his right to possess them privately and his right to avoid punishment under an overbroad law.[146]

ALTERNATIVE METHODS OF REGULATION

The difficulty in defining—and therefore regulating—obscenity prompted some states to experiment with techniques for sidestepping the problem of seeking a judicial determination of obscenity.[147] A variety of methods for controlling sexually explicit material without determining the material to be obscene arose. In *Bantam Books v. Sullivan*,[148] for example, the Court struck down attempts by a state commission in Rhode Island to control sexually explicit material by warning bookstores that certain books and magazines were inappropriate for young people. Brennan called the efforts "informal censorship" aimed at circumventing the criminal justice system.[149] And, in *Marcus v. Search Warrants of Property*,[150] the Court ruled that procedures for issuing search warrants in Missouri did not sufficiently protect bookstore owners. The warrants, Brennan wrote for the Court, were issued on the conclusions of one police officer that material was obscene. States may not do whatever they want in efforts to crack down on sexually explicit material, he wrote.[151] The Court reaffirmed the ruling a number of times, ensuring that states followed proper procedures to control obscene material.[152] In 1989, however, the Court ruled that state Racketeer-Influenced and Corrupt Organizations laws could be used to prosecute businesses dealing in obscene material even when those laws entailed significantly more severe penalties.[153]

Brennan also wrote the majority opinion in *Smith v. California*,[154] a case in which the Court held that bookstore operators cannot be held liable for knowing the contents of all the books they sell. The strict liability of the California statute that allowed prosecution of a bookstore operator for selling an obscene book would have the effect of seriously restricting nonobscene books, Brennan wrote.[155]

These efforts at regulation were often semi-veiled attempts to eliminate sexually explicit material. States were more successful in attempting to control how and where such material was disseminated, and often used liquor licensing and zoning to control the businesses disseminating the material. The Supreme Court, for example, allowed jurisdictions to ban topless dancing or other sexually explicit performances as well as sexually explicit films in bars as part of the state's control of the sale of alcoholic beverages,[156] even though a ban on all topless or nude dancing is unconstitutionally overbroad.[157] And the Court ruled that zoning ordinances regulating the location or number of bookstores or theaters disseminating sexually explicit material were constitutional because there was no denial of the marketplace to the businesses.[158]

Brennan found the restrictions unconstitutional. Liquor licenses, he wrote, cannot be used to inhibit speech because they allowed the impermissible regulation of protected speech.[159] And the zoning requirements were based solely on content and, therefore, were unconstitutional.[160]

In the 1980s, the Court faced the issue of closing as public nuisances theaters that showed sexually explicit films, and it issued some mixed signals. The Court held that to close a theater as a public nuisance because the theater had a history of showing obscene films amounted to unconstitutional prior restraint.[161] The Court held five years later, however, that statutes could exist that allowed for such theaters to be closed.[162] A year after that, the Court held that a bookstore could be closed because of activities occurring on the premises. In *Arcara v. Cloud Books*,[163] the Court upheld a New York statute that allowed the state to close a bookstore for one year because sexual acts occurred on the premises. Brennan joined Blackmun's dissent criticizing the majority for the ruling. The way to eliminate the sexual acts, Blackmun wrote, was to arrest those involved, not to close the bookstore.[164] The Court's action, Blackmun wrote, created a loophole for suppressing undesirable but protected speech without confronting the First Amendment.[165] In 1990, however, the Court ruled that businesses dealing in sexually explicit material could be regulated through governmental licensing, but that the licensing scheme could be no more onerous than licensing schemes for other businesses.[166]

Brennan would allow some restrictions on the distribution of sexually explicit material. He agreed with a majority of the justices that prohibitions against mailing[167] and importing[168] obscene material were constitutional, for example. A federal statute allowing the postmaster general to return obscene material to its sender was not constitutional, however, Brennan wrote for the Court, because it did not provide sufficient safeguards for the delivery of nonobscene material through the mails.[169] Brennan would also allow restrictions on companies that distributed pornographic messages over phone lines—dial-a-porn—but would not allow a ban on such messages.[170]

The Court also held, with Brennan again writing the majority opinion, that states can restrict the sale of sexually explicit material to children, even though the material may not be obscene. In *Ginzberg v. New York*,[171] the Court recognized the state interest in the welfare of children and upheld a New York law not allowing the sale of such material to persons under seventeen years of age.[172] White did not like what he perceived in Brennan's opinion to be a suggestion that the state might have a less stringent burden when minors were involved. He wrote to Brennan:

Perhaps you ride both horses in this case, that is, this junk is outside the First Amendment, but if it is not, it still may be kept from children because there is sufficient reason to do so which overrides both the minor's right to read and the right of the publisher to disseminate. This is admirable eclecticism if it gets four other guys. In the end, I shall probably be one of them. Although I would perhaps have preferred the "outside" course if a choice must be made, I have not, in theory or in practice, rejected the compelling state interest approach. Since the more one stirs, the more this pot boils to no good end, I am not moved to write separately, at least not for now. Good luck.[173]

Indeed, White did become one of the "four other guys" and abandoned his attempt to write separately, giving Brennan his essential fourth vote.[174]

CONCLUSIONS

On the surface, Brennan's dissent in *Paris Adult Theatre* might be seen as an abrupt change. No longer did he favor attempts to identify obscenity; instead, he advocated the elimination of criminal sanctions for the dissemination of obscene material. The opinion, however, should be seen as the conclusion to a long trek in which Brennan investigated the ways obscene material could be controlled without jeopardizing freedoms guaranteed to nonobscene, sexually explicit material. His conclusion was that the task is impossible, and that the constitutional guarantees are too precious to sacrifice in the name of controlling obscene material, absent a showing of actual harm. The stance Brennan took in *Paris Adult Theatre* was neither a change in his position on obscenity nor a surprise to his colleagues.

Brennan's opinion in *Roth* was premised on the notion that obscenity could be excluded from protections guaranteed by the constitution, not because its subject was sex, but because, historically, it was considered to be "utterly without redeeming social importance." If the expression of an idea had the "slightest redeeming social importance" it would be protected.[175] Sex, Brennan noted, "is one of the vital problems of human interest and public concern," and writings about sex, therefore, are not automatically excludable.[176]

Later Brennan substituted the word "value" for the word "importance" in the test of obscenity, a subtle, but important change.[177] The key to controlling obscenity in the Brennan paradigm was the ability to distinguish obscene material from nonobscene material. And that identification turned upon whether the material had any redeeming social value. A modicum of value, under the test, would save a distributor of sexually explicit material from jail.

The task of identifying obscenity became so onerous that a number of jurisdictions attempted to circumvent determinations of obscenity by finding alternative methods of controlling pornography. The methods usually did not pass constitutional muster, and Brennan often warned that methods of controlling pornography must provide sufficient guarantees so nonobscene expression would not be suppressed. "We risk erosion of First Amendment liberties," he wrote in one case, "unless we train our vigilance upon the methods whereby obscenity is condemned no less than upon the standards whereby it is judged."[178] The standards even applied when morally repugnant child pornography was involved.[179]

Indeed, in the long memorandum he wrote before the 1962 term—barely five years after his *Roth* opinion—Brennan, for the first time, expressed a theme that had previously been implied in his writings. Noting that even tawdry and vulgar material is protected,[180] he wrote that obscenity could not be regulated unless it could be identified.[181] He rejected the notion that political expression deserved more protection than artistic expression, arguing that the First Amendment protects aesthetics and politics equally.[182]

Brennan argued in the memorandum that there must be some category of material that can be identified as legally obscene before suppression of sexually explicit material can pass constitutional muster.[183] He also noted that obscenity is not a catchall classification for outlawing objectionable material. It did not apply, for example, to "unduly violent, gruesome or scatological expression,"[184] nor did it apply to mere nudity. Brennan recognized some twenty years before it became an issue in the social sciences, therefore, the potential problems with messages that juxtaposed sexual and violent images but were not obscene.[185]

In the memorandum, Brennan also rejected tests of obscenity that are based on the quality of the material. Tests must be based on the intent of the creator, he wrote, the ultimate test being whether the creator intended the work primarily as an aphrodisiac rather than as a work of art. Circumstantial evidence could be used to help make that determination, Brennan wrote.[186] Such evidence would include the manner in which the material was marketed, a criterion that drew support from at least four members of the Court in *Ginsburg v. U.S.*[187] In that case, the Court, with Brennan writing the majority opinion, held that pandering was evidence of the obscenity of material. In general, however, Brennan's aphrodisiac test never became part of obscenity law.

The basic point of the memorandum was that no work of art should be suppressed in the name of obscenity, no matter how repulsive it is to members of the community.[188]

Brennan made no point in the memorandum that contradicted his opinion in *Roth*. Indeed, the memorandum could have been an extension of *Roth*. The theme of the memorandum was that if artwork has the slightest redeeming value it must be protected; there must be no chill of protected expression in the name of obscenity.

That same theme extended into Brennan's *Jacobellis* opinion in 1964, where the "utterly without redeeming social importance" language became part of the test for obscenity. Attempts by the Ohio courts to weigh the social importance of the film in question against the appeal to the prurient interest in sex were improper, Brennan wrote. In order for the film to be unprotected it must be "utterly without redeeming social importance."[189]

Two years later, when that language, with the slight semantic change, became part of the tripartite test in *Memoirs,* Clark complained. The test had never been suggested, he wrote, and had only been referred to once previously by Brennan. Clark failed to follow the development of the test from *Roth* through *Jacobellis* to *Memoirs.* To Brennan, however, the progression was logical. Since obscenity was excluded from constitutional protection because historically it was seen as being without social value, if any social value attached to sexually explicit material, protection also attached; the standard was logical for determining when sexually explicit material was obscene. It was one method of ensuring that nonobscene material not be suppressed.

Finally, Brennan determined that it was impossible to distinguish between obscene and nonobscene material. Indeed, he returned to his theme that obscenity may not be a separate type of speech at all. Since words could not describe it, there was insufficient warning to protect the dissemination of nonobscene material so, therefore, obscenity could not be banned.[190] Sexually explicit material could be sufficiently described, however, to allow restrictions so that it would not be confronted by unwilling adults or juveniles.

Brennan made those points in the memorandum he circulated on *Miller* in 1972 and in his dissenting opinion in *Paris Adult Theatre* a year later. Ironically, the majority opinion in *Miller* drew upon Brennan's writings. First, Burger was obviously rejecting the key elements in the *Roth-Memoirs* test developed by Brennan: that "community standards" refer to the "society at large" rather than to local communities; and that obscene material is "utterly without redeeming social value." Second, although rejecting much of what Brennan had written, Burger apparently adopted Brennan's point that restrictions on sexually explicit material must include a precise description of what is proscribed. Brennan wrote in his *Miller* memorandum that the restricted expression would include

> representations of fundamentally offensive sexual acts that go beyond the mere depiction of nudity, . . . and that are described with particularity (for example, human sexual intercourse, masturbation, sodomy, and so forth).[191]

Brennan would only restrict such representations from display to consenting adults or to juveniles.[192] The tripartite test of obscenity Burger established in *Miller,* however, included the requirement for a similar description: "whether the work depicts or describes in a patently offensive way, sexual conduct specifically defined by the applicable state law."[193]

In *Paris Adult Theatre,* Brennan went even further than in his memorandum. He wrote that the state was attempting to establish a particular moral tone with its regulation of obscenity, and he challenged the right or authority of the state to do so. If the Constitution allows the state to limit certain materials in order to achieve that goal, "it would seem to follow that in pursuit of that same objective a State could decree that its citizens must read certain books or must view certain films."[194]

Such a notion was obnoxious to Brennan as directly *contra* to the tenets of a free society. Freedom means the right to choose material to read or view without state interference. In the area of obscenity, from the outset of the Court's attempts to resolve the problem, Brennan supported controlling material that was utterly without redeeming social value. He maintained that view throughout his writings and, indeed, there is no indication that he has abandoned it. Brennan recognized, however, that the task of determining when material crossed from the realm of tawdry and vulgar into the realm of the obscene was very nearly impossible. The rights of free expression are too precious to sacrifice without sufficient cause, and, therefore, it becomes better to let obscene material exist under specific guidelines than to chance suppressing speech that is not obscene. Only evidence of harm would be sufficient cause for attempts wholly to proscribe obscene material.

NOTES

1. The term "pornography" is used herein to mean sexually explicit material; it may or may not be obscene. "Obscenity," on the other hand, describes pornography that has met or could meet a test that would exclude it from First Amendment protection.

2. 354 U.S. 476 (1957).

3. Osborne v. Ohio, 110 S.Ct. 1691 (1990). Although the Court held that an individual could be convicted under the Constitution for mere possession of child pornography, the conviction in *Osborne* was vacated on due process grounds, and the case was remanded for a new trial.

4. 378 U.S. 174 (1964). In fact, Justice Byron R. White concurred in the judgment without opinion, but since his refusal to join a colleague indicates some difference of opinion, although one not stated, he is counted here as having a different opinion on the issue.

5. Memoirs v. Massachusetts, 383 U.S. 413 (1966); Pope v. Illinois, 481 U.S. 497 (1987).

6. Smith v. California, 361 U.S. 147 (1959); Mishkin v. New York, 383 U.S. 502 (1966); Ginzburg v. U.S., 383 U.S. 436 (1966); U.S. v. Thirty-Seven Photographs, 402 U.S. 363 (1971); California v. La Rue, 409 U.S. 109 (1972); Schad v. Borough of Mt. Ephraim, 452 U.S. 61 (1981); New York v. Ferber, 458 U.S. 747 (1982); FW/PBS, Inc. v. Dallas, 110 S.Ct. 596 (1990).

7. *See, for example,* the cases at 388 U.S. 431–54 (1967); and cases listed in Paris Adult Theatre I v. Slaton, 413 U.S. 49, 82, note 8, Justice Brennan dissenting.

8. Brennan Papers, Box 101, Obscenity Memorandum, 138–40. A duplicate is in Box 134. The memorandum is undated, but makes reference to the oral arguments in *Jacobellis* to be heard in the upcoming term. *Jacobellis* was argued in the 1962 term of the Court. Hereafter it will be cited as "Obscenity Memorandum."

9. Brennan Papers, Box 77, Manual Enterprises v. Day, memorandum of Justice Brennan to Justice Harlan, July 9, 1962.

10. 378 U.S. at 198, Justice Stewart concurring.

11. Memorandum to Justice Harlan, *supra* note 9.

12. Interstate Circuit v. Dallas, 390 U.S. 676, 704 (1968), opinion of Justice Harlan.

13. *Id.* at 707, opinion of Justice Harlan.

14. Memoirs v. Massachusetts, 383 U.S. 413, 441 (1966), Justice Clark dissenting.

15. 352 U.S. 380 (1957).

16. *Id.* at 383.

17. Kingsley Books v. Brown, 354 U.S. 436 (1957).

18. N. Hentoff, The Constitutionalist, The New Yorker, March 12, 1990, at 49.

19. R. Del Guidice, Justice Brennan and Freedom of Expression, unpublished Ph.D. dissertation, University of Massachusetts, 1975, at note 4.

20. 354 U.S. at 480.

21. Brennan Papers, Box 6.

22. 354 U.S. at 484.

23. *Id.* at 485.

24. *Id.* at 487.

25. *Id.* at 488.

26. *Id.* at 488–89.

27. *Id.* at 489.

28. *Id.* at 492.

29. Brennan Papers, Box 6, memorandum of Justice Whittaker to Justice Brennan, June 6, 1957.

30. Brennan Papers, Box 6, memoranda of June 6, June 10, June 12, and June 13, 1957. The term "Court" is used as a synonym for "majority" during the deliberations on a case.

31. 370 U.S. 478 (1962).

32. 378 U.S. 184 (1964).

33. 370 U.S. at 490.

34. *Id.* at 486–87.

35. *Id.* at 488.

36. *See quotation at supra* note 9.

37. Memorandum to Justice Harlan, *supra* note 9.

38. *Id.*

39. 383 U.S. 502 (1966).

40. *Id.* at 508.

41. *Id.*

42. 390 U.S. 629 (1968).

43. *Jacobellis* was delivered in 1964, two years after *Manual,* but it was first argued in October 1962.

44. Obscenity Memorandum, *supra* note 8, at 3.

45. *Id.* at 4.

46. *Id.* at 30–31.

47. *Id.* at 7.

48. *Id.* at 31–32.
49. *Id.* at 33–34.
50. *Id.* at 49–55.
51. *Id.* at 53.
52. *Id.* at 36–37.
53. *Id.* at 37.
54. *Id.* at 39–40.
55. *Id.* at 59–60.
56. *Id.* at 60–80.
57. *Id.* at 41.
58. *Id.* at 111–12.
59. *Id.* at 113–15.
60. *Id.* at 121–22.
61. *Id.* at 124–25.
62. *Id.* at 130.
63. *Id.* at 132.
64. *Id.* at 136.
65. *Id.* at 140.
66. 378 U.S. at 191.
67. *Id.* at 192–93.
68. *Id.* at 200, Chief Justice Warren dissenting.
69. 383 U.S. 413 (1966).
70. *Id.* at 418.
71. *Id.* at 419.
72. *Id.*
73. *Id.* at 442, Justice Clark dissenting.
74. 383 U.S. 463 (1966).
75. *Id.* at 467.
76. Brennan Papers, Box 137, memorandum of Justice Fortas to Justice Brennan, March 21, 1966.
77. *Id.*, memorandum of Chief Justice Warren to Justice Brennan, undated but probably March 21, 1966.
78. *Id.*, memorandum to Justice Brennan, undated, but probably March 21, 1966, signature undecipherable.
79. 386 U.S. 767 (1967).
80. *See* cases listed at 413 U.S. 49, 82, note 8.
81. During the 1971–72 term, Justices Marshall, Stewart, and Douglas would have voted to de-criminalize obscenity law, so Justice Brennan would have had to have picked up the votes of either Justice Powell or Justice Blackmun for a majority. During 1970–71, however, he would have received the support of Justice Black, for a solid majority.
82. Brennan Papers, Box 283, memorandum of Chief Justice Burger to the Conference, at 3.
83. *Id.* at 5–6.
84. *Id.* at 13.
85. *Id.*
86. Brennan Papers, Box 283, memorandum of Justice Brennan to the Conference, May 22, 1972.

87. 394 U.S. 557 (1969).

88. 413 U.S. 123 (1973).

89. Brennan Papers, Box 283, memorandum of Justice Brennan to the Conference, June 23, 1972. A copy of the first draft of this memorandum, which was circulated in early June, is not among Brennan's papers. Quotations herein are from his second draft, circulated with a note to the effect that since the cases were to be held over to the 1972–73 term, the memorandum is for the files of the justices.

90. *Id.* at 2.

91. *Id.* at 3–4.

92. *Id.* at 4–6.

93. *Id.* at 10.

94. *Id.* at 12–13.

95. *Id.* at 14.

96. *Id.* at 15.

97. *Id.* at 20.

98. *Id.* at 20–21.

99. *Id.* at 25.

100. *Id.* at 28–29.

101. *Id.* at 30.

102. *Id.* at 30–31.

103. Brennan Papers, Box 283, memorandum of Chief Justice Burger to Justice Brennan, with copies to the Conference, June 14, 1972.

104. *Id.* at 2–3.

105. *Id.* at 3.

106. *Id.*, memoranda of Justices Stewart and Marshall, June 15, 1972.

107. Brennan Papers, Box 28, memorandum of Justice Brennan, June 23, 1972.

108. Brennan Papers, Box 283, memorandum of Chief Justice Burger, November 13, 1972.

109. *Id.*, memorandum of Justice Stewart, November 13, 1972.

110. *Id.*, memorandum of Justice Powell, November 14, 1972.

111. *Id.*, memorandum of Justice Blackmun, November 20, 1972.

112. *Id.*, memorandum of Justice White, November 16, 1972.

113. *Id.*, memorandum of Justice Rehnquist, November 27, 1972.

114. *Id.*, memorandum of Chief Justice Burger, November 20, 1972.

115. Three other cases were decided the same day as *Miller* and *Paris Adult Theatre:* Kaplan v. California, 413 U.S. 115 (1973); U.S. v. 12 200-Ft. Reels of Film, 413 U.S. 123 (1973); and U.S. v. Orito, 413 U.S. 139 (1973). One case was delivered four days later: Heller v. New York, 413 U.S. 483 (1973). All four were vacated and remanded in light of the finding in *Miller.*

116. 413 U.S. 15, 24 (1973).

117. *Id.* at 27.

118. *Supra* note 89, at 25.

119. 413 U.S. at 30.

120. *Id.* at 32.

121. 413 U.S. 49 (1973).

122. *See* text accompanying *supra* notes 89–102.

123. 413 U.S. at 103, Justice Brennan dissenting.

124. *Id.* at 83–84, Justice Brennan dissenting.
125. *Id.* at 85, Justice Brennan dissenting.
126. *Id.* at 87, Justice Brennan dissenting.
127. *Id.* at 94, Justice Brennan dissenting.
128. *Id.* at 96, Justice Brennan dissenting.
129. *Id.* at 98, Justice Brennan dissenting.
130. *Id.* at 97, Justice Brennan dissenting.
131. *Id.* at 101–2, Justice Brennan dissenting.
132. *Id.* at 102–3, Justice Brennan dissenting.
133. *Id.* at 107–8, Justice Brennan dissenting.
134. *Id.* at 108, Justice Brennan dissenting.
135. *Id.* at 110, Justice Brennan dissenting.
136. *Id.* at 112, Justice Brennan dissenting.
137. *Id.* at 113, Justice Brennan dissenting.
138. Justice Brennan became the senior associate justice in the 1975 term of the Court, following the retirement of Justice Douglas.
139. Brennan Papers, Box 283, memorandum of Justice Brennan to Chief Justice Burger, June 6, 1973.
140. Justice Brennan usually wrote the dissents and, indeed, was responsible for streamlining a standard dissent to use in federal cases and a second dissent for state cases; Brennan Papers, Box 492, memorandum of Justice Brennan to Justices Stewart and Marshall, September 28, 1978.
141. See, e.g., Jenkins v. Georgia, 418 U.S. 153, 162 (1974), Justice Brennan dissenting; Hamling v. U.S., 418 U.S. 87, 141 (1974), Justice Brennan dissenting; McKinney v. Alabama, 424 U.S. 669, 678 (1976), Justice Brennan concurring and dissenting; Marks v. U.S., 430 U.S. 188, 197 (1977), Justice Brennan concurring and dissenting; Smith v. U.S. 291, 310 (1977), Justice Brennan dissenting; Pinkus, dba Rosslyn News Co. v. U.S., 436 U.S. 293, 305 (1978), Justice Brennan dissenting; Pope v. Illinois, 481 U.S. 497, 506 (1987), Justice Brennan dissenting.
142. 458 U.S. 747 (1982).
143. *Id.* at 775, Justice Brennan concurring in the judgment.
144. 109 S.Ct. 2633 (1989).
145. 110 S.Ct. 1691 (1990).
146. *Id.* at 1717, Justice Brennan dissenting.
147. *See, for example,* Grunes, Obscenity Law and the Justices: Reversing Policy on the Supreme Court, 9 Seton Hall L. Rev. 473 (1978); Collins, Beitler and Osborne, Miller and Its Progeny: Foreseeing Problems with the Foreseeability Issue, Communication Yearbook 3, 304 (1979); Mott and Kellett, Obscenity, Community Standards and the Burger Court: From Deterrence to Disarray, 13 Suffolk U. L. Rev. 15 (1979).
148. 372 U.S. 58 (1963). *Bantam Books* is also discussed *infra* Chapter 4, at notes 33–40.
149. *Id.* at 69.
150. 367 U.S. 717 (1961).
151. *Id.* at 732.
152. *See, e.g.,* A Quantity of Copies of Books v. Kansas, 378 U.S. 205 (1964); Lee Art Theatre v. Virginia, 392 U.S. 636 (1968); Roaden v. Kentucky, 413 U.S. 496 (1973); Dyson v. Stein, 401 U.S. 200 (1971).

153. Ft. Wayne Books v. Indiana, 489 U.S. 46 (1989).

154. 361 U.S. 147 (1961).

155. *Id.* at 152.

156. California v. LaRue, 409 U.S. 109 (1972); New York State Liquor Authority v. Dennis Bellancer, 452 U.S. 714 (1981).

157. Doran v. Salem Inn, 422 U.S. 922 (1975); Schad v. Borough of Mt. Ephraim, 452 U.S. 61 (1981).

158. Young v. American Mini Theatres, 427 U.S. 50 (1976); Renton v. Playtime Theatres, 475 U.S. 41 (1986).

159. California v. LaRue, 409 U.S. at 123, Justice Brennan dissenting.

160. Renton v. Playtime, 475 U.S. at 55, Justice Brennan dissenting. *See also* the dissent of Justice Stewart in Young v. American Mini Theatres, 427 U.S. at 86 (joined by Justice Brennan).

161. Vance v. Universal Amusement Co., 445 U.S. 308 (1980).

162. Brockett v. Spokane Arcades, 472 U.S. 491 (1985).

163. 478 U.S. 697 (1986).

164. *Id.* at 711, Justice Blackmun dissenting (joined by Justice Brennan).

165. *Id.* at 711–12, Justice Blackmun dissenting (joined by Justice Brennan).

166. FW/PBS, Inc. v. Dallas, 110 S.Ct. 596 (1990).

167. U.S. v. Reidel, 402 U.S. 351 (1971).

168. U.S. v. Thirty-Seven Photographs, 402 U.S. 363 (1971).

169. Blount v. Rizzi, 400 U.S. 410 (1971).

170. Sable Communications v. FCC, 109 S.Ct. 2829 (1989), Justice Brennan concurring and dissenting.

171. 390 U.S. 629 (1968).

172. *But see* Rabeck v. New York, 391 U.S. 462 (1968) and Interstate Circuit v. Dallas, 390 U.S. 676 (1968), where similar restrictions were struck down as impermissibly vague.

173. Brennan Papers, Box 169, memorandum of Justice White to Justice Brennan, March 4, 1968.

174. Justice Stewart concurred in the result, 390 U.S. at 648.

175. 354 U.S. at 484.

176. *Id.* at 487.

177. *Memoirs,* 383 U.S. at 418.

178. *Manual,* 370 U.S. at 497, opinion of Justice Brennan.

179. Massachusetts v. Oakes, 109 S.Ct. 2633 (1989); Osborne v. Ohio, 110 S.Ct. 1691 (1990).

180. Obscenity Memorandum, *supra* note 8, at 44.

181. *Id.* at 47.

182. *Id.* at 49–51.

183. *Id.* at 31–32.

184. Brennan Papers, *supra* note 89, at 25.

185. *See, e.g.,* N.M. Malmuth and E. Donnerstein, Pornography and Sexual Aggression (1983).

186. Obscenity Memorandum, *supra* note 8, at 52.

187. 383 U.S. 463 (1966).

188. Brennan Papers, *supra* note 8, at 140.

189. 378 U.S. at 191.

190. 413 U.S. at 110, Justice Brennan dissenting.
191. Brennan Papers, *supra* note 89, at 25.
192. *Id*. at 28–29.
193. 413 U.S. at 24.
194. *Id*. at 132.

3

"Close Analysis and Critical Judgment"

The 1950s saw an increase in national anxiety over communism, a result of increased tension between the United States and communist countries, and increased publicity about subversives, various espionage activities, and anti-communist activists.[1] Because of this anxiety, in the mid-twentieth century companies and even public employers increasingly were requiring employees and potential employees to swear their allegiance to the United States and to certify that they were not members of subversive organizations. In addition, investigatory committees—often with congressional approval—were attempting to root from American society communists and communist sympathizers. Increasingly, then, as prerequisites for employment individuals were asked to sign oaths of allegiance or were asked questions about their private lives.

Many people objected. As a result, the anxiety over communism spilled over into the courts. Indeed, twenty-eight times between 1957 and 1977 the Supreme Court resolved disputes growing out of attempts to require loyalty or to investigate the possible lack of loyalty. Most of the cases fell into two categories: employment cases and investigation cases.[2] Employment cases involved persons who refused to take loyalty oaths to gain employment or to continue employment. In some instances they also involved persons who refused to answer questions from potential employers about their beliefs or their associational ties. Investigation cases involved refusals to answer questions posed by investigatory bodies, usually un-American activities committees.

To be constitutional, the Supreme Court has ruled, oaths of allegiance must be narrowly tailored and must fit specific circumstances. And, the Court has ruled, one cannot be required to answer questions about personal beliefs, activities, or associations unless the questions are specific and pertinent to some proper investigation. The key, then, in both loyalty oath and refusal-to-answer cases was precision and relevance. Those requirements were rarely met. In only six of the twenty-eight cases did the Court rule against claimants making First Amendment arguments, and in each of those six cases, Justice Brennan wrote or joined a dissent. During the period, Brennan wrote four majority opinions, one concurring opinion, and five dissenting opinions, all in favor of claimants making First Amendment arguments.

The leading cases in this area were *Konigsberg v. State Bar of California,*[3] decided in 1957, and *Speiser v. Randall,*[4] decided a year later.

In *Konigsberg* a law-school graduate was denied admission to the California bar because he did not show he was of good moral character and that he did not advocate the violent overthrow of the government. The finding was based on the refusal of Raphael Konigsberg to answer certain questions put to him by a bar association committee. The Court held that, despite Konigsberg's refusal to answer, there was ample evidence in the record that he was of good moral character, and there was no evidence of any advocacy to the violent overthrow of the government. Therefore, Konigsberg could not be denied admission to the bar for refusing to answer additional questions on those subjects. Nothing in the California statutes or rules of the California Bar Association allowed denial of admission to the bar based on refusal to answer.[5] The Court did not address the First Amendment issues involving refusal to answer, but indicated in *dicta* that Konigsberg also had First Amendment arguments.[6]

Four years later, however, the Court allowed the California bar to refuse Konigsberg admission because of his refusal to answer questions about his membership in certain organizations.[7] In 1961, the Court held that Konigsberg's refusal to respond obstructed a full investigation of his qualifications.[8] The record was left incomplete because of the refusal, the Court held; the questions were not arbitrary, and Konigsberg was warned of the consequences should he refuse to answer.[9] The denial, therefore, was proper.

Brennan dissented on grounds that the committee presented no evidence that Konigsberg unlawfully advocated the overthrow of the government. Therefore, Brennan wrote, the Court's opinion in *Speiser v. Randall* protected him from being denied admission to the bar because of refusal to answer.[10]

Speiser was one of Justice Brennan's earliest and most significant free-speech cases. Like *Konigsberg,* it came out of California, where the state had denied property tax exemptions to veterans who had refused to sign the oath on the required application forms swearing that they would not advocate the overthrow of the government and would not support foreign governments against the United States.[11] The California Supreme Court had ruled against the veterans on grounds that any limitation on speech caused by the oath was insubstantial.[12]

Brennan, writing for six of the eight participating justices, disagreed.[13] He found that the veterans had been penalized for their speech. In addition, he held that the procedure for determining who may not receive tax-exempt status was fatally flawed and could further infringe upon the free-speech rights of the applicants.

Brennan did not dispute the argument that California could deny tax exemptions to persons who could legally be punished for their speech. What he disputed was the method the state used in determining speech that may be proscribed:

> When we deal with the complex strands in the web of freedoms which make up free speech the operation and effect of the method by which speech is sought to be restrained must be subjected to close analysis and critical judgment in light of the particular circumstances to which it is applied.[14]

Any attempt to proscribe speech, therefore, must be accompanied by procedural safeguards, upon which the validity of the restraint may turn.[15] A major problem with the California procedure was that it required a challenged applicant to prove that he deserved the tax exemption but did not provide sufficiently sensitive tools for determining the line between the types of speech that may and may not be regulated. A danger existed, therefore, that legitimate speech might be penalized.[16] "The man who knows that he must bring forth proof and persuade another of the lawfulness of his conduct," Brennan wrote, "necessarily must steer far wider of the unlawful zone than if the State must bear these burdens."[17] Therefore, due process requires that when a state taxing program deters speech, the state bears the burden of justifying the inhibition.[18]

Konigsberg and *Speiser,* then, established that a person could not be punished for refusing to speak within certain parameters. First, a person could not be punished for refusing to respond to questions that are intrusive or offensive. Second, a person could not be punished for refusing to take a loyalty oath. The Court reinforced those themes through the 1970s.

LOYALTY OATHS

Under *Speiser,* a person could not be punished for failure to adhere to a loyalty oath in the absence of safeguards to protect against intrusions on free speech and against due process violations. A person, therefore, could not be punished for refusing to adhere to vague or overbroad oaths[19] or for refusing to declare a belief in God.[20] The Court, however, allowed states to require public employees to take oaths of allegiance to state and federal constitutions.[21] Brennan, however, distinguished between oaths in which support for state and federal constitutions was required and oaths requiring support for any constitutional means in opposing the overthrow of the government. He found oaths of the latter vein to be vague and overbroad.[22]

Even when there is a prohibition against uttering words that are "treasonable or seditious," Brennan noted in his 1967 majority opinion in *Keyishian v. Board of Regents*,[23] there must be more specific definitions. "Our experience under the Sedition Act of 1798," he wrote, "taught us that dangers fatal to First Amendment freedoms inhere in the word 'seditious.' "[24] In *Keyishian,* faculty members of public universities in New York, for continued employment, were required to sign oaths certifying that they were not and had never been members of the Communist Party. Noting that the classroom "is peculiarly the 'marketplace of ideas,' " Brennan wrote that "our Nation is deeply committed to safeguarding academic freedom, which is of transcendent value to all of us and not merely to the teachers concerned."[25] Brennan found the oaths overbroad.[26]

Also found to be overbroad was a law denying to a political party a position on the state ballot unless the party certified that it did not advocate the violent overthrow of the government.[27] Brennan, in his majority opinion, noted that the Court had often held that mere advocacy of violence may not be proscribed unless the advocacy was directed to inciting imminent lawless action.[28] There was no reason to make access to the ballot an exception to the rule, he wrote.[29]

Brennan's opinions in cases involving communists often brought the justice mounds of hate mail. In fact, Brennan's opinion in *Keyishian* resulted in as much hate mail as he received on any free-expression case. "You are to be damned for this decision," one person wrote. "God have mercy and take you away." Accompanying the letter was a newspaper clipping on the decision with a photograph of Brennan. The word "stupid" was scrawled across the photograph.[30] Another person wrote "I believe you have struck the worst blow, the death blow, the final take-over blow to our form of government."[31]

In a related case, the Court found that a post office requirement came dangerously close to requiring an oath before certain types of mail could be delivered. The Court did not call the requirement attacked in *Lamont v. Postmaster General*[32] an oath, but used the same rationale in striking down the requirement that it had used in striking down some loyalty oaths: An affirmative statement was required in return for some privilege. In the oath cases the privilege was usually a job; in *Lamont* the privilege was the receipt of mail.

The post office regulation under attack required that an individual sign and return a card requesting mail from so-called subversive organizations before the post office would make delivery. Justice William O. Douglas ruled that the system "requires an official act . . . as a limitation on the unfettered exercise of the addressee's First Amendment Rights" and was, therefore, unconstitutional.[33] Douglas's opinion was short and only addressed the narrow question of whether an addressee must take some affirmative action—in this case to request it in writing—in order to receive mail. Douglas found that the requirement would have a deterrent effect on the receipt of information and, therefore, was at odds "with the 'uninhibited, robust, and wide-open' debate and discussion that are contemplated by the First Amendment."[34]

Brennan joined Douglas, but wrote a concurring opinion going a bit further. The addressees in the case, Brennan noted, rightly argued that the government is powerless to interfere with the delivery of material because of a First Amendment right to receive information:

> It is true that the First Amendment contains no specific guarantee of access to publications. However, the protection of the Bill of Rights goes beyond the specific guarantees to protect from congressional abridgment those equally fundamental personal rights necessary to make the express guarantees fully meaningful. . . . I think the right to receive publications is such a fundamental right.[35]

The government, Brennan noted, argued that the card system was only a minor inconvenience, did not abridge speech, and was not intended to control the content of speech. Brennan, however, replied that the "inhibition as well as prohibition against the exercise of precious First Amendment rights is a power denied to government." Failure to return the card, he wrote, would not only deny the addressee the delivery of the specific mail listed, but all similar publications. "In any event," he noted, "we cannot sustain an intrusion on First Amendment rights on the ground that the intrusion is only a minor one."[36]

Brennan originally joined Douglas only in the result. Shortly after Brennan circulated his opinion concurring in the judgment, Douglas wrote him:

> I liked your opinion in *Lamont* very much. But since you do not join my opinion, there must be something in it that stands in the way. If there is, and it is remedial, I would be very happy to circulate the necessary revision in order to accommodate your needs and to get a Court for the opinion.[37]

Brennan's papers contain no indication of a reply to Douglas,[38] but Brennan eventually joined Douglas's opinion.

REFUSAL TO RESPOND

Congress's power to investigate is important, Chief Justice Earl Warren wrote in *Watkins v. U.S.*,[39] and it is the duty of all citizens to cooperate with congressional investigations. But, he noted, Congress must also respect individual constitutional rights during investigations.[40]

Watkins was delivered in 1957, the same year as *Kongisberg,* and during the height of congressional investigations into un-American activities. Watkins, testifying before the House Un-American Activities Committee, admitted cooperating with the Communist Party and supporting some communist causes during his term as an officer in a labor union. He denied he was ever a member of the party, however, and refused to answer some questions by committee members as being outside the scope of the investigation. He was found guilty of contempt of Congress, fined $100 and given a one-year suspended jail term.[41]

Warren took the opportunity in *Watkins* to express his disdain for the way the House Un-American Activities Committee operated. While citizens must cooperate with congressional investigatory committees, Warren wrote, those committees must also respect the constitutional rights of each citizen. And "when First Amendment rights are threatened, the delegation of power to the committee must be clearly revealed in its charter."[42] The charter of the House Un-American Activities Committee failed, Warren wrote: "It would be difficult to imagine a less specific authorizing resolution."[43] The committee "conceived of its task in the grand view of its name," and seemed in the business of collecting information only for the sake of collecting. Watkins had not understood the purpose of the inquiry, nor had he been given fair opportunity to determine whether he was within his right to refuse to answer, and, therefore, his conviction for contempt of Congress was invalid.[44]

Watkins was the first in a number of cases in which the Court upheld the right of an individual to refuse to answer questions by investigatory bodies. The Court held, for example, that persons need not answer questions that are not clearly pertinent to the purpose of the investigation,[45] or questions that invade an individual's political freedom, specifically the right to associate with others or to give lectures.[46] And the Court would not allow a lawyer to be denied admission to the bar for refusing to answer questions about personal beliefs. Individual beliefs, the Court held, "are immune from bar association inquisitions."[47]

The right to refuse to answer questions by investigatory committees is not absolute, however. In *Barenblatt v. U.S.*[48] the Court held that the balance between individual rights and state interests may be struck for the state. If the investigation is valid and there is no pertinent objection to the questions, an individual has the responsibility to cooperate with the committee and respond to the questions.[49] The Court reinforced the ruling two years later in *Wilkinson v. U.S.*[50] Brennan dissented in both cases, arguing that the purpose of the questioning in both cases was harrassment and exposure for the sake of exposure.[51]

CONCLUSIONS

The Supreme Court has repeatedly said that the refusal to speak—in cases involving overbroad oaths of allegiance and overbroad questions by investigatory committees—may not be punished under the First Amendment. Oaths of allegiance must be narrowly tailored to fit certain circumstances—as with oaths by public employees that they will support state and federal constitutions—and investigatory committees may not be in the business of collecting information merely for the sake of collecting.

When the oaths proscribed certain types of speech, Brennan wrote that the methods of identifying those types of speech "must be subjected to close analysis and critical judgment."[52] It was insufficient, Brennan wrote, to proscribe speech using general terms, such as "sedition"[53] or advocacy of the violent overthrow of the government.[54]

In addition, Brennan agreed with Douglas that the right to receive information is fundamental and cannot be limited by requiring the recipient to take an affirmative action in order to benefit from the right.[55] Interference with the right to receive information through the mails, Douglas wrote, quoting Brennan's opinion in *New York Times Co. v. Sullivan*, was at odds "with the 'uninhibited, robust, and wide-open' debate and discussion that are contemplated by the First Amendment."[56]

Brennan was also with the Court when it held that investigatory committees could not infringe upon First Amendment rights by requiring responses to questions that were overbroad or irrelevant to specific issues under investigations. Brennan was often more protective than his colleagues, however, finding vague provisions where a majority found none.[57]

NOTES

1. *See, for example,* E. Bayley, Joe McCarthy and the Press (1981), specifically Chapter 1, "When It All Started," at 3–38.

2. Two cases were unrelated to employment or investigatory committees, but were tantamount to requiring oaths. Lamont v. Postmaster General, 381 U.S. 301 (1965), is discussed at *infra* notes 32–38. In Wooley v. Maynard, 430 U.S. 705 (1977), the Court held that New Hampshire could not force a person to disseminate, by license-plate motto, a message with which the person disagreed.

3. 353 U.S. 252 (1957).

4. 357 U.S. 513 (1958).

5. 353 U.S. at 270–73.

6. *Id.* at 260–61

7. Konigsberg v. State Bar of California, 366 U.S. 36 (1961). *See also,* In re Anastapolo, 366 U.S. 82 (1961).

8. *Id.* at 39.

9. *Id.* at 45–49.

10. *Id.* at 80, Justice Brennan dissenting. *See* text accompanying *infra* notes 35–38.

11. 357 U.S. at 514–15.

12. *Id.* at 518.

13. Chief Justice Earl Warren did not participate.

14. 357 U.S. at 520.

15. *Id.* at 521.

16. *Id.* at 525–26.

17. *Id.* at 526.

18. *Id.* at 529. *See also* First Unitarian Church v. Los Angeles, 357 U.S. 545 (1958).

19. Cramp v. Board of Public Instruction of Orange County, Florida, 368 U.S. 278 (1961); Keyishian v. Board of Regents of University of New York, 385 U.S. 589 (1967); Baggett v. Bullitt, 377 U.S. 360 (1974). *See also* Connell v. Higginbotham, 403 U.S. 207 (1971).

20. Torcaso v. Watkins, 367 U.S. 488 (1961).

21. Cole v. Richardson, 405 U.S. 676 (1972). *See also* Connell v. Higginbotham, 403 U.S. 207 (1971).

22. *Cole,* 405 U.S. at 691, Justice Marshall dissenting (joined by Justice Brennan).

23. 385 U.S. 589 (1967).

24. *Id.* at 598.

25. *Id.* at 603.

26. *Id.* at 609.

27. Communist Party of Indiana v. Whitcomb, 414 U.S. 441, 442–44 (1974).

28. *Id.* at 448.

29. *Id.* at 449.

30. Brennan Papers, Box 155.

31. *Id.*

32. 381 U.S. 301 (1965).

33. *Id.* at 304.

34. *Id.* at 307, quoting New York Times Co. v. Sullivan, 376 U.S. 254, 270 (1964).

35. *Id.* at 308, Justice Brennan concurring.

36. *Id.* at 309, Justice Brennan concurring.

37. Brennan Papers, Box 129, May 17, 1965, memorandum from Justice Douglas to Justice Brennan.

38. Brennan Papers, Box 129.

39. 354 U.S. 178 (1957).

40. *Id.* at 187–88.

41. *Id.* at 181–86.

42. *Id.* at 198.

43. *Id.* at 202.

44. *Id.* at 414–15. *See also* Scull v. Virginia, 359 U.S. 234 (1957).

45. Sacher v. U.S. 356 U.S. 576 (1958).

46. Sweezy v. New Hampshire, 354 U.S. 234 (1957). *See also* Shelton v. Tucker, 364 U.S. 479 (1960); and Schneider v. Smith, 390 U.S. 17 (1968).

47. Baird v. State Bar of Arizona, 401 U.S. 1, 8 (1971). *See also,* In re Stolar, 401 U.S. 23 (1971).

48. 360 U.S. 109 (1959).

49. *Id.* at 123–34.

50. 365 U.S. 399 (1961). *See also,* Braden v. U.S. 365 U.S. 431 (1961).

51. *Barenblatt,* 360 U.S. at 166, Justice Brennan dissenting; *Wilkinson,* 365 U.S. at 429, Justice Brennan dissenting.

52. *Speiser,* 357 U.S. at 520.

53. *Keyishian,* 385 U.S. at 598.

54. *Whitcomb,* 414 U.S. at 448–49.

55. *Lamont,* 381 U.S. at 308, Justice Brennan concurring.

56. 381 U.S. at 307, quoting New York Times Co. v. Sullivan, 376 U.S. 254, 270 (1964).

57. *Barenblatt,* 360 U.S. at 166, Justice Brennan dissenting; *Wilkinson,* 365 U.S. at 429, Justice Brennan dissenting.

4

"A Heavy Presumption"

The intent of the framers of the Bill of Rights in writing "Congress shall make no law . . . abridging the freedom of speech or of the press" has long been hotly debated by journalists, attorneys, judges, and scholars.[1] Upon one point, however, there seems to be almost uniform agreement: At a minimum, the First Amendment was intended to forbid prior restraint.[2] Most writers who have addressed the issue also agree on a second point: The prohibition against prior restraint is not absolute; the Constitution permits censorship in some circumstances.[3] The question is where the line is to be drawn.

Justice Brennan believed the line should be drawn to grant the sturdiest protection possible. He found that the chief purpose of the First Amendment was to protect against prior restraint.[4] For that reason, any system of prior restraint comes to the Court "bearing a heavy presumption against its constitutional validity."[5] He would allow prior restraint only in exceptional cases,[6] and only then when the system of restraint assured "an almost immediate judicial determination of the validity of the restraint."[7] Otherwise, prior restraint was among the most obnoxious methods of restricting expression.

It is not allowed, Brennan believed, when it is based on the content of the expression[8] or when it is arbitrarily applied by government,[9] even when the rationale for the restraint is to protect citizens or organizations.[10] Such a "paternalistic premise" is unsound.[11] Prior restraint could not be used to ban a play because it was controversial,[12] a film because it espoused unorthodox ideas,[13] or information about contraceptives because it may be embarrassing or offensive.[14] Nor could it be used to keep white supremacists from holding a rally even when they advocated violence as a means of accomplishing political reform.[15] Prior restraint is never permissible when applied to halt information about judicial proceedings, "no matter how shabby the means by which the information is obtained,"[16] Brennan wrote, nor is it permissible to stop the activities of critics of the government, even if those activities might be "perceived as harming national security."[17] Only when a publication causes an inevitable danger to national security, he indicated, may it be censored.[18]

Brennan also believed, although he was in the minority, that it was unconstitutional prior restraint for the government to halt its employees from participating in political campaigns,[19] to halt prisoners from forming unions[20] or granting interviews to the press,[21] or to halt students from publishing unpopular ideas in a high school newspaper.[22]

This is not to say that Brennan believed the government had no censorship authority at all. Indeed, his primary thesis regarding prior restraint—that there is a heavy presumption against its constitutionality—implicitly indicates that there are instances in which the heavy presumption can be met and restraint would be allowed. It could be met, for example, if the government showed that a publication would cause a direct and immediate harm to national security.[23] And, while Brennan never voted in support of film censorship boards, his writings indicated that if procedural safeguards are met and the burden of proof is placed on the censor, the boards may pass constitutional muster.[24] He has also indicated that some prior restraint in schools and prisons would be constitutional. He has written that the First Amendment rights of students at school are not coextensive with the rights of adults in other settings[25] and must be accorded in light of the special circumstances of the school.[26] And he has agreed that mail to and from prisoners may be censored under certain circumstances.[27]

Brennan has also indicated that the right to distribute information must be balanced against the individual's right to be left alone. He joined an opinion in which Chief Justice Warren Burger wrote that there is no constitutional right for a person to send unwanted material into the home of another. To rule otherwise, Burger wrote, would be to license a form of trespass. "If this prohibition operates to impede the flow of even valid ideas," Burger wrote, "the answer is that no one has a right to press even 'good' ideas on an unwilling recipient."[28] Brennan wrote a short concurrence emphasizing that parents may not have the right to prevent adult children living at the same address form receiving mail.[29] He had attempted to have Burger add the statement to the majority opinion, but the chief justice refused, prompting the concurrence.[30]

Although he would allow some prior restraint, Brennan was one of the Court's staunchest defenders against attempts to censor. Only three times in fifty-one cases did Brennan vote to allow some prior restrictions on publications, and none of those votes can be seen as restrictive of speech.[31] Brennan wrote eight majority, one plurality, and three *per curiam* opinions in prior-restraint cases.[32] In addition, he wrote five concurring opinions and five dissenting opinions.

THEORIES OF PRIOR RESTRAINT

Brennan began developing his theories on prior restraint early on. In 1963 he wrote his first majority opinion in a censorship case and established the doctrine that there is a heavy burden to overcome before the government can keep material from being published. In the line of cases that followed, Brennan fleshed out criteria according to which the burden may—and may not—be met.

The 1963 case was *Bantam Books v. Sullivan*.[33] Four book publishers were challenging the constitutionality of the Rhode Island Commission to Encourage Morality in Youth, an organization created by the Rhode Island Legislature to attempt to control material that tended to corrupt young people. The commission would notify distributors when they were disseminating material the commission determined to be questionable.

Brennan, writing for seven members of the Court, identified the practice as informal censorship[34] that allowed the government to circumvent established obscenity law.[35] He found the system to be unconstitutional and, in what would become an oft-quoted passage in later prior restraint cases, wrote that "any system of prior restraints of expression comes to this Court bearing a heavy presumption against its constitutional validity."[36]

This is not to say that there could never be prior restraint by the government, Brennan indicated. A system of prior restraint could only be tolerated, he wrote, if it "operated under judicial superintendence and assured an almost immediate judicial determination of the validity of the restraint."[37] A system of prior restraint, therefore, had to meet certain criteria, none of which the Rhode Island system met. It had no provision for judicial superintendence, no notice of hearing before the publications became identified as objectionable, and no definition of "objectionable." In addition, the statute was vague, and, although it was aimed at protecting youth, it also deprived adults of opportunities to purchase the publications. It was, therefore, "radically deficient."[38]

In an early draft of his opinion, Brennan showed his contempt for the manner in which members of the commission attempted to circumvent obscenity law by intimidation. He wrote that they had "threatened, cajoled, and misrepresented their powers and acted as an agency not to advise but to suppress."[39] Brennan cut the language from the final draft of his opinion, however, upon the suggestion of Justice Byron White.[40]

Two years later, Brennan had the opportunity once again to address criteria under which prior restraint would be allowed. *Freedman v. Maryland*[41] involved a film exhibitor who refused to submit a film to the Maryland

film review board, as required by state law. The facts in the case were
similar to those of *Times Film Corp. v. Chicago*,[42] which had been settled
four years earlier. The Court, in *Times Film,* ruled that Chicago was correct in its assertion that it had a "duty to protect its people against the
dangers of obscenity in the public exhibition of motion pictures."[43] Brennan joined a dissent written by Chief Justice Earl Warren complaining that
the Court was granting the city the unlimited power to censor motion
pictures. The opinion, Warren wrote, "presents a real danger of eventual
censorship for every form of communication, be it newspapers, journals,
books, magazines, television, radio or public speeches."[44]

The Court had also ruled that motion pictures could not be denied licenses because of the ideas they espoused. *Lady Chatterly's Lover* had been
denied a license because it purportedly portrayed adultery as acceptable.[45]
The Court reversed the denial. Wrote Justice Potter Stewart for the majority:

> What New York has done, therefore, is to prevent the exhibition of a mo-
> tion picture because that picture advocates an idea—that adultery under cer-
> tain circumstances may be proper behavior. Yet the First Amendment's basic
> guarantee is of freedom to advocate ideas. The state, quite simply, has thus
> struck at the very heart of constitutionally protected liberty.[46]

Freedman, however, could be distinguished from the two previous cases.
The license in *Freedman* was denied not because of the content of the film,
but because the film was not submitted for review. And the film exhibitor
in *Freedman* did not challenge film review boards, but argued that the
Maryland statute was unconstitutional because it was procedurally flawed.[47]
The Court agreed. "Applying the settled rule of our cases," Brennan wrote,
"we hold that a noncriminal process which requires the prior submission
of a film to a censor avoids constitutional infirmity only if it takes place
under procedural safeguards designed to obviate the dangers of a censorship system."[48] What that meant, Brennan wrote, was that, first, the burden of proving that the film was not protected expression must rest on
the censor, and, second, the censor may not have final determination.[49]
"To this end," Brennan wrote, "the exhibitor must be assured, by statute
or authoritative judicial construction, that the censor will, within a speci-
fied brief period, either issue a license or go to court to restrain showing
the film."[50]

In these early cases, therefore, Brennan began to establish a theory of
prior restraint that he would apply to later cases: Prior restraint, although
allowed under the constitution, is presumptively unconstitutional, and the
government faces a heavy burden when it attempts to act as a censor. In
some cases the burden is virtually insurmountable—when the government

requires licensing, bans commentary on matters of public concern, or otherwise restricts speech based on the content of that speech.

An example of Brennan's hard-line approach to prior restraint is *Nebraska Press Association v. Stuart*.[51] The case began when Erwin Charles Simants was arraigned for the murder of six members of the Henry Kellie family in Sutherland, Nebraska. Upon the request of the county prosecutor and Simants's attorney, Judge Hugh Stuart entered an order restraining the press from reporting on any testimony or other evidence taken during a preliminary hearing.

Writing for the majority, Burger, after a dissertation on the importance of fair trials and a free press, and citing Brennan's language in *Bantam Books,* found the gag order to be unconstitutional.[52] Burger wrote, however, that under some circumstances the necessity of guaranteeing a fair trial might make a gag order justifiable. Before a gag order would be constitutional, Burger wrote, the trial judge must determine "(a) the nature and extent of pretrial news coverage; (b) whether other measures would be likely to mitigate the effects of unrestrained pretrial publicity; and (c) how effectively a restraining order would operate to prevent the threatened danger."[53]

Brennan would have nothing to do with formulas on the reporting of judicial proceedings. Acknowledging that the right to a fair trial is precious and sacred, Brennan wrote, in his opinion concurring with the judgment, that "resort to prior restraints on the freedom of the press is a constitutionally impermissible method for enforcing that right."[54] The press guards against miscarriages of justice, he noted, and "commentary and reporting on the criminal justice system is at the core of First Amendment values, for the operation and integrity of that system is of crucial import to citizens concerned with the administration of government."[55] Therefore, there can be no prior restraints on press for the publication of information pertaining to pending judicial proceedings or the operation of the criminal justice system, he wrote, "no matter how shabby the means by which the information is obtained."[56]

Justices Thurgood Marshall and Potter Stewart joined Brennan's opinion, and Justices Lewis Powell and John Paul Stevens came close to joining, but were unwilling to accept Brennan's bar on prior restraint. The bar had been a sticky point in the early discussions on the case. A month before the opinion was delivered, Brennan indicated in a memorandum that he believed the consensus of the Conference had been "forever to bar prior restraint against pretrial publicity."[57] Burger responded "If the Conference consensus was as you suggest, to 'forever bar prior restraint' on pretrial publicity, I would be prepared to articulate that, but that is not my recollection. I will await other responses."[58] Powell responded that he could not accept the rule,[59] as did Stevens, who noted, however, that Brennan's opinion "comes closer to expressing my views than does the opinion prepared by the Chief Justice."[60] The bar did not make it into the majority opinion, therefore.

The restraints imposed in *Nebraska Press Association* were particularly obnoxious to Brennan because they restricted information and commentary about an area of public importance. Since the business of the press was to report on matters of public importance, therefore, rarely could restraints on the press stand.[61] A prime example is *New York Times Co. v. U.S.*[62] Brennan's short *per curiam* opinion for six members of the Court[63] allowed the *New York Times,* the *Washington Post,* and other newspapers to continue publishing a series of articles based on a top secret government report that had been surreptitiously copied by Pentagon employee Daniel Ellsberg and provided to the *Times.* There was little agreement, however, as to why the newspapers could continue publishing: Nine opinions accompanied the *per curiam.*

Justices Hugo L. Black and William O. Douglas were most adamant in their opinions, arguing that the government could never restrain the press.[64] Brennan came next. He would allow restraint, but only in certain circumstances, and not in the Pentagon Papers case. In his concurring opinion he wrote that none of the injunctions against the newspapers should have been granted. "The First Amendment," he wrote, "stands as an absolute bar to the imposition of judicial restraints in circumstances of the kind presented by these cases."[65] Wrote Brennan:

> The entire thrust of the Government's claim throughout these cases has been that publication of the material sought to be enjoined "could," or "might," or "may" prejudice the national interest in various ways. But the First Amendment tolerates absolutely no prior judicial restraints of the press predicated upon surmise or conjecture that untoward consequences may result.[66]

Restraint, therefore, is only permitted when the government can prove "that publication must inevitably, directly, and immediately cause the occurrence of an event kindred to imperiling the safety of a transport already at sea."[67]

Brennan made a similar point in his dissent to *Haig v. Agee.*[68] In that case, the passport of Philip Agee had been revoked because Agee had vowed to take whatever action necessary to disrupt U.S. intelligence operations abroad. The sweep of the action was too broad, Brennan wrote, and would encompass persons who disagree with government foreign policy as well as persons whose activities might actually damage national security. "Philip Agee is hardly a model representative of our Nation," Brennan wrote, "but just as the Constitution protects both popular and unpopular speech, it likewise protects both popular and unpopular travelers."[69]

THEORIES OF PRIOR RESTRAINT APPLIED

Except for Black and Douglas, the members of the Court agreed that prior restraint, although presumptively unconstitutional, was to be tolerated in some circumstances. They agreed, for example, that time, place, and manner restrictions were acceptable, and that speech within certain identifiable contexts—the speech of prison inmates and school students, for example—could be restricted. The disagreement came when members began drawing the restrictive lines. Brennan would typically grant more protection than his colleagues.

Such was the case in *Pell v. Procunier*[70] and *Saxbe v. Washington Post.*[71] Brennan recognized that the unique setting of the prison required limitations on prisoners' rights, but maintained that First Amendment rights still attached, particularly when representatives of the press were seeking interviews with named prisoners who wanted to be interviewed. The question in both cases was whether the press has the First Amendment right to interview specific prisoners who sought to be interviewed. In addition, in *Pell* the Court faced a second question of whether the prisoners themselves enjoyed the First Amendment right of access to the press in such situations. The Court ruled against the press and the prisoners, dismissing the First Amendment claims in favor of the need by prison officials to maintain order and discipline.

In *Saxbe,* Brennan joined Powell's dissent, which noted that neither news organizations nor reporters have constitutional rights that are not enjoyed by other persons,[72] but recognized the role of the press as an agent of the public, providing essential information that enabled the public "to assert meaningful control over the political process."[73] Unrestrained public access to prisons is not allowed for good reason, Powell wrote, but the absolute ban of prisoner press interviews negates the ability of the press to discharge its constitutionally established role.[74]

Douglas, who Brennan joined in *Pell,* took a similar tack. He called the restrictions "grossly overbroad."[75] The interest of a free press is enjoyed by society as well as the media, he wrote, and "the right of the people, the true sovereigns under our constitutional scheme, to govern in an informed manner" is at stake.[76] The operations of the prisons are the responsibility of the public, he wrote, and since the public will not be able to inspect the prisons, it is left for the press to inspect and inform so the public can act.[77]

In *Jones v. North Carolina Prisoners' Union,*[78] the Court held that prison officials could deny prisoners the right to establish a union because the union might be disruptive. Brennan joined Marshall, who dissented on grounds that the record contained no evidence of an intent to disrupt prison operations or of possible disruption, and that prisoners' First Amendment rights had been violated.[79] Marshall, again joined by Brennan, also took a narrower view than the Court in *Procunier v. Martinez* as well,[80] a case involving the censorship of prisoner mail. Marshall agreed that the mail of prisoners could be censored in some circumstances, but wrote that prison officials have no right to open and read all incoming and outgoing prisoner mail as a matter of course.[81]

Similarly, Brennan was willing to acknowledge that the free-speech rights of students were not coextensive with those of adults outside the schools, but found the threshold for implementing restraint to be higher than that of his colleagues.

In *Hazelwood School District v. Kuhlmeier*,[82] the Court ruled that a principal had a right to censor a school newspaper because he did not believe material published in the newspaper fit with the goals of the school. Robert E. Reynolds, principal of Hazelwood East High School in St. Louis, unilaterally cut two pages from an issue of the school newspaper because he believed two articles were inappropriate for students at the school. One article dealt with teenage pregnancy, the other with divorce.

White, writing for five members of the Court, found no First Amendment violation. He wrote: "We hold that educators do not offend the First Amendment by exercising editorial control over the style and content of student speech in school-sponsored expressive activities so long as their actions are reasonably related to legitimate pedagogical concerns."[83]

The First Amendment, Brennan responded, allows "no such blanket censorship" of student speech simply because the speech might be incompatible with the school's pedagogical message.[84] Even though the First Amendment rights of students are not automatically coextensive with the rights of adults in other settings, "public educators must accommodate some student expression even if it offends them or offers views or values that contradict those the school wishes to inculcate."[85] Brennan found that the *Hazelwood* opinion overruled *Tinker v. Des Moines School District*,[86] the 1969 case in which the Court held that students do not "shed their constitutional rights to freedom of speech or expression at the schoolhouse gate."[87]

In *Tinker*, three students were suspended from school because they wore black armbands in protest of the Vietnam War and in violation of a hastily approved school policy against such displays. Justice Abe Fortas, writing for the majority, held that the action was "closely akin to 'pure speech' "[88] and could not be restricted without some showing of a likelihood of disruption.[89]

Both *Hazelwood* and *Tinker* dealt with student expression. The Court addressed another aspect of prior restraint in the schools in *Board of Education, Island Trees v. Pico*,[90] a case that aptly demonstrates the vociferousness with which the justices could discuss this issue.

In July 1976, the school board of the Island Trees Union Free School District No. 26 in New York ordered nine books removed from school libraries. The board took the action after rejecting the recommendations of a committee it had appointed to examine library books that were possibly objectionable and ignoring school system policy on dealing with objectionable books. Students brought action asking for declaratory and injunctive relief. The district court dismissed the case, but the Second U.S. Circuit Court of Appeals reversed and remanded the case for trial.[91] The Supreme Court affirmed the circuit court's ruling, but there was no majority opinion.

Brennan, in an opinion joined by Marshall and Stewart, found that the school board violated the First Amendment rights of the students. Justices Harry Blackmun and Byron White concurred in the judgment, Blackmun writing that the First Amendment issues should be more narrowly addressed,[92] and White agreeing that the case should be remanded for trial, but writing that the First Amendment issues need not be addressed at all.[93]

School boards have broad discretion, Brennan wrote, but must operate within the guarantees of the First Amendment.[94] Students retain their First Amendment rights, he noted, even though those rights must be accorded in light of the special circumstances of the school setting.[95] "The right to receive ideas is a necessary predicate to the recipient's meaningful exercise of his own rights of speech, press, and political freedoms,"[96] Brennan wrote, and the school library is the "primary locus" of the freedom to inquire.[97]

While school systems have the right to determine the content of school libraries, Brennan wrote, the discretion may not be exercised in a narrowly partisan or political manner,[98] and officials may not suppress ideas. Therefore, the motives for removing books from a school library are important.[99] It would be permissible to remove books that are "pervasively vulgar" or because they are not educationally suitable.[100]

"This would be a very different case of the record demonstrated that petitioners had employed established, regular, and facially unbiased procedures for the review of controversial materials," Brennan wrote, but just the opposite had occurred.[101] The school board ignored the advice of literary experts, teachers, librarians, and the superintendent of schools.[102] The board also ignored the superintendent's advice to go through an in-place policy to handle such situations, and it rejected, without explanation, the recommendations of the committee it had appointed.[103]

Justices Warren Burger, Lewis Powell, William Rehnquist, and Sandra Day O'Connor filed dissenting opinions, Rehnquist's being the most virulent.

Rehnquist wrote that Brennan had launched "into a confusing, discursive exegesis on . . . constitutional issues as applied to junior high and high school libraries" before addressing the record. Brennan also violated the Court's practice "not to decide abstract, hypothetical or contingent questions, or to decide any constitutional question in advance of the necessity for its decision"[104] and only addressed "snippets and excerpts of the relevant facts."[105]

Rehnquist spent sixteen pages attacking the plurality opinion, referring to Brennan by name in almost every paragraph. He concluded that the actions of the school board were "hard to distinguish from the myriad of choices made by school boards in the routine supervision of elementary and secondary schools," interference from which the Court should abstain.[106] He found no infringement of First Amendment rights and wrote that, by the admission of the students, no ideas had been suppressed.[107]

The virulence of the dissent is due to the maneuvering that occurred in deliberations on the case, which resulted in the dissenters being foiled in their effort to find for the school board. The Court accepted the case upon the vote of the dissenters—Rehnquist, Burger, Powell, and O'Connor— who obviously believed they could swing a fifth vote, probably Blackmun or White. Brennan, Stevens, Marshall, Blackmun, and White had voted to deny *certiorari*. Only after considerable juggling and finger-pointing— some of which very nearly became public—did the justices who voted to deny *certiorari* end up together on the judgment, while the justices who voted to grant ended up dissatisfied with the outcome and, therefore, critical of their colleagues.

On May 4, 1982, Brennan circulated a draft of his opinion to Stevens, Marshall, Blackmun, and White, asking for their reactions before he circulated it to the Conference, and indicating that it was an "effort to write as narrowly as the case permits. That was the desire of the five of us, as I recall it."[108] Stevens and White had problems with the opinion.[109] Brennan redrafted, eventually satisfying Stevens, but White's concerns remained. He indicated to Brennan that he wanted to settle the issue on procedural rather than constitutional grounds. And he questioned Brennan's presumption that the school library was essentially different from other aspects of the educational system: "I also doubt that the standard you propose for the school library in which a student could independently browse could be so easily isolated from the question of what books may be used in the school curriculum or for assigned outside reading."[110]

In response, Brennan wrote that he found it essential to settle the case on First Amendment grounds so the district court would have a standard to use on remand.[111] Brennan suggested a change in his opinion, however, focusing on the point that school boards could not constitutionally remove books for partisan or political reasons, but that they retained discretion in the addition of books.[112] The changes did not satisfy White, who eventually concurred in the judgment.

In the meantime, Burger circulated an opinion with a memorandum soliciting four joiners.[113] He was unsuccessful. Powell, Rehnquist, and O'Connor all indicated they would write separately,[114] leaving Burger without the majority he sought.

Failing to derail a finding for the students through opinion-writing, Burger attempted another tack. Brennan had suggested to the chief justice in a telephone conversation that the Court expedite the case because the remaining student involved was soon to graduate; graduation might make the case moot. The possibility of mootness had been raised during oral arguments in the case on March 2, but Burger had forgotten this, until Brennan's call. He wrote Brennan:

> This raises another question, at least for me, but since I am in the minority the majority position controls. Is it not a bit odd that the Court strains so mightily to get down a plurality opinion on an important constitutional question 24–48 hours before it is mooted? I may add a footnote observation on this score to my dissent.[115]

The proposed footnote, which Burger circulated to the Conference June 22, purported to remind the justices of two long-standing tenets of the Court: that constitutional issues should be avoided when possible, and that the Court should practice self-restraint. Burger also wrote in the footnote:

> The sole surviving plaintiff has therefore either recently been graduated from high school or is within days or even hours of graduation. Yet the plurality strains mightily to reach out to express its views on a very important constitutional issue. . . . Far from exercising self-restraint, the plurality races to reach, although happily cannot resolve in any binding way, the critical constitutional issues initially raised.[116]

The added footnote brought an immediate response from Brennan. The record was void as to the graduation of the remaining plaintiff, Brennan wrote in a memo he circulated to the Conference. He wrote:

> I have always thought that we decided cases on the basis of the record before us, not on the basis of vague references at oral argument. The plain fact of the matter is that we just do not know whether the case will be moot "hours" from Friday, as you suggest. . . . and it would simply be an abdication of our constitutional responsibility to sit around waiting for the case to become moot.[117]

As for determining the constitutional issue in the case, Brennan wrote that Burger indicated his willingness to do so when he voted—with Powell, Rehnquist, and O'Connor—to grant *certiorari*. "Thus," Brennan wrote, "it seems to me strange that you should now take the view that the issue has somehow become too important to decide: especially strange since you are now in dissent."[118] The Court had possessed information about the possible graduation of the final plaintiff and had known the importance of the case for many months, Brennan wrote, concluding: "In my view, nothing has changed since then except that time has passed—and that you, who voted to grant, are now in dissent." [119]

In addition, the day after Burger's circulation, Stevens circulated a concurring opinion he proposed to deliver in response to Burger's footnote. The opinion read:

> When the Court acted on the petition for certiorari in this case, it was apparent that two reasons, both unrelated to the merits, would have justified a denial of the petition. First, the case was in an interlocutory posture, since it had not yet been tried; second, there was a possibility that it might become moot before final decision. One of those reasons prompted me to vote to deny certiorari. I find it ironic that the four members of the Court who voted to grant certiorari now elect to criticize the Court for discharging its responsibilities after taking jurisdiction in the case. [120]

In a footnote to the concurrence Stevens also reported that one method of avoiding a constitutional question—a method the justices do not consider acceptable—is simply to delay a decision until the case becomes moot—an apparent suggestion to the effect that Burger was proposing just such an avenue. [121]

In his memorandum, Brennan had named the four justices who had voted to accept the case, but the memorandum was circulated only to the Conference. Stevens, on the other hand, proposed to make public through his concurring opinion the justices voting to accept the case, a rare action and one that brought an immediate response from the chief justice. There should be no public disclosure of a vote on *certiorari,* Burger wrote Stevens the same day. Burger offered, therefore, to alter his footnote if Stevens withdrew his concurrence. The redrafted footnote still called for judicial restraint but eliminated the biting language critical of the majority. [122] Stevens withdrew his concurrence. [123]

Although the case was delivered without a majority opinion, five members of the Court voted against the school board, so that the four justices who thought they would be able to give the students their come-uppance were disappointed.

A key point in Brennan's *Island Trees* opinion was the arbitrary action of the school board. Brennan made a special point of noting that had the board acted within its established procedure, the outcome might have been different. It was a point Brennan had made in other cases as well. In *Lehman v. Shaker Heights* [124] the Court ruled that a city had a right to deny a political candidate advertising space on city buses, just as a newspaper can decide what advertisements to accept and reject. [125] Brennan disagreed. When the city opened the buses for advertising, it created a public forum, and the arbitrary denial of space to a political candidate was content-based discrimination. [126] And, in *Lakewood v. Plain Dealer Publishing Co.,* [127] Brennan, for the Court, held that a city's unbridled discretion in allowing newsracks was tantamount to prior restraint.

REPRISALS FOR SPEECH

Punishing a speaker for publishing a message that has been deemed improper is a method of controlling expression closely akin to prior restraint. Prior restraint kills a message before it is heard; reprisals punish for the publication of the message. In the second case, therefore, the material has at least seen the light of day—it is in the marketplace of ideas. The purpose of punishing expression goes beyond the single publication in question, however; the primary purpose for the punishment is often to keep similar expressions from the marketplace. Both philosophically and practically, then, prior restraint and postpublication reprisals are forms of censorship.

Stevens made just this point in his dissenting opinion to *Snepp v. U.S.*[128] The Court had upheld a district court's ruling that proceeds from a book written by Frank W. Snepp, III, be placed in a constructive trust for use by the government. The district court's rationale was that Snepp, a former CIA agent, had breached a contract with the agency when, without pre-publication review, he published *Decent Interval,* a book critical of the agency's activities in South Vietnam.[129]

Stevens, joined by Brennan and Marshall, argued that the Court had fashioned "a drastic new remedy . . . to enforce a species of prior restraint on a citizen's right to criticize his government."[130] Stevens wrote that the only purpose for the prior review of the book was to determine whether it included classified information. Since the CIA admitted that the book contained no classified information, the remedy was improper, even though Snepp admitted that he breached his duty to submit the manuscript.[131] That was not the only reason Stevens found the remedy improper: The contract Snepp signed with the CIA provided only that he could be terminated or incarcerated should he publish classified information, so those should have been the only allowable remedies.[132]

Snepp is one example of how reprisals can be successfully used to squelch criticism of the government. Because it was a successful attempt, the case is an aberration, but there have been many efforts. And, as with *Snepp,* most of the reprisals were in the form of depriving a speaker of something he had earned, usually a job or position. That happened twelve times during Brennan's term; in each case Brennan voted against allowing the reprisal to stand. In eight additional cases, other forms of punishment were meted out in response to the controversial speech. The Court held, for example, that a sheriff could not be held in contempt of court because of his out-of-court criticisms of a judge,[133] and that a newspaper could not be punished for publishing the name of a juvenile delinquent.[134] In all but one case Brennan would not have allowed the punishment to stand.[135]

The most common reprisal receiving Court attention during the Brennan years was dismissal from employment, usually dismissal from employment in a public agency. The Court was required to balance the state's interest in squelching speech against the employee's interest in exercising his free-speech rights. In most instances, the Court allowed the balance to swing to the employee.

The line of cases that determined when employees could be dismissed for speech-related activities began with *Pickering v. Board of Education,*[136] in which the Court held that there must be a balance between the interests of the employee, as a citizen, in commenting on matters of public concern and the interests of the state, as employer, in promoting the efficiency of the public services it performs through its employees. While the public employer must ensure that the operations of his office be maintained, "the threat of dismissal from public employment is . . . a potent means of inhibiting speech" and must not be abused.[137]

In *Pickering,* a schoolteacher had written a letter to the editor of a local newspaper critical of the school board's attempt to pass a bond referendum for additional funding and criticizing the board for appropriating too much money for athletics. The teacher had incorrectly stated the amount of the appropriation to athletics, but the Court held that the mistake was not reckless. Teachers, Marshall wrote for eight members of the Court, do not relinquish their First Amendment rights when they accept their positions,[138] and may not be proscribed from discussing matters of public concern.[139] The statements made by the teacher, he wrote, did not impede the proper performance of his duties or the regular operation of the schools.[140] Wrote Marshall:

> In these circumstances we conclude that the interest of the school administration is limiting teachers' opportunities to contribute to public debate is not significantly greater than its interest in limiting a similar contribution by any member of the general public.[141]

In *Pickering,* then, the dispositive issue was whether the speech in question involved matters of public concern. Marshall also noted that although false information was distributed by the speaker, there was no recklessness. The Court would later uphold the firing of an employee who made a recklessly false speech.[142]

In some cases, speech involving matters of public concern was easy to identify. The Court unanimously held, for example, that Julian Bond could not be denied his seat in the Georgia House of Representatives because he made statements critical of U.S. involvement in Vietnam.[143] In the opinion for the Court, Warren called on Brennan's opinion in a libel case to make his primary point:

> The central commitment of the First Amendment, as summarized in the opinion of the Court in *New York Times Co. v. Sullivan* . . . is that "debate on public issues should be uninhibited, robust, and wide-open." We think the rationale of the *New York Times* case disposes of the claim that Bond's statements fell outside the range of constitutional protections.[144]

Other cases were not so easy. Not all justices agreed with the Court's holding, for example, that speech intimating that the president of the United States should be shot was constitutionally protected because it involved matters of public concern.

Ardith McPherson was an employee of the constable's office of Harris County, Texas, when she learned on March 30, 1981, of an apparent attempt on the life of President Ronald Reagan. A coworker overheard her tell a friend that "if they go for him again, I hope they get him." The coworker reported the remark to the county constable, who fired McPherson.[145]

Marshall, writing for the majority, determined that the threshold question in applying the balancing test established in *Pickering v. Board of Education* was whether the comments constituted speech on a matter of public concern.[146] In doing so, Marshall, as had Warren, drew on Brennan's opinion in *New York Times v. Sullivan,* indicating that "debate on public issues should be uninhibited, robust, and wide-open, and . . . may well include vehement, caustic, and sometimes unpleasantly sharp attacks on government and public officials."[147] While a threat on the life of a president would not be protected, Marshall found that McPherson's statement was made in the course of a conversation addressing the policies of the Reagan administration and "plainly dealt with a matter of public concern."[148] He also found that the state's interest in discharging McPherson did not outweigh her First Amendment rights, particularly since there was no evidence that the statement interfered with the functioning of the office and since she made the statement in a private conversation with a close friend rather than in public.[149]

Justice Antonin Scalia, joined by Rehnquist, White, and O'Connor disagreed, arguing that the statement was not on a matter of public concern and that First Amendment rights were not implicated.[150]

Nineteen years earlier, the Court had drawn on the same language from Brennan's opinion in *Times v. Sullivan* to decide a similar case. During the turbulent Vietnam War era, a man had been convicted for saying that if he was drafted and made to carry a rifle, the first man he wanted to get in his sights was President Lyndon B. Johnson.[151] The Court said in a *per curiam* opinion joined by five justices that the language did not amount to a threat on the president's life and that the statute prohibiting presidential threats must be weighed "against the background of a profound national commitment to the principle that debate on public issues should be uninhibited, robust, and wide-open."[152]

Members of the Court also disagreed on whether speech involved matters of public concern in *Connick v. Myers*.[153] In that case, the Court allowed the dismissal of an assistant district attorney who had circulated a survey in the district attorney's office soliciting opinions on office policies and office morale. The Court found that the material addressed in the questionnaire was not public concern and that the dismissal did not violate the First Amendment. Brennan disagreed:

> We have long recognized that one of the central purposes of the First Amendment's guarantee of freedom of expression is to protect the dissemination of information on the basis of which members of our society may make reasoned decisions about the government.[154]

And, quoting *Mills v. Alabama,* he added:

> Whatever differences may exist about interpretations of the First Amendment, there is practically universal agreement that a major purpose of that Amendment was to protect the free discussion of governmental affairs. This of course includes discussions of candidates, structures and forms of government, the manner in which government is operated or should be operated, and all such matters relating to political processes.[155]

The questionnaire circulated by the assistant district attorney was related to the manner in which government operated. It was, therefore, material of public concern, which Brennan defined as "subjects that could reasonably be expected to be of interest to persons seeking to develop informed opinions about the manner in which the Orleans Parish District Attorney, an elected official charged with managing a vital governmental agency, discharges his responsibilities."[156]

Some twenty-four years earlier, Brennan had come to the defense of another attorney who was in trouble due to speech-related activity. The attorney had been suspended from the practices of law for a year because she made a speech critical of a judge.[157] Brennan, overturning the suspension, said the attorney had the right to criticize the judge and to say the judge was wrong in his view of the law. "Dissenting opinions in our reports are apt to make petitioner's speech look like tame stuff, indeed," he wrote.[158]

As previously indicated, the Court often allowed greater restrictions on the speech activities of certain groups. While the Court would not allow a college student to be expelled for distributing "indecent speech,"[159] for example, it allowed a high school student to be punished for making a lewd speech to an assembly.[160] Brennan concurred in the opinion on grounds that the student was punished not because of the ideas he expressed, but to maintain order in the school.[161]

And, in *Parker v. Levy*,[162] the Court held that an Army doctor could be punished for urging black soldiers not to go to Vietnam and for calling Special Forces personnel murderers. Military personnel maintain their First Amendment rights, Rehnquist wrote for the Court, but "the different character of the military community and of the military mission requires a different application of those protections."[163] Brennan joined Stewart's dissent, arguing that the statute under which the doctor was convicted was vague.[164]

Finally, it should be noted that a claim of a First Amendment violation is not always dispositive. In *Board of Regents v. Roth*,[165] the Court allowed the dismissal of a professor, even though the professor was not told the reason for the dismissal and alleged the dismissal was due to statements he had made critical of the college. David Roth had been hired for a one-year appointment and hiring procedures at the college did not require that he be given a reason for nonrenewal of his contract. The free-speech issue, the Court held, was not before the Court since the district court had yet to accept evidence on that point.[166] Brennan dissented, arguing that the professor's First Amendment and due process rights had been violated.[167]

CONCLUSIONS

Brennan often acknowledged that prior restraint may be allowed under the Constitution, but he rarely found cases in which the government could overcome the "heavy presumption against its constitutional validity."[168] Embarrassing material, unorthodox ideas, offensive conduct, advocacy of illegal action, even a possibility of danger to national security,[169] did not justify governmental censorship. As Brennan wrote in an unheralded 1988 case:

> The First Amendment mandates that we presume that speakers not the government know best what they want to say and how to say it. . . . To this end, the government, even with the purest of motives, may not substitute its judgment as to how best to speak for that of speakers and listeners; free and robust debate cannot thrive if directed by the government.[170]

Brennan's First Amendment theory regarding prior restraint was similar to that of most of his colleagues on the Court. He found the primary purpose of the First Amendment to be the prohibition of prior restraint.[171] But, like most of his colleagues, Brennan did not consider the prohibition on prior restraint to be absolute. So, while there can be no blanket censorship, some forms of speech can be restrained in some circumstances. To pass constitutional muster, the statutes proscribing speech must be nar-

rowly drawn,[172] procedural safeguards must ensure a quick judicial response of the censor's finding,[173] and the burden of proof must rest on the
censor to show that the material should be censored, rather than on the
speaker to prove it should not be censored.[174] The government could not
overcome the burden, therefore, when systems of prior restraint did not
contain proper procedural safeguards,[175] or when censorship laws were
vague.[176]

This formula presumed, of course, that the censorship was not based
merely on the content of the message, but on some government interest
unrelated to content; content-based regulations are always unconstitutional.[177]

Brennan, however, factored another element into his theory of prior
restraint: Speech involving matters of public concern should receive more
substantial protection than other forms of speech. If, as Brennan had written, the central commitment of the First Amendment was to ensure that
"debate on public issues should be ininhibited, robust, and wide–open,"[178]
it only made sense that protection for such speech should be substantial.
Brennan defined matters of public concern as "information on the basis of
which members of our society may make reasoned decisions about the
government,"[179] which included, "discussions of candidates, structures and
forms of government, the manner in which government is operated or
should be operated, and all such matters relating to political processes."[180]

Brennan's definition was broader than that of many of his colleagues.
Based on the definition, Brennan would hold that the government cannot
censor the bigoted speech of white supremacists because it constitutes political speech[181]; it cannot proscribe governmental employees from participating in political campaigns because "free discussion of governmental
affairs is basic in our constitutional system"[182]; and it cannot stop the speech-
related activity of critics of government, even if that activity would tend
to hamper governmental operations.[183] Only when the publication of information about government could be shown to cause an inevitable, direct, and immediate threat to national security could prior restraint be justified.[184]

Brennan's definition of matters of public concern is broader than political speech, however. It would include all forms of art,[185] for example, as
well as commentary on and discussions of sexual matters.[186] Brennan's
definition is broad enough to encompass almost any speech that would fall
into the category of "ideas," even though he admitted that "the line between ideological and nonideological speech is impossible to draw with
accuracy."[187] In *Bethel School District,* for example, Brennan voted to let
stand the punishment of a high school student for delivering a lewd speech
in a school assembly after the student was warned not to deliver the speech.
Brennan's rationale was that the student was punished not because of the
ideas he expressed, but to keep order at the school.[188]

Brennan also believed that the First Amendment established a right of an individual to receive ideas, since an individual's exercise of speech rights and political freedoms was predicated on the receipt of information.[189] The press fulfilled an important role in the receipt of ideas and, therefore, deserved added protection.[190]

Thus, Brennan, while in agreement with his colleagues on the Court on a First Amendment theory involving prior restraint, often disagreed on how that theory would be applied. He would only allow prior restraint that fit into the narrow formula described primarily in *Bantam Books* and *Freedman*. It would never be allowed when the government attempted to control the content of speech. In addition, regardless of the motives of government, prior restraint would not be allowed when the speech in question concerned matters of public concern.

NOTES

1. *See, for example,* D. Anderson, The Origins of the Press Clause, 30 U.C.L.A. L. Rev. 455 (1983); and L. Levy, Emergence of a Free Press (1985).

2. The concept came, in part, from the writings of Sir William Blackstone, who proposed that freedom of the press meant the absence of prior restraint, but that irresponsibility in publishing could be punished, 4 Commentaries 151, 152.

3. *See* Near v. Minnesota, 283 U.S. 697, 716 (1931). *See also* F. Haiman, Speech and Law in a Free Society 3–5 (1970).

4. Nebraska Press Association v. Stuart, 427 U.S. 539, 588–89 (1976), Justice Brennan concurring in judgment; New York Times v. U.S., 403 U.S. 713, 726 (1971), Justice Brennan concurring, quoting Near v. Minnesota, 382 U.S. 697, 713 (1931).

5. Bantam Books v. Sullivan, 372 U.S. 58, 70 (1963).

6. *Nebraska Press Association,* 427 U.S. at 590, Justice Brennan concurring in judgment.

7. *Bantam Books,* 372 U.S. at 70.

8. *See, for example,* Lehman v. Shaker Heights, 418 U.S. 298 (1974); and Widmar v. Vincent, 454 U.S. 263 (1981).

9. *See, for example,* Lehman v. Shaker Heights, 418 U.S. 298 (1974); and Staub v. Baxley, 355 U.S. 313 (1958).

10. Riley v. National Federation of the Blind of North Carolina, Inc., 108 S.Ct. 2667 (1988).

11. *Id.* at 2674.

12. Southeastern Promotions, Ltd. v. Conrad, 420 U.S. 546 (1975).

13. Kingsley International Picture Corp. v. Regents of New York University, 360 U.S. 684 (1959).

14. Carey v. Population Services International, 431 U.S. 678 (1977).

15. Carroll v. Princess Anne, 393 U.S. 175 (1968); Brandenburg v. Ohio, 395 U.S. 444 (1969).

16. *Nebraska Press Association,* 427 U.S. at 588, Justice Brennan concurring in judgment.

17. Haig v. Agee, 453 U.S. 280, 319 (1981), Justice Brennan dissenting.

18. New York Times Co. v. U.S., 403 U.S. 713, 725–27 (1971), Justice Brennan concurring.

19. Broadrick v. Oklahoma, 413 U.S. 601, 621 (1973), Justice Brennan dissenting; Civil Service Commission v. Letter Carriers, 413 U.S. 548, 595 (1973), Justice Douglas dissenting (joined by Justice Brennan).

20. Jones v. North Carolina Prisoner's Labor Union, 433 U.S. 119, 139 (1977), Justice Marshall dissenting (joined by Justice Brennan).

21. Pell v. Procunier, 417 U.S. 817, 837 (1974), Justice Douglas dissenting (joined by Justice Brennan); Saxbe v. Washington Post Co., 417 U.S. 843, 850 (1974), Justice Powell dissenting (joined by Justice Brennan).

22. Hazelwood School District v. Kuhlmeier, 484 U.S. 260 (1988).

23. New York Times Co. v. U.S., 403 U.S. 713, 726–27 (1971), Justice Brennan concurring.

24. *See, for example,* Freedman v. Maryland, 380 U.S. 51 (1965); and Teitel Film Corp. v. Cusack, 390 U.S. 139 (1968).

25. *Hazelwood,* 484 U.S. at 574, Justice Brennan dissenting.

26. Board of Education, Island Trees v. Pico, 457 U.S. 853, 868 (1982).

27. Procunier v. Martinez, 416 U.S. 396, 422 (1974), Justice Marshall dissenting (joined by Justice Brennan).

28. Rowan v. Post Office, 397 U.S. 728, 738 (1970).

29. *Id.* at 741, Justice Brennan concurring.

30. Brennan Papers, Box 216, memoranda of Justices Brennan and Burger, April 28, 1970.

31. In Pittsburgh Press v. Pittsburgh Commission on Human Resources, 413 U.S. 376 (1983), Justice Brennan agreed that a prohibition on references to sex in help-wanted classified advertisements was not a First Amendment violation; in Hoffman Estates v. Flipside, 455 U.S. 489 (1982), he voted to allow a prohibition on the display of literature encouraging illegal use of drugs adjacent to drug paraphenalia; and in Seattle Times v. Rhinehart, 467 U.S. 20 (1984), he voted to uphold a court order restraining a newspaper from publishing information a judge had ordered the plaintiff in a libel action to make available to the newspaper.

32. Teitel Film Corp. v. Cusack, 390 U.S. 139 (1968), Brennan Papers, Box 247; New York Times Co. v. U.S., 403 U.S. 713 (1971), Brennan Papers, Box 247; Brandenburg v. Ohio, 395 U.S. 444 (1969), Brennan Papers, Box 195.

33. 372 U.S. 58 (1963).

34. *Id.* at 67.

35. *Id.* at 69.

36. *Id.* at 70.

37. *Id.*

38. *Id.* at 71.

39. Brennan Papers, Box 94.

40. *Id.,* memorandum of Justice White, February 6, 1963.

41. 380 U.S. 51 (1965).

42. 365 U.S. 43 (1961).

43. *Id.* at 48–49.

44. *Id.* at 51, Chief Justice Warren dissenting.

45. Kingsley International Picture Corp. v. Regents of New York University, 360 U.S. 684 (1959).

46. *Id.* at 688.

47. 480 U.S. at 54.

48. *Id.* at 58

49. *Id.*

50. *Id.* at 58–59.

51. 427 U.S. 539 (1976). *See also* Oklahoma Publishing Co. v. District Court, 430 U.S. 308 (1977).

52. *Id.* at 556–61.

53. *Id.* at 562.

54. *Id.* at 572, Justice Brennan concurring in judgment.

55. *Id.* at 587, Justice Brennan concurring in judgment.

56. *Id.* at 588, Justice Brennan concurring in judgment.

57. Brennan Papers, Box 396, memorandum of Justice Brennan to the Conference, June 8, 1976.

58. *Id.,* memorandum of Chief Justice Burger, June 8, 1976.

59. *Id.,* memorandum of Justice Powell, June 8, 1976.

60. *Id.,* memorandum of Justice Stevens, June 9, 1976.

61. *See, for example,* Oklahoma Publishing Co. v. District Court, 430 U.S. 308 (1977).

62. 403 U.S. 713 (1971).

63. Brennan Papers, Box 247.

64. 403 U.S. at 714 (1971), Justice Black concurring; 403 U.S. at 720 (1971), Justice Douglas concurring.

65. 403 U.S. at 725 (1971), Justice Brennan concurring.

66. *Id.* at 725–26, Justice Brennan concurring.

67. *Id.* at 726–27, Justice Brennan concurring.

68. 453 U.S. 280 (1981).

69. *Id.* at 319.

70. 417 U.S. 817 (1974).

71. 417 U.S. 843 (1974).

72. *Id.* at 857, Justice Powell dissenting.

73. *Id.* at 863, Justice Powell dissenting.

74. *Id.* at 864, Justice Powell dissenting.

75. 417 U.S. at 837, Justice Douglas dissenting.

76. *Id.* at 839–40.

77. *Id.* at 840–41.

78. 433 U.S. 119 (1977).

79. *Id.* at 143–44, Justice Marshall dissenting.

80. 416 U.S. 396 (1974).

81. *Id.* at 422. *See also,* Bell v. Wolfish, 441 U.S. 520, 579 (1979), Justice Stevens dissenting (joined by Justice Brennan), and Thornburgh v. Abbott, 109 S.Ct. 1874, 1885 (1989), Justice Stevens dissenting (joined by Justice Brennan).

82. 484 U.S. 260 (1988).

83. *Id.* at 273.

84. *Id.* at 280, Justice Brennan dissenting.

85. *Id.,* Justice Brennan dissenting.

86. 393 U.S. 503 (1969).
87. *Id.* at 506.
88. *Id.* at 505.
89. *Id.* at 513.
90. 457 U.S. 853 (1982).
91. *Id.* at 860.
92. *Id.* at 875, Justice Blackmun concurring in judgment.
93. *Id.* at 883, Justice White concurring in judgment.
94. *Id.* at 863–66.
95. *Id.* at 868.
96. *Id.* at 867.
97. *Id.* at 868–69.
98. *Id.* at 870.
99. *Id.* at 871.
100. *Id.*
101. *Id.* at 874.
102. *Id.*
103. *Id.* at 875.
104. *Id.* at 905, Justice Rehnquist dissenting.
105. *Id.,* Justice Rehnquist dissenting.
106. *Id.* at 920, Justice Rehnquist dissenting.
107. *Id.,* Justice Rehnquist dissenting.
108. Brennan Papers, Box 594, memorandum of Justice Brennan, May 4, 1982.
109. *Id.,* memorandum of Justice White, May 10, 1982; memoranda of Justice Brennan, May 7–10, 1982.
110. *Id.,* memorandum of Justice White, May 10, 1982.
111. *Id.,* memorandum of Justice Brennan, May 19, 1982.
112. *Id.*
113. *Id.,* memorandum of Chief Justice Burger, June 7, 1982.
114. *Id.,* memoranda of Justices Powell and O'Connor, June 8, 1982.
115. *Id.,* memorandum of Chief Justice Burger, June 22, 1982.
116. *Id.*
117. *Id.,* memorandum of Justice Brennan, June 22, 1982.
118. *Id.*
119. *Id.*
120. *Id.,* circulation of concurring opinion by Justice Stevens, June 23, 1982.
121. *Id.*
122. *Id.,* memorandum of Chief Justice Burger, June 23, 1982. *See* 457 U.S. 886, note 2, Chief Justice Burger dissenting.
123. *Id.,* memorandum of Justice Stevens, June 24, 1982.
124. 418 U.S. 298 (1974).
125. *Id.* at 303.
126. *Id.* at 310, Justice Brennan dissenting.
127. 486 U.S. 750 (1988).
128. 444 U.S. 507, 516 (1980), Justice Stevens dissenting (joined by Justice Brennan).
129. *Id.* at 507–10; 456 F.Supp. 176 (E.D. Va. 1978).
130. *Id.* at 526, Justice Stevens dissenting.

131. *Id.* at 516–17, Justice Stevens dissenting.

132. *Id.* at 517, Justice Stevens dissenting.

133. Wood v. Georgia, 370 U.S. 375 (1962).

134. Smith v. Daily Mail Publishing Co., 443 U.S. 97 (1978). *See also* Landmark Communications v. Virginia, 435 U.S. 829; and Florida Star v. B.J.F., 109 S.Ct. 2693 (1988). Justice Brennan did not participate in *Landmark Communications*.

135. Bethel School District v. Fraser, 478 U.S. 675 (1986). *See* discussion accompanying *infra* note 160–61.

136. 391 U.S. 563 (1968). *See also* Givhan v. Western Line Consolidated School District, 439 U.S. 410 (1979); and Mt. Healthy City School District Board of Education v. Doyle, 429 U.S. 274 (1977).

137. 391 U.S. at 547.

138. *Id.* at 568.

139. *Id.* at 571–72.

140. *Id.* at 572–73.

141. *Id.* at 573.

142. Arnett v. Kennedy, 416 U.S. 134 (1974).

143. Bond v. Floyd, 385 U.S. 116 (1988).

144. *Id.* at 135–36.

145. Rankin v. McPherson, 483 U.S. 378 (1987).

146. *Id.* at 384.

147. *Id.* at 387.

148. *Id.* at 386.

149. *Id.* at 388–89. The Court has also held that First Amendment rights are not lost when speech is made in private rather than in public, Givhan v. Western Line Consolidated School District, 439 U.S. 410 (1979).

150. *Id.* at 394, Justice Scalia dissenting.

151. Watts v. U.S., 394 U.S. 705 (1968).

152. *Id.* at 708, quoting New York Times Co. v. Sullivan, 376 U.S. at 270.

153. 461 U.S. 138 (1983).

154. *Id.* at 161, Justice Brennan dissenting.

155. *Id.,* Justice Brennan dissenting, quoting Mills v. Alabama, 384 U.S. 214, 218–19 (1966).

156. *Id.* at 163, Justice Brennan dissenting.

157. In re Stolar, 360 U.S. 622 (1959).

158. *Id.* at 635.

159. Papish v. Board of Curators of University of Missouri, 410 U.S. 667 (1973).

160. Bethel School District v. Fraser, 478 U.S. 675 (1986).

161. *Id.* at 687, Justice Brennan concurring.

162. 417 U.S. 733 (1974).

163. *Id.* at 758.

164. *Id.* at 773, Justice Stewart dissenting (joined by Justice Brennan).

165. 408 U.S. 564 (1972).

166. *Id.* at 574–75.

167. *Id.* at 604, Justice Brennan dissenting.

168. Bantam Books v. Sullivan, 372 U.S. 58, 70 (1963).

169. *See supra* notes 12–18.

170. Riley v. National Federation of the Blind of North Carolina, Inc., 108 S.Ct. 2667, 2674 (1988).

171. Nebraska Press Association v. Stuart, 427 U.S. 539, 588–89 (1976), Justice Brennan concurring; New York Times v. U.S., 403 U.S. 713, 726 (1971), Justice Brennan concurring, quoting Near v. Minnesota, 382 U.S. 697, 713 (1931).

172. *See, generally, Bantam Books,* 372 U.S. 58 (1963); and Freedman v. Maryland, 380 U.S. 51 (1965).

173. 372 U.S. at 70. *See also Freedman,* 380 U.S. at 58 (1965).

174. 380 U.S. at 58–59.

175. *See, e.g., Bantam Books,* 372 U.S. 58 (1963); *Freedman,* 380 U.S. 51 (1965); Teitel Film Corp. v. Cusack, 390 U.S. 139 (1968); Southeastern Promotions, Ltd. v. Conrad, 420 U.S. 546 (1975).

176. *See, e.g.,* Interstate Circuit, Inc. v. Dallas, 390 U.S. 676 (1968); Broadrick v. Oklahoma, 413 U.S. 601, 621 (1973), Justice Brennan dissenting.

177. *See, e.g.,* Staub v. Baxley, 355 U.S. 313 (1958); Linmark Associates v. Willingboro, 413 U.S. 85 (1977); Widmar v. Vincent, 454 U.S. 264 (1981); Lehman v. Shaker Heights, 418 U.S. 298, 308 (1974), Justice Brennan dissenting.

178. *Times v. Sullivan,* 376 U.S. 254, 270 (1964).

179. Connick v. Meyers, 461 U.S. 138, 161 (1983), Justice Brennan dissenting.

180. *Id.,* Justice Brennan dissenting, quoting Mills v. Alabama, 384 U.S. 214, 218–19 (1966).

181. Carroll v. Princess Anne, 393 U.S. 175 (1968).

182. Civil Service Commission v. Letter Carriers, 413 U.S. 548, 598 (1973), Justice Douglas dissenting (joined by Justice Brennan); *see also* Broadrick v. Oklahoma, 413 U.S. 601, 621 (1973), Justice Brennan dissenting.

183. Haig v. Agee, 453 U.S. 280, 310 (1981), Justice Brennan dissenting.

184. New York Times v. U.S., 403 U.S. at 726–27, Justice Brennan concurring.

185. Brennan Papers, Box 101, Obscenity Memorandum at 36–40.

186. Roth v. U.S., 354 U.S. 476, 487 (1957).

187. *Lehman,* 418 U.S. at 319, Justice Brennan dissenting.

188. *Bethel School District,* 478 U.S. at 687, Justice Brennan concurring.

189. *Island Trees,* 457 U.S. at 867.

190. Pell v. Procunier, 417 U.S. at 837–41, Justice Douglas dissenting (joined by Justice Brennan); Saxbe v. Washington Post, 417 U.S. at 857–64, Justice Powell dissenting (joined by Justice Brennan).

5

"Debate . . . Should Be Uninhibited, Robust, and Wide-Open"

In 1964, Justice Brennan, writing for a unanimous Court, signaled a new era in libel law in the United States with his opinion in *New York Times Co. v. Sullivan*.[1] It was the most important libel opinion ever written and may be the most important free-expression opinion in U.S. jurisprudence. Both the law and the language of libel were changed, and a new course was cut—a course that, more than a quarter-century later, despite debate and criticism, is still the path of libel law in the United States.[2]

In addition, *Times v. Sullivan* might be Brennan's most important opinion not only because of its impact on the law, but also because of its impact on the justice's First Amendment theory. In that opinion, Brennan developed some First Amendment themes only hinted at in his earlier opinions[3]—themes that would guide him, and other members of the Court, in subsequent cases.

Brennan's leading theme in *Times v. Sullivan* was that the First Amendment's primary purpose is to guarantee protection when speech touches on areas of self-government. The theory had been espoused by Alexander Meiklejohn,[4] and while Brennan acknowledged Meiklejohn's influence,[5] the philosopher was not cited once in the opinion. Meiklejohn believed the First Amendment to be absolute in its protection of speech involving matters of self-government, which include the arts and education as well as politics.[6] The implications of the concept, as defined by Brennan, are far-reaching. For Brennan, the theory means that no individual or institution has greater or lesser free-speech protection than any other individual or institution. Therefore, when First Amendment rights come into conflict, those rights must be balanced. Because of the self-governing role of the First Amendment, Brennan's measure for balancing was often to consider the societal benefit of the conflicting speech. The First Amendment is more than an individual guarantee according to this theory; it is a societal guarantee. Society as a whole, not just an individual, benefits from free expression.

A second theme Brennan expanded in *Times v. Sullivan* was that the First Amendment is vital for more than philosophical reasons; it is vital because its practical application works for the benefit of society. That is, Brennan demonstrated through his opinions and votes his obvious belief that the marketplace of ideas theory described by John Milton[7] and Justice Oliver Wendall Holmes[8] genuinely worked to improve society and to fulfill one of its basic purposes. Therefore, speech involving matters of self-government deserved broad protection.

Ironically, while Brennan's contributions to the law of libel, privacy, and related torts are staggering, the justice rarely wrote for the majority in such cases. His opinion in *Times v. Sullivan* was followed the same year by a majority opinion in *Garrison v. Louisiana,*[9] and two years later by a majority opinion in *Rosenblatt v. Baer.*[10] He also wrote the plurality opinion in *Rosenbloom v. Metromedia*[11] in 1971 and a majority opinion in the invasion of privacy case of *Time, Inc. v. Hill*[12] in 1967. After 1967, however, Brennan wrote no majority opinion in libel or invasion of privacy cases.[13]

From the time Brennan joined the Court until 1971, therefore, the Court decided eleven libel cases and one invasion-of-privacy case. Brennan wrote one plurality and four majority opinions; he wrote one dissenting opinion[14] and one opinion concurring and dissenting.[15] From 1974, however, when the Court decided *Gertz v. Robert Welch, Inc.,*[16] through the end of the 1989–90 term, the Court decided fifteen libel cases and four invasion-of-privacy cases. Brennan wrote no majority or plurality opinions and dissented nine times, writing opinions in eight of the nine cases. In only four libel cases and three privacy cases did he agree with the majority without additional comment.

One reason for the dearth of majority opinions by Brennan in the last twenty years is the Court's retrenchment, beginning in 1974. For the ten years following *Gertz v. Welch,* therefore, Brennan found himself at odds with a majority of his colleagues on the Court. During his tenure on the Court, opinions in thirty-three libel, privacy, and related cases were delivered. Only once did Brennan deliver what might be considered an anti-expression vote.[17]

It all began, of course, in 1964, with *Times v. Sullivan.*

TIMES V. SULLIVAN AND SELF-GOVERNMENT

Prior to 1964, a libel plaintiff in the United States could recover damages by proving identification in a defamatory publication.[18] Falsity and damages were presumed, although in some cases malice, usually defined as ill-will or spite, was required.[19] The Supreme Court changed all that when it handed down its ruling in *Times v. Sullivan.*

The case began with a full-page advertisement, placed in the *New York Times* by a civil rights group, criticizing official activity in several southern cities, among them Montgomery, Alabama. The ad spawned several libel actions. The first to reach trial was that brought by L. B. Sullivan, a Montgomery commissioner. Sullivan, although not named in the ad, claimed that the criticism of police activity in Montgomery was based on false statements and, therefore, was also false criticism of him, as the commissioner responsible for the police. Sullivan won $500,000 in a verdict upheld by the Alabama Supreme Court.[20] The U.S. Supreme Court overturned the verdict, however, and constitutionalized the law of libel.

In essence, Justice Brennan saw the case as one of seditious libel: The *New York Times* was being punished for its criticism of governmental conduct. Such criticism, Brennan wrote, was at the heart of the First Amendment,[21] and deserved protection, even though the criticism might be based on false statements: Falsity alone is insufficient for liability.[22] Since error is inevitable during public debate, Brennan noted, to punish simple mistakes would chill the debate. The defense of truth would be of little consolation; a speaker might hush his criticisms unless he was convinced he could prove the truth of his charges in a court.[23] Therefore, Brennan wrote, to ensure robust public debate, liability would only attach to criticism of public officials if those officials could prove actual malice, defined as knowledge of falsity or reckless disregard for the truth.[24] "Actual malice" was not a new term in libel law by any means, and even Brennan had used the term in a previous case:[25] in *Times v. Sullivan,* however, Brennan had expanded some of the earlier definitions of the term to fit the case's particular circumstances.[26]

The rationale of Brennan's opinion in *Times v. Sullivan* was that the *rasion d'être* of the First Amendment is to advance self-government. He wrote: "The general proposition that freedom of expression upon public questions is secured by the First Amendment has long been settled."[27] And, he added, an essential element of self-government is criticism of those in power. There is a "profound national commitment," he wrote, "to the principle that debate on public issues should be uninhibited, robust, and wide-open, and that it may well include vehement, caustic, and sometimes unpleasantly sharp attacks on government and public officials."[28]

Such was the lesson, Brennan wrote, from "the great controversy over the Sedition Act of 1798, which first crystallized a national awareness of the central meaning of the First Amendment."[29] Brennan quoted James Madison's premise that the Constitution created a form of government in which "the people, not the government, possess the absolute sovereignty,"[30] and twice quoted Madison's assertion that "the censorial power is in the people over the Government, and not in the Government over the people."[31] Therefore, Brennan wrote, "the right of free public discussion of the stewardship of public officials was, . . . in Madison's view, a fundamental principle of the American form of government."[32] It was a principle Brennan adopted and applied in *Times v. Sullivan,* by way of the Court's 1959 ruling in *Barr v. Matteo.*[33] In that case, the Court held that utterances of a federal official are absolutely privileged if made even "within the outer perimeter" of the official's duties.[34] Brennan dissented in the opinion, arguing that officials deserve a qualified, not absolute, privilege,[35] and held in *Times v. Sullivan* that the "citizen-critic" deserves the same privilege: "It is as much his duty to criticize as it is the official's duty to administer."[36] Justice Louis Brandeis, Brennan had noted earlier in his opinion, had written that "public discussion is a public duty" and was "a fundamental principle of the American government."[37]

A year after the case was delivered, Brennan, in a speech at Brown University, acknowledged Meiklejohn's theory that the First Amendment is absolute when speech involves matters of self-government. Brennan said[38]:

> The first amendment, in his view, is the repository of these self-governing powers that, because they are exclusively reserved to the people, are by force of that amendment immune from regulation by the agencies, federal and state, that are established as the people's servants.[39]

And *Times v. Sullivan,* Brennan wrote, "presented a classic example of an activity that Dr. Meiklejohn called an activity of 'governing importance' within the powers reserved to the people and made invulnerable to sanctions imposed by their agency-governments."[40]

While it is clear that a number of states were granting much the same protection Brennan advocated in *Times v. Sullivan,*[41] to constitutionalize a portion of tort law that had previously been within the purview of the states was revolutionary. "The legal world was stunned," the *Kentucky Law Journal* noted.[42] Another critic wrote that the Court had fashioned "a nuclear blunderbuss with which to swat a gnat."[43] And, while Brennan spoke for a unanimous Court when he read the opinion March 9, 1964, it was a struggle for him to win a unanimous court: At one point in the deliberations over the case, there had been some concern that Brennan's opinion would not even win a bare majority.

Following the circulations of Brennan's initial drafts of the opinion in February, five justices were unwilling to join, but for different reasons. Hugo Black, William O. Douglas, and Arthur Goldberg believed Brennan's opinion did not grant sufficient protection to criticisms of public officials; they had specific complaints with the actual-malice rule, which they eventually voiced in their concurring opinions.[44] Tom C. Clark and John M. Harlan, on the other hand, had complaints with Brennan's evaluation of the evidence to determine whether publication was made with actual malice.[45]

The importance of the issues in *Times v. Sullivan* was obvious, however, and more than one justice recognized the need for a strong opinion. "I think it is desirable to get a Court opinion whenever we can," Douglas wrote Brennan, "and perhaps you have some other ingenious method of indicating properly what the position is."[46] Goldberg agreed. "It would be very bad if you didn't get a court," he wrote Brennan.[47] And he suggested a scenario for getting a Court:

> Why don't you just say in your opinion all justices agree to page 25. All justices agree on your malice test except Black, Douglas & Goldberg. All justices agree on your analysis of the malice evidence except Harlan & Clark. This gives you a majority on your opinion on all issues. Then all of the concurring opinions can be labelled concurring—not just in result.[48]

Goldberg, Black, and Douglas, as it turned out, joined Brennan's opinion with little additional persuasion. Goldberg wrote Brennan:

> As you know I am enthusiastic about your opinion which I regard to be the most outstanding of the term. You know my view that your evidence warrants the rule of an absolute privilege for comment on official conduct. I reserve private libels to unprotected speech. . . . I don't know about Hugo but I am certainly agreeable to joining your excellent opinion and then writing very briefly that I would go beyond to the extent that I have indicated. You can count on my vote for your opinion.[49]

Hugo Black eventually joined as well, although there is no official notification in Brennan's case file as to when he did so. One note, however, from Black expresses the justice's support for Brennan's opinion:

> You know of course that despite my position and what I write I think you are doing a wonderful job in the *Times* case and however it finally comes out it is bound to be a very long step towards preserving the right to communicate ideas.[50]

And later, apparently after the opinion was delivered, Black again expressed his satisfaction:

> In getting [Harlan] to agree to your opinion as it is you have done a great service to the freedoms of the First Amendment. For your opinion, I believe, will inevitably lead to a later holding that people have complete immunity from having to pay damages for criticism of government or its officials in the performance of their public duties. Most inventions even of legal principles come out of urgent needs. The need to protect speech in this area is

so great that it will be recognized and acted upon sooner or later. The ratio-
nalization for it is not important—the result is. What counts in your opinion
I think will be the point from which this result will be achieved.[51]

In order to win the votes of Harlan and Clark, however, Brennan decided to effect a compromise. He began by changing part of his reasoning
in the third section of the opinion. In Part III, Brennan examined the evidence in the case to determine whether the *Times* had published with actual malice. Brennan concluded that the evidence did not support a finding
of actual malice[52]; at most, it supported a finding of negligence.[53] Clark
and Harlan were opposed to the section on grounds that the examination
was unnecessary; they disagreed with Brennan's initial presumption that
the Alabama jury had awarded punitive damages.

Harlan attempted to resolve his differences on Part III by submitting a
revision to Brennan,[54] which eliminated much of Brennan's examination
of the evidence. Brennan decided against the changes, explaining his rationale to Harlan in a memorandum on March 2, 1964:

> I think we should retain the analysis of the constitutional insufficiency of the
> proofs of actual malice and connection even if this has the effect of "chilling"
> the possibility of a new trial. I think we are justified in doing this on two
> counts: (a) the profession should be apprised now that we are going to ex-
> amine evidence in this area as we have in others, and (b) because the analysis
> of the proofs to demonstrate their insufficiency will be both illustrative of
> how we do this and also informative to the parties in this case of a void in
> the proofs that would have to be filled if a new trial is had.[55]

Chief Justice Earl Warren agreed with Brennan, noting that the section
gave meaning to the rest of the opinion. If it were excluded, Warren wrote,
"we will merely be going through a meaningless exercise. The case would
be remanded, another improvisation would be devised and it would be
back to us in a more difficult posture."[56] Harlan, however, was disappointed and, the day after receiving Brennan's memorandum, announced
that he would write a short "Separate Memorandum" stating that he was
joining the opinion except for Part III.[57] Harlan wrote that the Court should
not examine the evidence and that he was not "intimating any view as to
whether the existing evidence would have sufficed constitutionally had these
cases been tried in accordance with the governing constitutional principles
announced in the Court's opinion."[58]

Black also had reservations about Brennan's examination of the evidence, but for different reasons. Although he believed that examining the
evidence "is fully justifiable" he wrote Brennan that he would not do so
in the *Times* case, partly because "I think that under the definition you
give malice the evidence (so far as I read it) would prove malice."[59]

Brennan refused to eliminate his discussion of the evidence in *Times v. Sullivan,* but he compromised with Harlan on one important point, and with Clark on a second. Brennan's previous opinion denied Alabama the right to grant Sullivan a new trial. On March 3, Brennan sent a memorandum to the Conference announcing that he was eliminating that language, based on discussions with Harlan. Brennan wrote that he and Harlan agreed that, "even assuming constitutional power to deny a state the right to apply its new trial rules, it would not be wise to use this case as a vehicle for saying so for the first time."[60] The change, however, made the examination of the evidence by the Court even more important. In the same memorandum, Brennan explained his rationale for retaining that portion of the opinion:

> I am convinced, however, that the analysis of the evidence to show its insufficiency under the constitutional rule we lay down is essential to the opinion. Since Sullivan did undertake to prove actual malice as a predicate for punitive damages, we of necessity must demonstrate the insufficiency of his evidence under the constitutional test of actual malice. Moreover, if Alabama should give Sullivan a new trial the parties should know that the evidence in this record will not support a judgment—that there is a large void to be filled. If we said nothing and we later overturned another judgment entered on this record, we might be rightly accused of having second thoughts because of the implication from our silence here that the application of the valid rule to this evidence would be sustained. Finally, there are a number of other libel suits pending both in Montgomery and in Birmingham and those concerned should know what to expect in the way of judicial superintendence from this Court over those proceedings.[61]

Brennan made one additional change at the suggestion of Tom Clark. As indicated, a primary basis of his review of the evidence initially had been that the verdict of the Alabama jury must have been for punitive damages. On Clark's suggestion, Brennan altered the opinion to find that the review of the evidence was justified only "in the interest of effective judicial administration." Brennan wrote Potter Stewart that, "Personally I think this is a slight change. . . . Tom also thought that this basis might appeal to John Harlan, although I have not had any reaction as yet from John."[62] Clark must have been right. Harlan announced to the Conference on March 9—the day the opinion was delivered—that he was withdrawing the separate memorandum and was "unreservedly joining the majority opinion."[63]

The last-minute announcement, therefore, meant that the only point of disagreement in *Times v. Sullivan* was on the actual-malice qualification for criticism of public officials. Black, Goldberg, and Douglas remained convinced that criticism of public officials should have absolute protection.

Brennan, however, not willing to give absolute protection to officials in the conduct of the official tasks—as expressed in his dissenting opinion in *Barr v. Matteo*[64]—was not willing to give critics absolute immunity in their criticism of those same officials. To Brennan's way of thinking, there were few absolutes under the First Amendment. The free-expression guarantee, being as much for the benefit of society as for the benefit of the individual, meant that rights must be balanced to ensure the greatest possible benefit for both society and the individual. That was the essence of self-government, and no justice disagreed with the concept that the First Amendment protections of expression were established first and foremost to provide for effective self-governance.

THEMES IN LIBEL LAW

Libel law took a serpentine path after *Times v. Sullivan,* but Brennan's path remained constant. And the prevalent theme in his writings was that freedom of expression should receive sturdy protection because, in a government based upon participation of the governed, such protection is essential.

As indicated, during the ten years following *Times v. Sullivan,* the Court continued to expand the protections established in that landmark opinion. In *Garrison v. Louisiana*[65] the Court ruled that the actual-malice standard applied to criminal as well as civil libel actions, and in *Curtis Publishing Co. v. Butts*[66] the Court ruled that public figures as well as public officials must prove actual malice. Then, in *Rosenbloom v. Metromedia,*[67] the Court established that actual malice must be proved by private-person libel plaintiffs if the material upon which they based their libel suits involved matters of public concern. Brennan wrote the plurality opinion, which was joined only by Chief Justice Warren Burger and Justice Harry Blackmun. Since Black adhered to his position that news media are insulated from libel judgments under the First Amendment,[68] however, the rule was put into effect.[69]

The Court backed off the *Rosenbloom* rule in *Gertz v. Welch,*[70] ruling that while there could be no liability without fault in libel actions, actual malice should not be required of all private persons involved in matters of public concern.[71] Instead, the Court held that the states would determine the degree of fault private persons would be required to prove in libel actions so long as there was no liability without some degree of fault.[72] Elmer Gertz, the well-known Chicago attorney who brought the action, was not a public figure, the Court held, even though he was widely published and was active in public affairs.[73]

In the cases that followed, the Court limited even further the definition of public figures,[74] limited occasions when privilege attached to publications,[75] expanded jurisdictions in which libel cases could be filed,[76] and required journalists to describe their conversations and state of mind when compiling and writing material for publication.[77]

Brennan often dissented from opinions in these cases, and often couched his dissents in terms of the importance of freedom of expression to self-governance and to the benefit of society.

Garrison v. Louisiana was delivered barely eight months after the decision in *Times v. Sullivan,* even though the case was decided in the next term of Court. Brennan wrote the opinion in *Garrison,* a case in which a district attorney had been convicted of criminal libel because of his criticism of eight judges. The Court reversed the conviction. Brennan, echoing terminology he had used in *Times v. Sullivan,* wrote that neither the protection of private reputation nor an interest in the motivation of the speaker was sufficient to inhibit robust and wide-open debate on public issues. "Where the criticism is of public officials and their conduct of public business, the interest in private reputation is overborne by the larger public interest, secured by the Constitution, in the dissemination of truth," he wrote.[78] Nor should the debate be inhibited by a requirement that it be made with good motives:

> Debate on public issues will not be uninhibited if the speaker must run the risk that it will be proved in court that he spoke out of hatred; even if he did speak out of hatred, utterances honestly believed contribute to the free interchange of ideas and the ascertainment of truth.[79]

Finally, Brennan concluded that "speech concerning public affairs is more than self-expression; it is the essence of self-government."[80]

In *Rosenblatt v. Baer,*[81] two years later, Brennan wrote that society has "a pervasive and strong interest in preventing and redressing attacks upon reputation."[82] But, he noted, the Court in *Times v. Sullivan* recognized that "when interests in public discussion are particularly strong . . . the Constitution limits the protections afforded by the law of defamation."[83] And, in an invasion–of–privacy case a year later, Brennan wrote that protections for the press in invasion–of–privacy actions "are not for the benefit of the press so much as for the benefit of all of us. A broadly defined freedom of the press assures the maintenance of our political system and an open society."[84]

Four years later Brennan wrote the plurality opinion in *Rosenbloom v. Metromedia* and once again expressed the view that the First Amendment guarantees expression on matters of self-governance. Indeed, in a draft of his opinion circulated February 17, 1971, Brennan went further and wrote that the First Amendment is the cornerstone of a free government. Citing Meiklejohn, he wrote:

> The guarantees secured by the First and Fourteenth Amendments for speech and press constitute the cornerstone of a government "of the people, by the

people, and for the people," ensuring a free flow of information and a free marketplace of ideas competing for popular acceptance.[85]

Brennan eliminated the sentence, however, in order to win Blackmun's vote.[86]

Rosenbloom began when a distributor of nudist magazines sued a radio station for calling him a smut-peddler. While it was relatively clear that George Rosenbloom brought the suit as much to get back at the radio station as to recoup his reputation,[87] Brennan saw the case as one involving self-governance through debate on matters of public concern. "Self-governance in the United States," he wrote, "presupposes far more than knowledge and debate about the strictly official activities of various levels of government"[88] and included proper enforcement of laws, particularly in the area of obscenity.[89] Noting that the distinction between public and private individuals was artificial[90] and made no sense in terms of First Amendment guarantees,[91] Brennan wrote that a better distinction was that speech about matters of public concern should have the greater protection of actual malice:

> If a matter is a subject of public or general interest, it cannot suddenly become less so merely because a private individual is involved, or because in some sense the individual did not "voluntarily" choose to become involved. The public's primary interest is in the event; the public focus is on the conduct of the participant and the content, effect, and significance of the conduct, not the participant's prior anonymity or notoriety.[92]

In addition, Brennan wrote, the purpose of providing sturdy protection to discussion of public officials and public figures was not because public persons have any less interest in protecting their reputations than private persons, but "to encourage ventilation of public issues."[93] Therefore, Brennan wrote,

> we honor the commitment to robust debate on public issues, which is embodied in the First Amendment, by extending constitutional protection to all discussion and communication involving matters of public or general concern, without regard to whether the persons involved are famous or anonymous.[94]

Plaintiffs bringing libel suits based on discussion of matters of public or general concern, therefore, were required to prove that the material was published with knowledge of falsity or with reckless disregard for the truth. Brennan's opinion did not command a Court. It was joined only by Burger and Blackmun.

The web of protection Brennan had helped fashion in libel law began to unravel in 1974, with *Gertz v. Welch,* the first of five libel cases in which the justice dissented.

Elmer Gertz had sued the publishers of *American Opinion* magazine for an article in which he was linked with a communist conspiracy to undermine police in the United States. He was identified as a Leninist, a Marxist, and a communist-fronter.[95] Gertz won a $50,000 jury verdict, but the trial judge overturned the verdict on the grounds that, under the *Rosenbloom* rule, the actual-malice standard should have been applied.[96] The Seventh U.S. Circuit Court of Appeals agreed.[97]

The Supreme Court, however, in a 5-4 opinion written by Powell, found that actual malice was too stringent a test for private-person libel plaintiffs to meet, and overturned the *Rosenbloom* rule. The Court held that each state would determine the degree of fault private persons must prove in libel actions, with the stipulation that there would be no liability without some degree of fault.[98] The Court also established that no libel plaintiff could win punitive damages without proving actual malice.[99] Elmer Gertz, the Court held, was a private person.[100]

Powell began an important section of the opinion with broad language about freedom of expression:

> Under the First Amendment there is no such thing as a false idea. However pernicious an opinion may seem, we depend for its correction not on the conscience of judges and juries but on the competition of other ideas.[101]

The passage, however, was only an introduction to a series of restrictions on debate that Powell delineated. He noted that, while the Court's decisions in *New York Times v. Sullivan* and *Curtis Publishing Co. v. Butts* were correct,[102] the need to avoid self-censorship by the news media was not the only societal value at issue.[103] State interests in libel actions must also be accommodated, he wrote,[104] and those state issues demanded additional protection for the reputations of private persons.

Private persons, Powell wrote, are at a disadvantage when they believe they have been wronged by defamatory publications. They are less able to respond than public persons who "enjoy significantly greater access to the channels of effective communication."[105] They are more vulnerable to injury and deserve more protection since they have not exposed themselves to such public scrutiny by accepting public office or assuming roles of especial prominence.[106]

The opinion was possible because Blackmun, who had joined Brennan's *Rosenbloom* opinion, abandoned that position in *Gertz*. Blackmun would have adhered to the *Rosenbloom* rule, he wrote, but he believed it to be "of profound importance for the Court to come to rest in the defamation area and to have a clearly defined majority position that eliminates the unsureness engendered by *Rosenbloom's* diversity."[107] He also wrote that he believed the *Gertz* requirement that actual malice be present for an award of punitive damages eliminated "significant and powerful motives for self-censorship."[108]

Brennan adhered to the rule he enunciated in *Rosenbloom*. Under the *Gertz* ruling, he argued, the free and robust debate "essential to the proper functioning of our system of government" was not permitted adequate breathing space.[109] Self-governance "perseveres because of our 'profound national commitment to the principle that debate on public issues should be uninhibited, robust, and wide-open.' "[110] Brennan was alone in his dissent.

Gertz was followed by four libel cases in five years, all of which the defendants lost. Three of the cases turned on the public-figure status of the plaintiffs. The Court ruled that a socialite involved in a scandalous divorce action,[111] a man who had once been convicted of contempt of court in connection with an espionage investigation,[112] and a researcher who received public funding[113] were not public persons. Brennan dissented in all three cases.

In the fourth case, *Herbert v. Lando*,[114] the Court further defined the parameters within which the actual-malice rule operated. Barry Lando, a producer for the CBS television program *60 Minutes*, refused to testify about his reasons for using certain material for a segment on Col. Anthony Herbert. Herbert had brought a defamation action and was attempting, through depositions, to determine how CBS had edited the program. Lando complained that the questions invaded the editorial process, which was protected by the First Amendment.

The Court agreed that the questions explored the editorial process, but held that such exploration was demanded by the actual malice rule. "*New York Times* and its progeny," Justice Byron White wrote for the majority, "made it essential to proving liability that the plaintiff focus on the conduct and state of mind of the defendant."[115] He found it to be "only common sense" that the author of an alleged defamation be questioned as to why he may have used certain material and excluded other material.[116] White found it difficult to believe that "error-avoiding procedures" would be eliminated or reduced because of the likelihood that they would be examined in court.[117]

In his dissent, Brennan argued for a privilege for conversations between journalists unless the public-figure plaintiff could establish that the publication constituted a defamatory falsehood.[118] The privilege was necessary, Brennan argued, for the benefit of society as well as for the benefit of the press. The First Amendment, he wrote, is not solely for the good of the individual, but for the good of society as well.[119] It would shield the press in its role as agent of the public at large.[120] Absence of the privilege, Brennan wrote, would not chill a journalist's thought process, but would chill the statement of doubts in the newsroom. In the absence of the privilege, therefore, accuracy and thoroughness might be diminished, which affects the public's interest in accurate and effective reporting by the news media.[121]

Brennan made a similar argument in his dissent to *Time, Inc. v. Firestone*.[122] In that case, he argued that *Time* magazine should not be legally liable for mistakes it made in reporting on the divorce of Mary Alice and Russell Firestone. He noted:

> The Court has emphasized that the central meaning of the free expression guarantee is that the body politic of this Nation shall be entitled to the communications necessary for self-governance, and that to place restraints on the exercise of expression is to deny the instrumental means required in order that the citizenry exercise that ultimate sovereignty reposed in its collective judgment by the Constitution.[123]

The press, Brennan argued, is an essential part of the self-governing process and should have a sturdy privilege to report on governmental matters. He used a long quote from *Cox Broadcasting Corp. v. Cohn* to buttress his argument:

> In a society in which each individual has but limited time and resources with which to observe at first hand operations of his government, he relies necessarily upon the press to bring to him in convenient form the facts of those operations. Great responsibility is accordingly placed upon the news media to report fully and accurately the proceedings of government, and official records and documents open to the public are the basic data of governmental operations. Without the information provided by the press most of us and many of our representatives would be unable to vote intelligently or to register opinions on the administration of government generally. With respect to judicial proceedings in particular, the function of the press serves to guarantee the fairness of trials and to bring to bear the beneficial effects of public scrutiny upon the administration of justice. . . . The freedom of the press to publish that information appears to us to be of critical importance to our type of government in which the citizenry is the final judge of the proper conduct of public business.[124]

For the first time since the retrenchment of *Gertz v. Welch,* the Supreme Court in 1984 reaffirmed, as one Court-watcher wrote, in ringing terms, the concepts established in *Times v. Sullivan*.[125] The case was *Bose Corporation v. Consumers Union*[126] and involved a review in *Consumer Reports* of a stereo speaker system marketed by the Bose Corporation. The district court concluded that the author of the review, Arnold Seligson, misled readers of the magazine by using language that intentionally exaggerated the points Seligson was making about the speakers. Therefore, the court concluded, since he knew the report would be misread, he was guilty of publishing with actual malice.[127]

The Supreme Court, however, rejected the conclusions drawn from the semantic evaluation. While Seligson's testimony did not rebut any inference of actual malice, neither did it constitute clear and convincing evidence of the existence of actual malice. Justice John Paul Stevens wrote:

> Seligson displayed a capacity for rationalization. He had made a mistake and when confronted with it, he refused to admit it and steadfastly attempted to maintain that no mistake had been made—that the inaccurate was accurate. That attempt failed, but the fact that he made the attempt does not establish that he realized the inaccuracy at the time of publication.[128]

The sort of language used in the review, Stevens concluded, represented the sort of inaccuracy that is commonplace in the forum of robust debate to which the *New York Times* rule applied and "fits easily within the breathing space that gives life to the First Amendment."[129]

In reaching his conclusion, Stevens pointed out that "the First Amendment presupposes that the freedom to speak one's mind is not only an aspect of individual liberty—and thus a good unto itself—but also is essential to the common quest for truth and the vitality of society as a whole."[130]

The importance of free speech to society was also one of the rationales used a year later when the Court decided *Dun & Bradstreet v. Greenmoss*,[131] but the rationale was used in finding for a plaintiff rather than for a defendant. Justice Lewis F. Powell reiterated the importance of free debate on matters of public concern, citing a number of cases to make the point that it was "at the heart of the First Amendment's protection."[132] But, he held, a credit report sent by Dun & Bradstreet to five subscribers was not a matter of public concern because it was "solely in the individual interest of the speaker and its specific business audience," the five subscribers were not allowed to disseminate the report further, and the dissemination was based solely on the desire for profit.[133] Therefore, Powell wrote, the plaintiff was not required to prove actual injury, as required in *Gertz,* in order to win damages.

Brennan, joined by Justices Thurgood Marshall, Harry Blackmun, and John Paul Stevens disagreed, finding that the credit-reporting "surely involves a subject matter of sufficient public concern to require the comprehensive protections of *Gertz.*"[134] Brennan argued that the majority was wrong to consider the source of the allegedly defamatory message; the source of the message was irrelevant in the assignment of First Amendment protections, he wrote. *Times v. Sullivan* held that the First Amendment protected "all who speak in good faith"[135] on matters of public concern. The First Amendment requires protection of expression "far broader than simply speech about pure political issues,"[136] and the cases since *Sul-*

livan had proceeded from the general premise that all libel law implicates First Amendment values to the extent it deters true speech that would otherwise be protected by the First Amendment."[137]

Dun & Bradstreet should be protected, Brennan wrote, because each citizen is guaranteed an equal right to free speech:

> We protect the press to ensure the vitality of First Amendment guarantees. This solicitude implies no endorsement of the principle that speakers other than the press deserve less First Amendment protection. . . . [T]he rights of the institutional media are no greater and no less than those enjoyed by other individuals or organizations engaged in the same activities.[138]

When Brennan first wrote his opinion in the spring of 1984, he was writing what was to be a majority opinion, but could not garner a fifth vote.[139] In June, as the term neared its end, Powell wrote a memorandum to the Conference, in which he and Brennan suggested the case be held over and reargued with regard to two specific issues: whether the constitutional rule with respect to presumed and punitive damages established in *New York Times* and *Gertz* applies to nonmedia defendants, and whether the rule applies to commercial speech.[140]

After reargument, Brennan again wrote an opinion for the Court, but, as before, only Stevens, Blackmun, and Marshall joined him,[141] and even Stevens had reservations, writing that Brennan's "extensive and passionate discussion of the importance of public debate" might be counterproductive since the arguments might shed little light "on the question whether commercial credit reports are entitled to special protection."[142] Brennan did not tone down his argument.

Six months after Brennan circulated his first draft, Burger reassigned the opinion to Powell.[143] In the end, however, Powell could not win a Court either, being joined only by Justices William H. Rehnquist and Sandra Day O'Connor, with Burger and White concurring in the judgment.

Matters of public concern were also at issue a year later when the Court delivered its opinion in *Philadelphia Newspapers v. Hepps*.[144] O'Connor, who was appointed to write the majority opinion by Brennan, wrote that public-figure plaintiffs would be required to prove falsity in libel actions when the published material was on issues of public concern. The rule was necessary, she wrote, "to ensure that true speech on matters of public concern is not deterred. . . . To do otherwise could 'only result in a deterrence of speech which the Constitution makes free.'"[145]

Just as Brennan, in *Dun & Bradstreet,* had found the source of a message irrelevant in the determination of First Amendment protections, he found the receiver of the message irrelevant in *McDonald v. Smith*.[146] Robert McDonald was sued for defamation because of a letter he wrote to government officials disputing the qualifications of a candidate for United States

Attorney. He claimed that the petition clause of the First Amendment gave him absolute immunity from liability when he was communicating directly with the government. When the citizen is speaking directly to the government, McDonald claimed, rather than to the public at large, he is performing a self-governing function.

Brennan disagreed, arguing for a qualified privilege. In his concurring opinion, he wrote: "Such a distinction is untenable. The Speech and Press Clauses, every bit as much as the Petition Clause, were included in the First Amendment to ensure the growth and preservation of democratic self-governance."[147]

One additional dissent by Brennan—the last he ever wrote in a libel case—is worthy of mention. In his dissent to *Milkovich v. Lorain Journal Co.,*[148] Brennan wrote that Rehnquist's majority opinion had settled the question of how opinion should be treated under the First Amendment "cogently and almost entirely correctly."[149] Brennan agreed with the Court's determination of how opinion should be treated under the constitutional rules of libel law; he disagreed, however, with the application of the rules to the facts in *Milkovich.*[150] Brennan's was an odd dissent, but Rehnquist's was an odd majority opinion, as well.

Michael Milkovich, the wrestling coach at Maple Heights High School in Maple Heights, Ohio, sued the *Lorain Journal* and sports writer Theodore Diadiun for a column Diadiun wrote criticizing Milkovich. The Ohio High School Athletic Association had investigated a brawl during a wrestling match between Maple Heights and Mentor High School. The organization issued sanctions against Maple Heights and censured Milkovich, but a county court overturned the sanctions on due process grounds. The day after the court issued its ruling, the *Lorain Journal* published Diadiun's column under the headline "Maple beat the law with the 'big lie.' " In the column, Diadiun suggested that Milkovich had lied during the court hearing. Milkovich sued, claiming the column accused him of having committed perjury.[151] The case took a convoluted path to the Court, which granted *certiorari* to determine whether the Ohio court was correct in recognizing a "constitutionally required 'opinion' exception to the application of its defamation laws."[152]

Rehnquist noted that a number of courts had determined that opinion was protected from defamation actions, using as their basis the oft-cited passage from *Gertz:*

> Under the First Amendment there is no such thing as a false idea. However pernicious an opinion may seem, we depend for its correction not on the conscience of judges and juries, but on the competition of other ideas. But there is no constitutional value in false statements of fact.[153]

But read in context, Rehnquist wrote, the passage equated the word "opinion" in the second sentence with the word "idea" in the first sentence and, therefore, "was merely a reiteration of Justice Holmes' classic 'marketplace of ideas' concept. . . . Thus," Rehnquist wrote, "we do not think this passage from *Gertz* was intended to create a wholesale defamation exemption for anything that might be labeled 'opinion.' "[154] To rule otherwise, he wrote, would be contrary to "the tenor and context of the passage" and would ignore the fact that expressions of opinion "often imply an assertion of objective fact."[155]

Rehnquist then launched into a series of examples, however, that seem to demonstrate that pure opinion is, indeed, protected from libel actions. The prefacing of a statement like "Jones is a liar" with the disclaimer "In my opinion" does not eliminate the assertion of the objective fact, Rehnquist noted, and does not eliminate the actionable quality of the statement. The Court, therefore, would not create "an artificial dichotomy between 'opinion' and fact" that would protect the second of the statements because it was opinion. But, Rehnquist added, sufficient breathing space for freedom of expression "is adequately secured by existing constitutional doctrine."[156]

First and foremost, Rehnquist wrote, under *Philadelphia Newspapers, Inc. v. Hepps,* before statements on matters of public concern can be actionable, they must be provably false: "*Hepps* ensures that a statement of opinion relating to matters of public concern which does not contain a provably false factual connotation will receive full constitutional protection."[157] Next, the Court, in a series of cases,[158] had not allowed public debate to suffer for lack of imaginative expression or rhetorical hyperbole "which has added much to the discourse of our Nation."[159] Finally, the actual-malice rule ensures that debate on public issues remains uninhibited, robust, and wide-open.[160]

The question in *Milkovich,* therefore, becomes whether the defendants published a statement that is "sufficiently factual to be susceptible of being proved true or false." The Court found that the defendants charged Milkovich with perjury, which was such a statement of fact.[161]

It was only this final holding with which Brennan took issue. "No reasonable reader," he wrote, "could understand Diadiun to be impliedly asserting—as fact—that Milkovich had perjured himself."[162] Brennan agreed that standing alone, a statement like "In my opinion John Jones is a liar" would be a statement of fact. In certain contexts, however, such a statement could be recognized as opinion.[163] Such circumstances exist in the Milkovich case.

The format, placement, and headline of the column signal the reader that Diadiun was writing an opinion, Brennan noted.[164] In addition, the organization and language demonstrate that the author is asserting his opinions rather than stating what he believes to be a fact.[165] Diadiun "is guilty of jumping to conclusions, of benightedly assuming that court decisions are always based on the merits, and of looking foolish to lawyers," Brennan wrote. "He is not, however, liable for defamation."[166]

There seemed to be no disagreement, then, on the point that a statement is not actionable unless it is provably false. A statement not provably false— or not provably true—is necessarily a statement of opinion. Brennan makes this point in his dissent:

> While the Court today dispels any misimpression that there is a so-called opinion privilege *wholly in addition* to the protections we have already found to be guaranteed by the First Amendment, it determines that a protection for statements of pure opinion is dictated by *existing* First Amendment doctrine.[167] (emphasis in the original)

Pure opinion, therefore, would seem to have constitutional protection. The Court does libel law a disservice by not stating so outright, however, because a number of judges will doubtless use *Milkovich* to rule against defendants in summary judgment actions when defamation actions are obviously based on statements of opinion.

CONCLUSIONS

In his writings on libel, Brennan fully developed his theme that the primary purpose of the First Amendment is to protect speech that touches on areas of self-government. Such speech should receive almost absolute protection because it is essential to the workings of a democratic society. And he defined areas of self-government broadly, not limiting them to political speech but encompassing almost any matter of public concern. It was a theory that spilled over into other areas of free-expression law.

The seminal expression in this area of the law was Brennan's opinion in *Times v. Sullivan*. The opinion was premised on the theory that free speech is a fundamental guarantee essential to a democratic society,[168] that the discussion of matters of public concern is a public duty,[169] and that citizens are duty-bound to criticize those who govern them.[170] Since error is inevitable in such debate, even false statements are protected, if made without actual malice, in order to ensure that the debate of public matters remains uninhibited, robust and wide-open.[171]

Brennan continued to espouse those principles, sometimes in even stronger terms, in later cases. He found, for example, that speech concerning public affairs was "the essence of self-government,"[172] and that self-government, which is essential to democracy, only perseveres because of a "profound national commitment to the principle that debate on public issues should be uninhibited, robust, and wide-open."[173] Indeed, Brennan believed First Amendment speech and press rights to be "the cornerstone of a government 'of the people, by the people, and for the people.' "[174] Therefore, Brennan advocated special protection for communications necessary for self-governance.[175]

Brennan believed that this special protection applies directly to the press, which has an important societal role to play in a democracy. The press is guaranteed protection not simply for the benefit of the press, he wrote, but also for the benefit of society, since the press acts as the agent of the public.[176] A free press assures "the maintenance of our political system and an open society,"[177] Brennan wrote. This does not mean, however, that the press has rights above those of individuals. Indeed, Brennan wrote that every person has the same rights of free expression under the First Amendment: "We protect the press to ensure the vitality of First Amendment guarantees. This solicitude implies no endorsement of the principle that speakers other than the press deserve less First Amendment protection. . . . The free speech guarantee gives each citizen an equal right."[178]

Free speech is essential to a democratic society, Brennan believed, because the marketplace of ideas is more than a philosophical metaphor, it is a functioning model. For the model to work properly, public debate must be robust. Truth can only win out in the marketplace if it is competing in that marketplace. To limit any speech threatens the model, since the speech that is restricted might be that true speech destined to overcome the false ideas in the market.

NOTES

1. 376 U.S. 254 (1964).
2. *See, for example,* W. W. Hopkins, Actual Malice Twenty-Five Years after Times v. Sullivan (1989).
3. *See, for example,* discussion accompanying *supra* Chapter 3, notes 15–18.
4. Meiklejohn, The First Amendment Is an Absolute, 1961 Sup. Ct. Rev. 245.
5. Brennan, The Supreme Court and the Meiklejohn Interpretation of the First Amendment, 79 Harv. L. Rev. 1 (1965).
6. Meiklejohn, *supra* note 4.
7. J. Milton, Complete Poems and Major Prose 746–47 (M. Hughes ed. 1957).
8. "The ultimate good desired is better reached by free trade in ideas . . . the best test of truth is the power of the thought to get itself accepted in the competition of the market." Abrams v. U.S., 250 U.S. 616, 630 (1919), Justice Holmes dissenting.
9. 379 U.S. 64 (1964).
10. 383 U.S. 75 (1966).
11. 403 U.S. 29 (1971).
12. 385 U.S. 374 (1967).
13. He appointed the majority-opinion writers in Letter Carriers v. Austin, 418 U.S. 264 (1974); and Philadelphia Newspapers v. Hepps, 475 U.S. 767 (1986).
14. Barr v. Matteo, 360 U.S. 564 (1959).
15. Curtis Publishing Co. v. Butts, 388 U.S. 130 (1967).
16. 418 U.S. 323 (1974).
17. In Keeton v. Hustler, 465 U.S. 770 (1984), Brennan voted to allow Kathy Keeton to bring suit against *Hustler* magazine in New Hampshire even though the

only connection either party had with New Hampshire was that the magazine circulated in that state. *See also* Anderson v. Liberty Lobby, 477 U.S. 242 (1986); Calder v. Jones, 465 U.S. 783 (1984); and Harte-Hanks Communications v. Connaughton, 109 S.Ct. 2678 (1989).

18. W. Prosser, The Law of Torts 790–92 (3d ed., 1964).

19. Actual malice had a variety of meanings under the common law, but was often defined as ill-will or spite. *See* Hopkins, *supra* note 2, at 48–58.

20. 273 Ala. 656, 144 So. 2d 25 (1962).

21. 376 U.S. at 273.

22. *Id*. at 271–72.

23. *Id*. at 279.

24. *Id*. at 279–80.

25. *See* Barr v. Matteo, 360 U.S. 564, 586, note 2, Justice Brennan dissenting.

26. *See, for example,* Hopkins *supra* note 2, at 91–111.

27. 376 U.S. at 269.

28. *Id*. at 270.

29. *Id*. at 273.

30. *Id*. at 274.

31. *Id*. at 275, and at 282.

32. *Id*. at 275.

33. 360 U.S. 564 (1959).

34. *Id*. at 575.

35. *Id*. at 586, Justice Brennan dissenting.

36. 376 U.S. at 282.

37. *Id*. at 270.

38. Brennan, *supra* note 5. The speech was delivered April 14, 1965, as the Alexander Meiklejohn Lecture at Brown University.

39. *Id*. at 11–12.

40. *Id*. at 14.

41. *See, for example,* Hopkins, *supra* note 2, at 75–86.

42. The New York Times Rule—The Awakening Giant of First Amendment Protection, 62 Ky. L. J. 824, 827 (1974).

43. Green, The New York Times Rule: Judicial Overkill, 12 Vill. L. Rev. 730, 735 (1967).

44. 376 U.S. at 293, Justice Black concurring, joined by Justice Douglas; 376 U.S. at 297, Justice Goldberg concurring, joined by Justice Douglas.

45. Brennan Papers, Box 107, memoranda of Justice Harlan, February 20, 1964, and March 3, 1964; memorandum of Justice Brennan, March 6, 1964.

46. Brennan Papers, Box 107, memorandum of Justice Douglas, March 3, 1964.

47. Brennan Papers, Box 107, handwritten, undated note from Justice Goldberg.

48. *Id*.

49. Brennan Papers, Box 107, handwritten, undated note from Justice Goldberg.

50. Brennan Papers, Box 107, handwritten, undated note from Justice Black.

51. *Id*.

52. 376 U.S. at 286.

53. *Id*. at 288.

54. Brennan Papers, Box 107, memorandum of Justice Harlan, February 26, 1964. The suggested revision is not included in Brennan's case file.

55. Brennan Papers, Box 107, memorandum of Justice Brennan, March 2, 1964.

56. Brennan Papers, Box 107, handwritten, undated note from Chief Justice Warren.

57. Brennan Papers, Box 107, memorandum of Justice Harlan, March 3, 1964.

58. Brennan Papers, Box 107, "Separate Memorandum" of Justice Harlan, March 3, 1964.

59. Brennan Papers, Box 107, handwritten, undated note from Justice Black.

60. Brennan Papers, Box 107, "Memorandum to the Conference" from Justice Brennan, March 3, 1964.

61. *Id.*

62. Brennan Papers, Box 107, memorandum of Justice Brennan, March 6, 1964.

63. Brennan Papers, Box 107, "Memorandum to the Conference" from Justice Harlan, March 9, 1964.

64. 360 U.S. at 586, Justice Brennan dissenting.

65. 379 U.S. at 64 (1964).

66. 388 U.S. 130 (1967).

67. 403 U.S. 29 (1971).

68. *Id.* at 57, Justice Black concurring in the judgment.

69. Justice Douglas took no part in the case, and Justice White concurred in the judgment.

70. 418 U.S. 323 (1974).

71. *Id.* at 347.

72. *Id.*

73. *Id.* at 351–52.

74. *See* Time, Inc. v. Firestone, 424 U.S. 448 (1976); Wolston v. Reader's Digest Association, 443 U.S. 157 (1979).

75. Hutchinson v. Proxmire, 442 U.S. 111 (1979).

76. Keeton v. Hustler Magazine, 465 U.S. 770 (1984); Calder v. Jones, 465 U.S. 783 (1984).

77. Herbert v. Lando, 441 U.S. 153 (1979).

78. 379 U.S. at 72–73.

79. *Id.* at 73.

80. *Id.* at 74–75.

81. 383 U.S. 75 (1966).

82. *Id.* at 86.

83. *Id.*

84. Time, Inc. v. Hill, 385 U.S. 374, 389 (1967).

85. Brennan Papers, Box 234, draft opinion of Rosenbloom v. Metromedia, circulated February 17, 1971.

86. Brennan Papers, Box 234, memorandum of Justice Blackmun, March 22, 1971.

87. 403 U.S. at 35.

88. *Id.* at 41.

89. *Id.* at 43.

90. *Id.* at 41.

91. *Id.* at 46.

92. *Id.* at 43.
93. *Id.* at 46–47.
94. *Id.* at 43–44.
95. 418 U.S. at 327.
96. *Id.* at 329.
97. 471 F.2d 801 (1972).
98. 418 U.S. at 347.
99. *Id.* at 349.
100. *Id.* at 351–52.
101. *Id.* at 339–40.
102. *Id.* at 343.
103. *Id.* at 341.
104. *Id.* at 343.
105. *Id.* at 344.
106. *Id.* at 345.
107. *Id.* at 354, Justice Blackmun concurring.
108. *Id.*
109. *Id.* at 361, Justice Brennan dissenting.
110. *Id.* at 361–62, Justice Brennan dissenting.
111. Time, Inc. v. Firestone, 424 U.S. 448 (1976).
112. Wolston v. Reader's Digest Association, 443 U.S. 157 (1979).
113. Hutchinson v. Proxmire, 443 U.S. 111 (1979).
114. 441 U.S. 153 (1979).
115. *Id.* at 169.
116. *Id.* at 173.
117. *Id.* at 174.
118. *Id.* at 181, Justice Brennan dissenting.
119. *Id.* at 187–88, Justice Brennan dissenting.
120. *Id.* at 189, Justice Brennan dissenting.
121. *Id.* at 194, Justice Brennan dissenting.
122. 424 U.S. 448 (1976).
123. *Id.* at 471, Justice Brennan dissenting.
124. *Id.* at 473–74, Justice Brennan dissenting, quoting Cox Broadcasting Corp. v. Cohn, 420 U.S. 469, 491–92, 495 (1985).
125. Winfield, The Sound of Libel in the Key of B(ose) Goes Flat, Com. Law., Fall 1984, at 8.
126. 466 U.S. 485 (1984).
127. *Id.* at 491.
128. *Id.* at 512.
129. *Id.* at 513.
130. *Id.* at 503–4.
131. 472 U.S. 749 (1979).
132. *Id.* at 759.
133. *Id.* at 762.
134. *Id.* at 786, Justice Brennan dissenting.
135. *Id.* at 776, Justice Brennan dissenting.
136. *Id.* at 777, Justice Brennan dissenting.
137. *Id.* at 778, Justice Brennan dissenting.

138. *Id.* at 783, Justice Brennan dissenting.

139. Brennan Papers, Box 673, draft opinion circulated May 29, 1984.

140. Brennan Papers, Box 673, "Memorandum to the Conference" from Justice Powell, June 27, 1984.

141. Brennan Papers, Box 673, opinion circulated October 30, 1984; memoranda of Justice Stevens, October 30, 1984, Justice Blackmun and Justice Marshall, October 31, 1984.

142. Brennan Papers, Box 673, memorandum of Justice Stevens, March 21, 1985.

143. Brennan Papers, Box 673, memorandum of Chief Justice Burger, April 22, 1985.

144. 475 U.S. 767 (1986).

145. *Id.* at 776–77.

146. 472 U.S. 479 (1985).

147. *Id.* at 489.

148. 110 S.Ct. 2695 (1990).

149. *Id.* at 2708, Justice Brennan dissenting.

150. *Id.* at 2709, Justice Brennan dissenting.

151. *Id.* at 2699.

152. *Id.* at 2701.

153. *Id.* at 2705, quoting *Gertz,* 418 U.S. at 339–40.

154. *Id.*

155. *Id.*

156. *Id.* at 2705–6.

157. *Id.* at 2706.

158. *See* Greenbelt Cooperative Publishing Assn., Inc. v. Bresler, 398 U.S. 6 (1970); Letter Carriers v. Austin, 418 U.S. 264 (1974); and Hustler Magazine v. Falwell, 108 S.Ct. 876 (1988).

159. 110 S.Ct. at 2706.

160. *Id.* at 2707.

161. *Id.*

162. *Id.* at 2711, Justice Brennan dissenting.

163. *Id.* at 2709–10, Justice Brennan dissenting.

164. *Id.* at 2712, Justice Brennan dissenting.

165. *Id.* at 2713, Justice Brennan dissenting.

166. *Id.* at 2714, Justice Brennan dissenting.

167. *Id.* at 2708, Justice Brennan dissenting.

168. 376 U.S. at 275.

169. *Id.* at 270.

170. *Id.* at 282.

171. *Id.* at 270.

172. *Garrison,* 279 U.S. at 74–75.

173. *Gertz,* 418 U.S. at 361–62, Justice Brennan dissenting.

174. Brennan Papers, *supra* note 85.

175. Time v. Firestone, 424 U.S. at 471, Justice Brennan dissenting.

176. Time, Inc. v. Hill, 385 U.S. at 389.

177. *Herbert,* 441 U.S. at 181, Justice Brennan dissenting.

178. *Dun & Bradstreet,* 472 U.S. at 783.

6

"Closely Akin To 'Pure Speech' "

The First Amendment guarantee that "Congress shall make no law abridging . . . the freedom of speech" is generally thought to refer to spoken words.[1] Some actions are singularly communicative, however, in that their primary function is to express ideas. The Supreme Court has recognized that such actions constitute protected speech under the Constitution. The Court has held, for example, that the wearing of armbands is conduct "closely akin to 'pure speech.' "[2] To remain standing in "silent, reproachful presence" after having been ordered to leave a segregated public library, the Court has said, is also protected speech,[3] as is wearing a jacket with an offensive message,[4] displaying a U.S. flag upside down with a peace symbol attached,[5] and burning the U.S. flag.[6] In addition, picketing has been recognized as a unique form of speech.[7]

The Court has also recognized, however, that some types of expressive conduct are not protected under the First Amendment. While burning the American flag may be protected expression, for example, burning a draft card is not.[8] And, while the Court assumed that sleeping, in some circumstances, may be expression, it is not protected expression in light of a federal restriction against camping on the mall in Washington, D.C.[9] In addition, speech itself, when it becomes so abusive that it takes on the characteristics of action, may also be restricted.[10]

The Court's varied rulings on expressive conduct, then, raise a number of questions. When is conduct protected by the First Amendment? When is picketing protected? When is abusive speech protected? The Court faced those questions some fifty-three times between 1957 and 1990, most often finding in favor of free-speech positions.[11] Justice Brennan was more protective than his colleagues. Only twice in the fifty-three cases did he vote against claimants making First Amendment arguments, and neither of those votes can be seen as serious First Amendment infringements.[12]

The cases in this area of the law can be divided into three groupings: expressive conduct in general, picketing, and abusive speech, that is, speech that takes the form of conduct.

EXPRESSIVE CONDUCT

In 1968 the Court enunciated the test it would use to determine when First Amendment protection attaches to expressive conduct. And in 1974 the Court provided a test to determine what types of conduct could be classified as speech and, therefore, would implicate First Amendment protections. Not until 1989, however, were all these elements pulled together in a cogent explanation of the relationships among conduct, speech, and the First Amendment. That explanation was written by Brennan in his first majority opinion in the area of expressive conduct.[13]

The 1958 case was *U.S. v. O'Brien*[14] and involved the conviction of David Paul O'Brien for burning his draft card on the steps of the South Boston Courthouse. O'Brien did not deny burning the card; indeed, he told the jury at his trial he did so to influence others to reevaluate their positions on Selective Service and the armed forces.[15] He claimed that the federal statute under which he was convicted was unconstitutional because it was enacted to abridge free speech and had no legitimate legislative purpose.[16] O'Brien argued that freedom of expression included "all modes of 'communication of ideas by conduct.' "[17]

Chief Justice Earl Warren, writing for six members of the Court,[18] however, found that the Court could not "accept the view that an apparently limitless variety of conduct can be labeled 'speech' whenever the person engaging in the conduct intends thereby to express an idea."[19] When speech and nonspeech elements are combined, Warren wrote, "a sufficiently important governmental interest in regulating the nonspeech element can justify incidental limitations on First Amendment freedoms."[20] Therefore, he ruled, expressive conduct can be restricted if four criteria are met:

1. the government regulation is within the constitutional power of the government;

2. the regulation furthers an important or substantial governmental interest;

3. the governmental interest furthered is unrelated to the supression of free expression; and

4. the incidental restriction on free expression is no greater than is essential to the furtherance of that governmental interest.[21]

The 1974 case was *Spence v. Washington*,[22] a flag-misuse case. The defendant in the case, in front of his home, had flown the U.S. flag upside down with a peace symbol attached and was convicted for violating a state law prohibiting the display of the flag on which anything was attached. In a *per curiam* opinion, the Court overturned the conviction, finding that the display was protected speech. The Court reiterated that not all conduct can be considered speech, but stated that when the purpose of the conduct is to convey a particular message, and when the likelihood is great that witnesses of the conduct will understand the message, the conduct is speech.[23] In *Spence,* the Court held, the two symbols were used to make "a pointed expression of anguish" and "the likelihood was great that the message would be understood by those who viewed it."[24]

Brennan joined the majority without additional comment in both cases. In later cases, however, it became clear that Brennan adhered to more expansive applications of the two tests. For example, in *Clark v. Community for Creative Non-Violence*,[25] a 1984 case, he joined Justice Thurgood Marshall's dissent, arguing that sleeping to protest the plight of the homeless was unqualified speech and deserved protection.[26] The case began when members of the Community for Creative Non-Violence, joined by a number of homeless persons in Washington, D.C., protested the plight of the homeless by sleeping on the Washington Mall. The CCNV had received a permit allowing the protest, but the U.S. Park Service enforced a restriction disallowing camping on the mall. Justice Byron White, for the majority, applied the *O'Brien* test and found that sleeping on the mall could be prohibited. The Park Service restriction, he wrote, was a valid time, place, and manner limitation that focused on maintaining the parks. The requirement was content-neutral, and any restriction on speech was incidental.[27]

Marshall found otherwise. The majority, he argued, failed to recognize that every governmental abridgment of expression must be justified.[28] While the government contended that the ban on sleeping was necessary, there was no showing that there would be any substantial wear and tear on park property.[29]

Brennan had assigned the dissent to Marshall,[30] but wrote his own dissent as well, which he did not publish. He found it absurd that the U.S. Park Service would allow the group to pitch tents, lay down, and feign sleep, but would stop the protesters from actually falling asleep: "All that is accomplished by such application is squelching the particular form of symbolic conduct that the CCNV [Community for Creative Non-Violence] protesters most want to pursue."[31] The conduct involved, Brennan wrote, was not merely facilitative; it was

a powerful symbolic means of dramatizing the plight of the homeless in this country and of pricking the conscience of those who would normally ignore that plight. In this sense, the homeless people's act of sleeping represents a form of symbolic conduct no different from that of blacks standing in silent protest in a segregated library, or of someone placing a peace symbol on the American flag.[32]

Clark was one of few cases in which the Court did not rule in favor of plaintiffs making First Amendment arguments in expressive-conduct cases during the Brennan era. The Court overturned convictions of blacks for sitting at a segregated lunch counter[33] and, as indicated, of refusing to leave a segregated public library when ordered to do so.[34] The Court also found unconstitutional a statute prohibiting one from wearing a military uniform in a skit critical of U.S. involvement in Vietnam,[35] and overturned the conviction of a man for wearing in public a jacket bearing the slogan "Fuck the draft."[36] The state, the Court held in this second case, has no right to "cleanse public debate" of what it finds objectionable.[37]

Brennan joined the Court in all these cases. Indeed, he wrote only one published opinion—a concurrence in judgment disagreeing with the Court's rationale in *Brown v. Louisiana*[38]—before 1989, when he wrote the majority opinion in *Texas v. Johnson,*[39] the flag-burning case. This was not the Court's first case involving a conviction for misuse of the flag. As previously indicated, the Court had overturned a conviction for flying the flag upside down with a peace symbol attached.[40] The Court had also overturned convictions for treating a flag contemptuously by wearing it sewn into the seat of a pair of paints,[41] and, in *Street v. New York,*[42] of speaking ill of the flag.

In *Street,* Justice Brennan asked Justice John Marshall Harlan to remove from the majority opinion one sentence: "We add that disrespect for our flag is to be deplored no less in these vexed times than in calmer periods of our history." Brennan wrote Harlan, "I must tell you in all candor I have no idea what this means and secondly, if I did, I still wouldn't like it."[43] Harlan did not remove the sentence.[44]

Brennan may have presaged his opinion in the flag-burning case with his memorandum to Harlan, but only when he delivered his majority opinion in that case did Brennan fully delineate his views on expressive conduct. First, however, Brennan delineated the Court's methodology in handling cases in which elements of conduct and expression are combined.

Gregory Lee Johnson was convicted of desecrating the flag under Texas law rather than of simply insulting the flag with words or treating the flag contemptuously. First, Brennan noted, writing for a five-member majority,[45] the Court must determine whether Johnson's action was expressive conduct, allowing him to invoke the First Amendment. If the conduct is expressive, the Court must then decide whether the state regulation involved is related to the suppression of free expression or to some governmental interest.[46]

Johnson burned the flag as the culmination of a political rally protesting the renomination of Ronald Reagan as the Republican candidate for president. "The expressive, overtly political nature of this conduct was both intentional and overwhelmingly apparent," Brennan noted. The conduct, therefore was "sufficiently imbued with elements of communication . . . to implicate the First Amendment."[47]

While the government generally has a freer hand in restricting expressive conduct than in restricting the written or spoken word, conduct may not be proscribed because it has expressive elements, Brennan wrote. Only when there is a substantial governmental interest may the expressive conduct be restricted.[48] In *Texas v. Johnson,* Texas asserted two interests: preventing breaches of the peace and preserving the flag as a symbol of nationhood and national unity. The interest in preventing breaches of the peace was not implicated in the case, Brennan ruled. There was no disturbance and there was no evidence of a threatened disturbance because of the flag-burning. The government may not assume that every expression of a provocative idea will incite a riot and may not, therefore, automatically prohibit the expression of disagreeable ideas.[49] The state interest in preserving the flag as a national symbol is directly related to expression, Brennan held. The concerns over the effects of burning the flag "blossom only when a person's treatment of the flag communicates some message, and thus are related 'to suppression of free expression.' " Therefore, Brennan held, the case does not fulfill the criteria for the *O'Brien* test.[50]

The only remaining question, Brennan wrote, is whether the state interest in preserving the flag as a symbol of national unity justifies Johnson's conviction. It is important to the case, Brennan noted, that Johnson was convicted for his specific dissatisfaction with the policies of the United States—"expression situated at the core of our First Amendment values."[51] In addition, the Texas statute under which Johnson was convicted was content-based, since it only punished treatment of the flag that would be offensive to viewers. The state argued that any expressive conduct that cast doubt on the idea of national unity is a harmful message and may be prohibited. But, Brennan wrote, "if there is a bedrock principle underlying the First Amendment, it is that the Government may not prohibit the expression of an idea simply because society finds the idea itself offensive or disagreeable."[52]

When that rule is applied to the flag, Brennan wrote, it means that the government may not establish an orthodox way to use a symbol: "To conclude that the Government may permit designated symbols to be used to communicate only a limited set of messages would be to enter territory having no discernible or defensible boundaries."[53] The government has an interest in encouraging the proper treatment of the flag, but may not criminally punish one for burning a flag as a means of political protest.[54]

Brennan concluded the opinion with a treatise of support for the flag, noting that Johnson's action would not endanger "the special role played by our flag or the feelings it inspires." Wrote Brennan:

> We are tempted to say, in fact, that the flag's deservedly cherished place in our community will be strengthened, not weakened, by our holding today. Our decision is a reaffirmation of the principles of freedom and inclusiveness that the flag best reflects, and of the conviction that our toleration of criticism such as Johnson's is a sign and source of our strength. . . . It is the Nation's resilience, not its rigidity, that Texas sees reflected in the flag—and it is that resilience that we reassert today.[55]

A year later the Court reaffirmed *Texas v. Johnson* in a second flag-burning case, with Brennan again writing the majority opinion. In response to the Court's opinion in *Texas v. Johnson,* Congress passed the Flag Protection Act of 1989,[56] which made any type of physical defilement of the flag a crime. Prosecutors argued that two convictions under the act should be upheld because the act was not designed to control content. Instead, its purpose was to protect the physical integrity of the flag "as the unique and unalloyed symbol of the Nation," regardless of the motive for the abuse.[57]

Brennan, however, did not buy the argument. He wrote that the provisions of the Flag Protection Act made it clear that the government was attempting to suppress expression.[58] "Government may create national symbols," Brennan wrote, "promote them, and encourage their respectful treatment. But the Flag Protection Act goes well beyond this by criminally proscribing expressive conduct because of its likely communicative impact."[59] The act, therefore, was unconstitutional.

PICKETING

Picketing is a special activity the Court has long recognized as constitutionally protected expression.[60] As a form of expression, therefore, the Court held that peaceful picketing could not be licensed,[61] that restrictions could not be content-based,[62] and that it could not be banned from public property.[63] The Court also held that restrictions on related activities were unconstitutional. The nonviolent aspects of boycotts, for example, were protected[64]; the requirement that handbills contain the names and addresses of their sponsors was a free-speech violation[65]; and restrictions on the fees and expenses professional fundraisers could charge were disallowed.[66]

Even as these protections were being established, however, the Court was limiting some types of picketing. Protesters, for example, were not allowed to obstruct jails[67] or courthouses,[68] and picketing in some other public settings could be restricted as well.[69] The Court also held that picketing in shopping malls[70] and other private property, including private residences, could be restricted,[71] and that distribution of literature or petitions on military bases—even those portions of the bases open to the public—could be regulated.[72]

Brennan agreed with only one of these restrictions, and his agreement there was because the ordinance involved was narrowly drawn and, he wrote, content-neutral. The case was *Cameron v. Johnson*.[73] Writing for seven members of the Court, Brennan upheld a Mississippi anti-picketing ordinance that prohibited picketing that obstructed traffic in and out of courthouses. Although Justices Abe Fortas and William O. Douglas complained that the statute was specifically designed and enforced to hamper civil rights demonstrators,[74] Brennan found the statute precise and content-neutral.[75]

Cameron was one of only four majority opinions Brennan wrote on picketing, and two of the other three cases were settled on procedural rather than constitutional grounds.[76] Because Brennan wrote majority opinions so rarely, much of his philosophy on picketing issues was expressed in his separate writings, but there is a dearth there as well. Brennan wrote five dissents, one concurrence, and two concurrences and dissents between 1957 and 1990. Five other times he joined dissenters without writing.[77]

What is clear, however, is that Brennan found government restrictions on picketing as obnoxious as other attempts to restrain expression and, therefore, restrictions on such expression would have to be narrowly tailored. Speech, he wrote, can be prohibited only when the regulations are narrowly drawn to serve a compelling state interest or to prohibit speech that interferes with vital government facilities or is directed toward an illegal purpose. And there can be content-neutral time, place, and manner restrictions, which must also be narrowly drawn, to serve a significant government interest. These restrictions must leave open ample alternative channels of communication.[78]

Rarely did the government meet the formula. Brennan disagreed when the Court ruled that picketing at shopping malls could be banned because the malls, although open to the public for shopping, were private property.[79] He disagreed when the Court banned handbilling and petition–circulation on military bases,[80] restricted such activity at state fairs,[81] and allowed trespassing convictions for protesting on jail property.[82] He opposed ordinances requiring advance written notice before canvassing would be allowed[83] and that allowed only certain types of picketing.[84] And he believed persons should be allowed to violate a judge's injunction against picketing, if the order was unconstitutional.[85]

The high regard Brennan had for free expression through picketing is apparent in the first such case in which he wrote, *Walker v. Birmingham*.[86] In that case, the Court upheld a contempt-of-court conviction of civil rights marchers who violated a judge's injunction and marched on Good Friday in 1963. Brennan wrote one of three dissents, chiding the majority for letting loose "a devastatingly destructive weapon" for those who would infringe freedom of expression.[87]

The vitality of First Amendment protections, Brennan wrote, has rested in large part on one's ability to take one's chances and express oneself in the face of restrictions and, later, to challenge the constitutionality of those restraints. Were it not for the judge's order, he noted, the marchers might have taken that path in this case.[88] It should have been clear to the Court, which is charged with the responsibility of safeguarding constitutional freedoms, therefore, that injunctions are far more dangerous to First Amendment freedoms than statutes.[89] The danger is even more clear in this case, Brennan wrote, because the state appellate court had held that the ordinance the judge had incorporated into his injunction was unconstitutional.[90]

Brennan chided the majority again nine years later, writing, as one of two dissenters in *Greer v. Spock,*[91] that the Court was no longer allowing, under any circumstances, free expression on military bases.[92] Six members of the Court upheld a ban on political speech-making or distribution of literature on military bases. The Court found that the policy was objective and evenhanded and was designed to keep military personnel free of partisan entanglements.[93] "Such a policy," the Court ruled, "is wholly consistent with the American constitutional tradition of a politically neutral military establishment under civilian control."[94]

Brennan disagreed on both practical and philosophical grounds. It is naive, he wrote, to believe that any organization, including the military, is value-neutral. Because the military is affected by national affairs, he wrote, it is susceptible to politicization, and, therefore, the isolation that the restriction promoted "only erodes neutrality and invites the danger that neutrality seeks to avoid."[95] The regulation, therefore, was contrary to, rather than supportive of, its intent. Readiness to fight, Brennan argued, did not require the exclusion of ideas, and history teaches that "the First Amendment does not evaporate with the mere intonation of interests such as national defense, military necessity, or domestic security."[96]

Dr. Benjamin Spock and his colleagues did not claim that the First Amendment was unbending or that military bases were public forums, Brennan noted. They simply claimed the right to distribute literature on portions of Fort Dix that were open to the public.[97] The Court had allowed such action in a previous case involving Fort Sam Houston,[98] and Brennan argued that the two bases were significantly similar so that the distribution of literature should be allowed at Fort Dix.[99]

But, more important, Brennan complained, the Court's ruling deemed free expression to be detrimental to members of the armed forces, when the Court should have recognized that free expression is, in fact, beneficial. He argued for a flexible approach to determining when public expression should be limited. Otherwise, there would be a danger that certain forms of important public speech might be suppressed.[100]

Brennan renewed his argument four years later in *Brown v. Glines*,[101] in which a regulation required military personnel to receive command permission before they could circulate petitions. Brennan saw the case as one involving prior restraint. The regulations, he wrote, "plainly establish an essentially discretionary regime of censorship" that arbitrarily deprived military personnel of communicative rights.[102]

The regulations were invalid in three ways, Brennan wrote. First, the requirement for command approval was based on the military's interest in maintaining discipline and efficiency. Such interests are important, Brennan wrote, but are insufficient to warrant censorship.[103] Second, the command-approval procedure was seriously flawed because essential safeguards were absent: The censor was not required to justify the censorship; there was no guarantee of a speedy judicial review of the suppression; and there was no opportunity to be heard during suppression proceedings.[104] Third, the regulations did not demonstrably serve military interests.[105]

The regulations were invalid, Brennan argued, even in the face of *Greer*. At least under *Greer* the demonstrators had alternative avenues for expression. "For soldiers and sailors, as opposed to civilians," Brennan wrote, "military installations *must* be the place for 'free . . . communication of thoughts. . . .' Further, when service personnel are stationed abroad or at sea, the base or warship is very likely the *only* place for free communication of thoughts."[106]

In addition, the military officials involved refused to allow the circulation of petitions because they found the content of the petitions to be erroneous and misleading. That judgment was "quintessentially political," Brennan wrote, and, therefore, the "tradition of a politically neutral military" referred to in *Greer* was violated.[107]

The restrictions in *Greer* and *Brown* were doubly obnoxious because they violated two areas Brennan found to be virtually sacrosanct: freedom to assemble in a public place, and freedom to engage in political speech.

Brennan would allow time, place, and manner restrictions for picketing on public property.[108] Unless there was the threat of violence, disruption of the course of business, or obstruction of the public place to those who are conducting business, assembly and picketing must be allowed,[109] even if the public place is a jail:

> The jailhouse, like an executive mansion, a legislative chamber, a courthouse, or the statehouse itself is one of the seats of government, whether it be the Tower of London, the Bastille, or a small county jail. And when it houses political prisoners or those who many think are unjustly held, it is an obvious center for protest.[110]

Political speech, of course, was considered by Brennan to be "core conduct" protected by the First Amendment. Such conduct was at issue in *Hynes v. Mayor of Oradell*.[111] The Court struck down an ordinance that required advance written notice before political canvassing or soliciting. The ordinance was unconstitutionally vague, the Court held, although narrowly drawn restrictions would be allowed.

Brennan wrote separately to take issue with the notion that any such ordinance would be constitutional. Eliminating the possibility of anonymous political speech, he wrote, poses a threat to political expression, which is "the core conduct protected by the First Amendment."[112]

He made the same argument in his separate opinion to *Heffron v. International Society for Krishna Consciousness*.[113] The Court, in *Heffron*, ruled that a state could allow distribution of literature at a state fair only from a rented booth. The regulation was not content-based, the Court held. Brennan agreed that the solicitation or the sale of literature could be restricted to a booth, but disagreed that the distribution of free literature could be so restricted.[114]

Any person, Brennan wrote, could mill around at the fair, speak to others, or otherwise proselytize. As soon as that person gave out a piece of literature, however, the person could be arrested and removed, placing "a significant restriction on First Amendment rights."[115] The state argued that the regulation was necessary to keep order, but Brennan found no evidence that a relaxation of the rule would cause increased disorder. The state, he wrote, is "relying on a general, speculative fear of disorder" to place significant restrictions on Krishna's "ability to exercise core First Amendment rights."[116]

Fairgrounds, courthouses, jails, and military bases are public property, but Justice Brennan also believed that picketing was sometimes allowable on private property, particularly if the private property had a public use, as with a privately owned shopping mall.[117] And he disagreed with his colleagues that picketing aimed at private residences could be restricted.[118] While the law should not allow a crowd virtually to imprison a person in his or her home, Brennan wrote, "so long as the speech remains outside the home and does not unduly coerce the occupant, the government's heightened interest in protecting residential privacy is not implicated."[119]

ABUSIVE LANGUAGE

The Court had first dealt with abusive speech in the 1942 case of *Chaplinsky v. New Hampshire*.[120] In that case the Court allowed a Jehovah's Witness to be convicted for calling another person a "God damned racketeer" and "a damned Fascist,"[121] holding that fighting words—words that "by their very utterance inflict injury or tend to incite an immediate breach of the peace"—could be punished.[122] The words could be punished, not simply because they were abusive, but because they were directed at an individual and were so virulent that their very utterance might cause a physical, rather than verbal, response.

In the mid-1970s the Court faced a handful of abusive-language cases that took a different slant. Chaplinsky had been convicted under a statute that forbade a verbal assault on another person. The cases in the 1970s, however, although they involved speech, were often treated as conduct cases. Defendants were convicted of breach of the peace,[123] disorderly conduct,[124] or interfering with an officer in the performance of his duties[125] all because of the nature of the language they used.

Brennan usually found the convictions unconstitutional, and usually on the grounds that the statutes under which the defendants were convicted were overbroad. Brennan's opinions in abusive-language cases also demonstrate his resolve to accord speech a place of special prominence in society. The use of abusive language—even profanity aimed at a police officer in the performance of his duty—was insufficient, in Brennan's eyes, to warrant punishment for expression.[126] He wrote the majority opinions in three abusive language cases: *Gooding v. Wilson*[127] in 1972, *Lewis v. New Orleans*[128] in 1974, and *Houston v. Hill*[129] in 1987.

In *Gooding* a black man was convicted for telling a police officer, "White son of a bitch, I'll kill you. . . . You son of a bitch, I'll choke you to death," and for telling an accompanying officer, "You son of a bitch, if you ever put your hands on me again, I'll cut you all to pieces."[130] He was convicted under a Georgia statute making it a crime to use "opprobrious words or abusive language tending to cause a breach of the peace."[131]

The statute was invalid, Brennan wrote, because it punished only words without the requisite narrow construction. When a statute punishes words, it must be narrowly drawn so that protected speech is not also punished.[132] Under the definition placed on "breach of peace" by the Georgia courts, Brennan wrote, it would be a " 'breach of peace' merely to speak words offensive to some who hear them," so the statute was overbroad.[133]

Chief Justice Warren Burger dissented, arguing that previous cases under the Georgia statute demonstrated that protected speech would not be restricted and criticizing the majority for basing its decision on "a few isolated cases, decided as long ago as 1905 and generally long before this Court's decision in *Chaplinsky v. New Hampshire.*"[134] Burger had attempted to derail *Gooding* by setting the case for reargument, based on an abbreviated discussion of the case and his memory that no more than four of the seven participating justices favored overturning the conviction, with Justice Douglas undecided.[135] "The total time devoted to it at our conference was barely ten minutes," Burger wrote. "It was a case of major importance, and I do not believe it has had adequate exploration."[136]

Douglas responded the same day, indicating that he had worked through "the tangled materials" during the Conference and joined the majority. As a result, he wrote, he had assigned the opinion to Brennan.[137]

Burger responded that "there was no recorded vote of your position after your comment on the initial call that you were 'in doubt.' " He saw no harm in awaiting Brennan's opinion, but still recommended rearguing the case since only four members favored overturning the conviction. "I think it very likely this case will be reargued," he wrote. "I, for one, will not take part in overruling *Chaplinsky,* directly or indirectly, with a seven-member Court. I will await Bill Brennan's writing."[138] A month later Burger renewed his call for reargument, citing the 4-3 vote.[139] Brennan responded the same day, however, noting that *Gooding* was 5-2, with Marshall, White, Stewart, and Douglas joining the Brennan opinion.[140]

Lewis, decided in two years after *Gooding,* so greatly resembled the earlier case that Burger, who wrote biting dissents in both cases, called the cases blood brothers.[141] In *Lewis,* as in *Gooding,* a black man was convicted of violating state law by using profanity when responding to a police officer. The defendant in *Lewis,* however, denied using profane language.[142] Quoting *Gooding,* Brennan wrote that the New Orleans statute in question could be applied to protected speech and, therefore, was overbroad.[143]

Using *Lewis* as a basis, the Court struck down, without opinion, a number of convictions for the use of abusive language in 1974.[144] Then, in 1987, *Gooding* and *Lewis* were reinforced, with Brennan again writing the majority opinion. Wayne Hill was convicted of interfering with a police officer when, as the police officer arrested another man, he asked the officer, "Why don't you pick on somebody your own size?"[145] Once again, Brennan found that constitutionally protected speech might be prohibited by the ordinance under which Hill was convicted.[146] "The freedom of individuals verbally to oppose or challenge police action without thereby risking arrest is one of the principal characteristics by which we distinguish a free nation from a police state," he wrote.[147]

Except for Chief Justice William Rehnquist, all members of the Court agreed that the conviction should be overturned, although not all agreed with Brennan's reasoning. Powell and Scalia, for example, did not believe that the ordinance violated the First Amendment.[148]

CONCLUSIONS

Brennan's activity in expressive-conduct cases was not as pronounced as in other areas of free-expression law. In fifty-three cases he wrote only eight majority opinions, two concurring opinions, five dissents, and two opinions concurring and dissenting. It is clear, however, that the justice supported ample protection for expressive conduct. Two themes—common to much of Brennan's work in free expression areas—emerge in the expressive-conduct cases. First, expression is not a luxury in a free society; it is a right. And, because it is a right, free expression, in whatever form, deserves protection even when it inconveniences, embarrasses, or hampers. Second, free expression is a right because it benefits society. That is, the right exists for more than philosophical or esoteric reasons; it exists because, in a practical sense, it facilitates the proper workings of a free society.

Brennan recognized that expressive conduct might take the form of a slogan that offends,[149] of "silent, reproachful presence" that causes discomfort,[150] of action that causes anger,[151] or of activity that inconveniences government.[152] Such conduct was protected, however, in order to ensure robust speech. Expressive conduct in public places—except when there was an obstruction of business,[153] the threat of possible disruption,[154] or routine time, place, and manner restrictions—could not be halted, Brennan believed, even if the expressive conduct was aimed at private individuals.[155] Likewise, conduct that constituted political speech could not be banned, for it was "the core conduct protected by the First Amendment."[156]

In addition, while abusive language could be restricted, any restrictions must be narrowly drawn so that protected speech is clearly excluded. Even restrictions on language aimed at law-enforcement officers must fit within the formula. The freedom to oppose police action verbally without fear of imprisonment is basic to a free nation, Brennan wrote.[157]

In the cases involving expressive speech on military bases, Brennan made it clear that he believed free speech to be so essential to the proper operation of a free society that it could not be banned. Although he recognized that one purpose of the Constitution was to provide for the common defense, he found that an equally important purpose was to "secure the Blessings of Liberty to ourselves and our Posterity," for which the First Amendment is "both explicit and indispensable."[158] The Court, Brennan argued in his *Greer* dissent, assumed that free speech worked to the detriment of the armed forces, when it actually works to its benefit.[159] Because the military is not value-neutral, he wrote, and is affected by national affairs, it is susceptible to politicization. The isolation of military personnel from ideas, therefore, is dangerous to the concept of a politically neutral military.[160] Military installations, then, must be places for free communication of thoughts, Brennan wrote.[161] After all, he wrote, the significance of the First Amendment is so great that it "does not evaporate with the mere intonation of interests such as national defense, military necessity, or domestic security."[162]

Much of Brennan's theory on expressive conduct was expressed in the flag-burning cases. In *Texas v. Johnson,* Brennan found that, coming at the culmination of a political rally protesting the policies of President Ronald Reagan, the "expressive, overtly political nature" of the flag-burning was "both intentional and overwhelmingly apparent," therefore implicating First Amendment protections.[163] In addition, he found that, while the government has an interest in establishing and promoting national symbols, like the flag, that interest does not override First Amendment protections of expression.[164] "If there is a bedrock principle underlying the First Amendment," Brennan wrote, "it is that the Government may not prohibit the expression of an idea simply because society finds the idea itself offensive or disagreeable."[165]

NOTES

1. Justice Hugo Black was probably the Court's leading proponent of the theory that the First Amendment did not protect conduct because conduct was neither speech nor press. *See, for example,* his opinion in Adderly v. Florida, 385 U.S. 39 (1966); and his joiner of Justice Harry Blackmun's dissent in Cohen v. California, 403 U.S. 15 (1971).

2. Tinker v. Des Moines School District, 393 U.S. 503, 505 (1969).

3. Brown v. Louisiana, 383 U.S. 131, 141–42 (1966).

4. Cohen v. California, 403 U.S. 15 (1971).

5. Cowgill v. California, 396 U.S. 371 (1971).

6. Texas v. Johnson, 109 S.Ct. 2533 (1989); U.S. v. Eichmann, 110 S.Ct. 2404 (1990).

7. Cox v. Louisiana, 379 U.S. 559 and 379 U.S. 537 (1965); Shuttlesworth v. Birmingham, 394 U.S. 147 (1969); Gregory v. Chicago, 394 U.S. 111 (1969).

8. U.S. v. O'Brien, 391 U.S. 367 (1968).

9. Clark v. Community for Creative Non-Violence, 468 U.S. 288 (1984).

10. *See* discussion accompanying *infra* notes 120–25, *for example.*

11. The Court's rulings favored free expression in thirty-five cases, hampered free expression in sixteen cases, and were neutral in two cases.

12. In *O'Brien* Justice Brennan joined the Court's opinion holding that a conviction for burning a draft card was constitutional in light of the government's interest in maintaining a defensive force weighed against the incidental infringement on speech, 391 U.S. 367 (1968). In Cowgill v. California, the Court dismissed the appeal of a conviction for abusing the flag by wearing it fashioned into a vest, and Justice Brennan joined Justice John Marshall Harlan's concurring opinion in which Harlan stated he would dismiss the appeal on the basis of a record inadequate to determine the issue of whether wearing the flag as a vest is a symbolic message, 396 U.S. 371, 371 (1971), Justice Harlan concurring.

13. For purposes of this chapter, picketing is considered separately from other forms of expressive conduct. *See infra* notes 60–119. Justice Brennan, of course, had written earlier opinions in the area of picketing.

14. 391 U.S. 367 (1968).

15. *Id.* at 370.

16. *Id.*

17. *Id.* at 376.

18. Justice Thurgood Marshall did not participate; Justice William O. Douglas dissented on grounds that the case should be set for reargument, *id.* at 389.

19. 391 U.S. at 376.

20. *Id.*

21. *Id.* at 377.

22. 418 U.S. 405 (1974).

23. *Id.* at 411.

24. *Id.* at 410–11.

25. 468 U.S. 228 (1984).

26. *Id.* at 301, Justice Marshall dissenting.

27. *Id.* at 294–96.

28. *Id.* at 309, Justice Marshall dissenting.

29. *Id.* at 311, Justice Marshall dissenting.

30. Brennan Papers, Box 657, memorandum of Justice Brennan, April 2, 1974.

31. *Id.* Undated, unpublished opinion of Justice Brennan.

32. *Id.*

33. Garner v. Louisiana, 368 U.S. 157 (1961).

34. Brown v. Louisiana, 383 U.S. 131 (1966).

35. Schacht v. U.S., 398 U.S. 58 (1970).

36. Cohen v. California, 403 U.S. 15 (1971).

37. *Id.* at 25.

38. 383 U.S. 131, 144, Justice Brennan concurring in judgment. Justice Brennan found the statute under which five blacks were convicted of breach of the peace to be overbroad and a serious threat to the exercise of constitutional rights. Therefore, he found it unnecessary to determine whether the conduct involved was constitutionally protected.

39. 109 S.Ct. 2533 (1989).

40. Spence v. Washington, 418 U.S. 405 (1974).

41. Smith v. Goguen, 415 U.S. 566 (1974).

42. 394 U.S. 576 (1969).

43. Brennan Papers, Box 183, memorandum of Justice Brennan, December 2, 1968.

44. *See* 394 U.S. at 594.

45. Justice Brennan was joined by Justices Thurgood Marshall, Harry Blackmun, Antonin Scalia, and Anthony M. Kennedy, who also joined his opinion in U.S. v. Eichman, 110 S.Ct. 2404 (1990).

46. 109 S.Ct. at 2538–39.

47. *Id.* at 2540.

48. *Id.*

49. *Id.* at 2541.

50. *Id.* at 2541.

51. *Id.* at 2543.

52. *Id.* at 2544.

53. *Id.* at 2546.

54. *Id.* at 2547.

55. *Id.*

56. 18 U.S.C.A. sec 700 (Supp. 1990).

57. U.S. v. Eichman, 110 S.Ct. 2404, 2408 (1990).

58. *Id.* at 2408–9.

59. *Id.* at 2409.

60. Cox v. Louisiana, 379 U.S. 559, 379 U.S. 537 (1965); Gregory v. Chicago, 394 U.S. 111 (1969); Shuttlesworth v. Birmingham, 394 U.S. 147 (1969).

61. Edwards v. South Carolina, 372 U.S. 229 (1963); Henry v. Rock Hill, 376 U.S. 776 (1964); U.S. v. Grace, 461 U.S. 171 (1983).

62. Police Department of Chicago v. Mosely, 408 U.S. 92 (1972); Carey v. Brown, 447 U.S. 455 (1980).

63. Tally v. California, 362 U.S. 229 (1963); Shuttlesworth v. Birmingham, 394 U.S. 147 (1969); Hynes v. Mayor of Oradell, 425 U.S. 610 (1976); U.S. v. Grace, 461 U.S. 171 (1983); Board of Airport Commissioners v. Jews for Jesus, 482 U.S. 569 (1987).

64. NAACP v. Claiborne Hardware Co., 458 U.S. 886 (1982).

65. Tally v. California, 362 U.S. 60 (1960).

66. Schaumburg v. Citizens for a Better Environment, 444 U.S. 620 (1980); Secretary of the State of Maryland v. Joseph H. Munson Co., 467 U.S. 947 (1984).

67. Adderly v. Florida, 385 U.S. 39 (1966).

68. Cameron v. Johnson, 390 U.S. 611 (1968).

69. Heffron v. International Society for Krishna Consciousness, 452 U.S. 640 (1981). *See also* Teamsters Union v. Vogt, 354 U.S. 284 (1957).

70. Lloyd Corp. v. Tanner, 407 U.S. 551 (1972); Hudgens v. NLRB, 424 U.S. 507 (1976).

71. American Radio Association v. Mobile Steamship Association, 419 U.S. 215 (1974); Frisby v. Schultz, 487 U.S. 474 (1988).

72. Greer v. Spock, 424 U.S. 828 (1976); Brown v. Glines, 444 U.S. 348 (1980).

73. 390 U.S. 611 (1968).

74. *Id.* at 624–27, Justice Fortas dissenting, joined by Justice Douglas.

75. *Id.* at 616–17.

76. Zwickler v. Koota, 389 U.S. 241 (1967); Bachellar v. Maryland, 397 U.S. 564 (1970).

77. Justice Brennan joined dissents in Adderly v. Florida, 385 U.S. 39 (1966); Lloyd Corp. v. Tanner, 407 U.S. 551 (1972); American Radio Association v. Mobile Steamship Association, 419 U.S. 215 (1974); Hudgens v. NLRB, 424 U.S. 507 (1976); U.S. v. Albertini, 472 U.S. 675 (1985).

78. *Carey,* 447 U.S. at 470; Perry Education Association v. Penny Local Educators' Association, 460 U.S. 37 (1983) 45.

79. *Lloyd Corp.,* 407 U.S. at 571, Justice Marshall dissenting (joined by Justice Brennan); *Hudgens,* 424 U.S. at 525, Justice Marshall dissenting (joined by Justice Brennan).

80. *Greer,* 424 U.S. at 852, Justice Brennan dissenting; Brown v. Glines, 444 U.S. at 372, Justice Brennan dissenting.

81. *Heffron,* 452 U.S. at 656, Justice Brennan concurring and dissenting.

82. *Adderly,* 385 U.S. at 48, Justice Douglas dissenting (joined by Justice Brennan).

83. *Hynes,* 425 U.S. at 623, Justice Brennan concurring in part.

84. Carey v. Brown, 447 U.S. 455 (1980).

85. Walker v. Birmingham, 388 U.S. 307, 338 (1967), Justice Brennan dissenting.

86. 388 U.S. 307 (1967). In 1967 Justice Brennan also wrote the majority opinion in Zwickler v. Koota, 389 U.S. 241, but the case was settled on procedural

rather than constitutional grounds. Justice Brennan wrote that anonymous hand-billing was a First Amendment issue that should have been settled by the appellate court.

87. 388 U.S. at 349.

88. *Id*. at 345–47.

89. *Id*. at 346.

90. *Id*. at 342.

91. 424 U.S. 828 (1976).

92. *Id*. at 851, Justice Brennan dissenting.

93. *Id*. at 839.

94. *Id*.

95. *Id*. at 869, Justice Brennan dissenting.

96. *Id*. at 852, Justice Brennan dissenting.

97. *Id*. at 856–57, Justice Brennan dissenting.

98. Flower v. U.S., 407 U.S. 197 (1972).

99. 424 U.S. at 849–51, Justice Brennan dissenting.

100. *Id*. at 859–60, Justice Brennan dissenting.

101. 444 U.S. 348 (1980). Justice Brennan's dissent also applied to Secretary of the Navy v. Huff, 444 U.S. 353, in which the Court delivered a *per curiam* opinion citing Brown v. Glines and upholding a requirement that servicemen receive command permission before circulating petitions on military bases.

102. 444 U.S. at 362, Justice Brennan dissenting.

103. *Id*. at 365, Justice Brennan dissenting.

104. *Id*. at 366, Justice Brennan dissenting.

105. *Id*. at 367, Justice Brennan dissenting.

106. *Id*. at 372, Justice Brennan dissenting.

107. *Id*. at 373, Justice Brennan dissenting.

108. Cameron v. Johnson, 390 U.S. 611 (1968); Grayned v. Rockford, 408 U.S. 104 (1972). *See* discussion accompanying *supra* notes 73–75.

109. *Adderly,* 385 U.S. at 48, Justice Douglas dissenting (joined by Justice Brennan).

110. *Id*. at 49, Justice Douglas dissenting (joined by Justice Brennan).

111. 426 U.S. 610 (1976).

112. *Id*. at 626, Justice Brennan concurring in part.

113. 525 U.S. 640 (1981).

114. *Id*. at 657, Justice Brennan concurring and dissenting.

115. *Id*. at 660, Justice Brennan concurring and dissenting.

116. *Id*. at 662, Justice Brennan concurring and dissenting.

117. Lloyd Corporation, Ltd. v. Tanner, 407 U.S. 551 (1972).

118. Frisby v. Schultz, 487 U.S. 474, 491 (1988), Justice Brennan dissenting.

119. *Id*. at 493, Justice Brennan dissenting.

120. 315 U.S. 568 (1942).

121. *Id*. at 569.

122. *Id*. at 572.

123. Gooding v. Wilson, 405 U.S. 518 (1972).

124. Hess v. Indiana, 414 U.S. 105 (1973).

125. Norwell v. Cincinnati, 414 U.S. 14 (1973); Lewis v. New Orleans, 415 U.S. 130 (1974).

126. *See, e.g.,* Houston v. Hill, 482 U.S. 451 (1987), and Lewis v. New Orleans, 415 U.S. 130 (1974).

127. 405 U.S. 518 (1972).

128. 415 U.S. 130 (1974).

129. 482 U.S. 451 (1987).

130. 405 U.S. at 534.

131. *Id.* at 518–19.

132. *Id.* at 521–22.

133. *Id.* at 527.

134. *Id.* at 528–29, Chief Justice Burger dissenting.

135. Brennan Papers, Box 256, memorandum of Chief Justice Burger, December 17, 1971. Justices William Rehnquist and Lewis Powell did not participate.

136. *Id.*

137. *Id.,* memorandum of Justice Douglas, December 17, 1971.

138. *Id.,* memorandum of Chief Justice Burger, December 20, 1971.

139. *Id.,* memorandum of Chief Justice Burger, January 17, 1972.

140. *Id.,* memorandum of Justice Brennan, January 17, 1972.

141. 415 U.S. at 136, Chief Justice Burger dissenting.

142. *Id.* at 131, note 1.

143. *Id.* at 133–34.

144. *See, for example,* Karlan v. Chicago, 416 U.S. 924 (1974); Kelly v. Ohio, 416 U.S. 923 (1974); Lucas v. Arkansas, 416 U.S. 919 (1974); and Rosen v. California, 416 U.S. 924 (1974).

145. 482 U.S. at 454.

146. *Id.* at 462–67.

147. *Id.* at 462–63.

148. *See* Justice Blackmun concurring, *id.* at 472; Justice Powell concurring in judgment, joined in part by Justices O'Connor, Rehnquist, and Scalia, *id.* at 473; and Justice Rehnquist dissenting, *id.* at 481.

149. Cohen v. California, 403 U.S. 15 (1971).

150. Brown v. Louisiana, 383 U.S. 131 (1966).

151. Texas v. Johnson, 109 S.Ct. 2533 (1989).

152. Clark v. Community for Creative Non-Violence, 468 U.S. 288 (1984).

153. Cameron v. Johnson, 390 U.S. 611 (1968).

154. Adderly v. Florida, 385 U.S. 39, 48 (1966), Justice Douglas dissenting (joined by Justice Brennan).

155. *Carey,* 447 U.S. 455 (1980); *Frisby,* 487 U.S. at 491, Justice Brennan dissenting.

156. *Hynes,* 425 U.S. at 626.

157. *Houston,* 482 U.S. at 462–63.

158. *Greer,* 424 U.S. at 852, Justice Brennan dissenting.

159. *Id.* at 859–60, Justice Brennan dissenting.

160. *Id.* at 869, Justice Brennan dissenting.

161. Brown v. Glines, 444 U.S. at 372, Justice Brennan dissenting.

162. *Greer,* 424 U.S. at 852, Justice Brennan dissenting.

163. 109 S.Ct. at 2540.

164. *Id.* at 2542–43.

165. *Id.* at 2544.

7

"Free Trade in Ideas in a Competitive Market"

Few types of speech are completely unencumbered by some form of governmental regulation. Even speech on matters of public concern—that type of speech so often referred to by the Court as speech that is at the core of First Amendment protections and, therefore, worthy of that amendment's most sturdy protection—must fall within certain boundaries. It cannot be used to needlessly and knowingly harm through falsehoods, for example, nor can it needlessly invade an individual's privacy. Other types of speech are subject to greater regulation. Commercial speech, for example, because of its economic self-interest, is subject to stricter regulation than noncommercial speech, and speech over the airwaves falls under the control of the Federal Communication Commission because the airwaves ostensibly belong to the public.

The spectrum encompassing types of speech, therefore, has two poles. Speech that is presumptively open and enjoys the full protection of the First Amendment is at one pole; speech that, by its very nature, is subject to stricter regulation is at the other. Between these two poles fall a plethora of types of speech that are encumbered by varying degrees of governmental regulation. Many of the restrictions—restrictions often affirmed by the Court—were obnoxious to Justice Brennan. The restrictions were obnoxious whether they involved regulating a single word[1] or portions of a book,[2] whether they involved access to mailboxes[3] or billboards,[4] whether they involved the posting of signs on public property[5] or requirements on the use of public sound equipment for concerts.[6]

Brennan believed, of course, that some regulation of expression was necessary, particularly in the areas of commercial speech and broadcasting. He also believed, however, that any governmental intrusion on expression demanded strict scrutiny, and few intrusions could withstand such scrutiny. The justice, therefore, often found himself in the minority when the Court faced cases involving regulations on expression.

He dissented in 1959, for example, when a majority of the Court held that a political activist was required to produce the membership list for a summer camp he operated.[7] The camp was operated to promote the discussion of political ideas. When the operator refused to produce the membership lists, he was held in contempt of court. Brennan wrote that there was no showing of the requisite legislative purpose in order to infringe First Amendment rights, and that the record showed that the only purpose was exposure for the sake of exposure.[8] In an era of mass communication, Brennan wrote, association with dissident groups is fraught with serious consequences that would chill expression.[9]

Brennan also dissented in a second case involving controversial political expression. The Court ruled that an alien could be denied entry to the United States to speak to academic groups because of the nature of the lectures.[10] Brennan joined Justice Thurgood Marshall, who complained that Americans could not be denied the right to hear the speaker because the government disapproved of his ideas.[11]

The restrictions were obnoxious to Brennan, not simply because they related to political speech, but also because they turned on the government's approval or disapproval of the speaker or his message. Attempts by the government to control the method through which the speaker expressed his message were also obnoxious to the justice. Cases involving restrictions by three different cities are illustrative: San Diego restricted billboards, Los Angeles denied the use of public property for the posting of signs, and New York City required all organizations planning concerts in a city amphitheater to use city-owned equipment. Brennan found that the ordinances violated the First Amendment. In all three cases he was in the minority.

In a fourth case involving public access, however, Brennan found the regulations at issue to be narrowly tailored to address a substantial governmental interest and, therefore, constitutional. Brennan agreed with a majority of his colleagues that the postal service could limit the use of letterboxes to the receipt of material on which postage had been paid, but disagreed on the rationale.

The San Diego case began when the city adopted various restrictions on billboards, including a ban of commercial messages. A plurality struck down a portion of the ordinance as being violative of the First Amendment, but held that restrictions on billboards were allowed, particularly since the ordinance did not ban billboards altogether.[12] Brennan agreed with the plurality's finding that billboards "are a well-established medium of communication, used to convey a broad range of different kinds of messages."[13] He found, however, that the practical effect of the ordinance was to eliminate the billboard as a means of communication.[14] Therefore, Brennan said, the Court should determine whether the ban advanced a substantial governmental interest that could not be fulfilled by alternatives less intrusive of expression.[15] San Diego, Brennan wrote, had failed to provide adequate justification for the restriction, so the ordinance should be invalidated.[16]

Similarly, Brennan found that Los Angeles's interest in eliminating visual clutter was insufficient to allow a restriction banning signs on public property. The posting of signs is a cheap and "time-honored means of communicating a broad range of ideas and information,"[17] Brennan wrote. Los Angeles had failed to show that there were ample alternative means for effective communication of the message[18] or that the city was attempting to deal with the problem of visual clutter through some method other than a ban on signs.[19]

New York, because of complaints of excessive noise, adopted an ordinance requiring all organizations planning concerts for one of the city's outdoor amphitheaters to use city-owned sound equipment operated by a city employee. The Court found the ordinance to be a reasonable time, place, and manner restriction. Brennan joined Marshall's dissent complaining that the Court had abandoned its requirements that the government had an obligation to adopt the restriction that was least intrusive of expression and that the Court should defer to government's reasonable determination that the requirement was the best method of reducing noise.[20] Marshall found the Court's ruling troubling for another reason, however. He agreed with the Court that music is one of the oldest forms of human expression, but, he added, the New York ordinance, "is one of the oldest forms of speech repression."[21] He compared the city's monopoly on sound equipment to England's monopoly on printing presses in the sixteenth and seventeenth centuries, and found it to be unconstitutional prior restraint.[22]

The mailbox case grew out of a federal restriction against placing unstamped mailable material in mailboxes. The Greenburgh Civic Association distributed much of its literature by placing the literature in letterboxes.[23] Brennan found the regulation to be a legitimate time, place, and manner restriction,[24] but disagreed with the Court's finding that letterboxes are not public forums. The mail, he wrote, is and always has been a vital national medium of expression through which is transported material ranging from "the sublime to the ridiculous": newspapers, magazines, books, films, "and almost any type and form of expression imaginable."[25] Based on this history, he wrote, "it is extraordinary that the Court reaches the conclusion that the letterbox, a critical link in the mail system, is not a public forum."[26]

As indicated, Brennan recognized that few types of speech remain unencumbered by some form of regulation. Indeed, he recognized that each medium of communication has its own set of problems and must be treated differently.[27] Three types of regulation—copyright, restrictions on commercial speech, and restrictions on broadcasting—deserve special attention.

COPYRIGHT

The right of an artist to protect his or her creation is vital to the promotion of artwork in a free society. The framers of the Constitution recognized the essential nature of copyright protection when they gave to Congress the power to establish copyright laws.[28]

The Court resolved only a handful of cases involving the infringement of another's work while Brennan was a justice. Two of them—one that is trademark infringement rather than copyright infringement—are worthy of discussion here as part of an examination of the justice's free-expression jurisprudence.[29] Brennan dissented in both *San Francisco Arts & Athletics v. U.S.*[30] and *Harper & Row Publishers v. The Nation.*[31]

San Francisco Arts & Athletics, while not a copyright case, involved the exclusive use of the word "olympic" by the U.S. Olympic Committee. The San Francisco Arts & Athletics corporation, pursuant to the Amateur Sports Act,[32] was ordered by a federal judge in California to stop using the word in connection with an athletic event the organization was planning called the "Gay Olympic Games."[33] The athletic club appealed, claiming that the U.S. Olympic Committee had not shown that the club's use of the term caused confusion between the "Gay Olympic Games" and an event sanctioned by the U.S. Olympic Committee.[34] The athletic club also argued that "olympic" was a generic word that could not gain trademark protection,[35] and that by granting exclusive use of the word without proof that its use would cause confusion, Congress was suppressing political speech, a violation of the First Amendment.[36]

The Court rejected both arguments. First, Justice Lewis F. Powell wrote for the majority, "the history of the origins and associations of the word 'Olympic' demonstrates the meritlessness of the SFAA's contention that Congress simply plucked a generic word out of the English vocabulary and granted its exclusive use to the USOC."[37] The word had been used almost exclusively in connection with the Modern Olympic Games since the games were established in 1896, and Congress had the power to grant the Olympic Committee use of the word as a limited property right under trademark law.[38]

The claim of suppression of political speech was based on the athletic club's contention that it planned to use the word "olympic" to convey a political statement by demonstrating healthy and positive aspects of homosexuals.[39] Powell wrote that the Court, in such cases, was required to determine whether the incidental restrictions on protected expression were greater than necessary to further a substantial governmental interest.[40] He found that Congress's interest in promoting international amateur athletics through the U.S. Olympic Committee was substantial[41]; that the athletic club, through the use of the word "olympic," sought to exploit the image created by the U.S. Olympic Committee"[42]; and, therefore, that the Olympic Committee had the right to prohibit the use of the word in the promotion of athletic events.[43]

The Court also rejected the athletic club's claim that the Olympic Committee discriminated in enforcing the prohibition of the use of the word.[44] The Court held that the Olympic Committee was not a governmental entity and the claim must therefore fall.[45]

Brennan dissented. Much of this dissent was based on the argument that the Olympic Committee was a governmental body and, therefore, any action by the committee constituted a governmental action.[46] On that basis alone, he wrote, the case should be remanded for further action by the district court.[47] Brennan also argued, however, that the Court had misinterpreted trademark law and that the statute was overbroad. On that basis, the athletic club was entitled to use of the word " 'Olympic' in a nonconfusing and nonmisleading manner in the noncommercial promotion of a theatrical or athletic event, absent proof of resultant harm to the USOC."[48]

Trademark protection, Brennan wrote, has been confined to commercial speech, and specifically to speech that would tend to cause confusion between commercial products or their producers. The use of the word "olympic" by the athletic club might draw attention to similarities between the "Gay Olympic Games" and the "Olympic Games," but would not necessarily cause confusion between the games or between the athletic club and the Olympic Committee.[49] In addition, Brennan wrote, the Court had ruled that the athletic club could not use traditional defenses for trademark infringement, including the fair-use defense, which prevents regulation of noncommercial speech. The Court, therefore, improperly allowed the Olympic Committee to regulate the use of "olympic" in noncommercial as well as commercial speech.[50]

Brennan also had complaints with the contention of the Court that the prohibition of the use of the word "olympic" did not prevent the athletic club from conveying the message it was attempting to convey. The statute, Brennan wrote, "violates the First Amendment by prohibiting dissemination of a message for which there is no adequate translation."[51] "Olympic" is a word "with a deep history in the English language and Western culture,"[52] he wrote, and "because individual words carry 'a life and force of their own,' translations never fully capture the sense of the original."[53]

In addition, Brennan found that the Amateur Sports Act restricted speech in a way that was not content-neutral.[54] The Olympic Committee is encouraged by the statute to endorse certain messages while prohibiting others, a scheme that is unacceptable under the First Amendment.[55]

Harper & Row began when *The Nation* acquired a prepublication copy of former president Gerald Ford's memoirs, which were to be published by Harper & Row. The magazine published a 2,000-word excerpt of the 200,000-word manuscript, including a section in which Ford discussed his pardon of former president Richard Nixon. Harper & Row sued for copyright infringement. *The Nation* argued that it had a fair-use right to publish the excerpt. When the fair-use doctrine is invoked, the Court must apply a four-part test to determine whether copyright has been infringed. The Court must determine the purpose of the use, the nature of the copyrighted work, the amount and substance of the portion used, and the effect on the market of the use. The Court in *Harper & Row* went through the test point by point:

1. The purpose of the publication by *The Nation,* the Court held, "was to supplant the commercially valuable first publication."[56] Justice Sandra Day O'Connor, writing for the majority, admitted that *The Nation* has a right to first publication of newsworthy material. The magazine exceeded its right, however, by making a news event out of its first publication of the copyrighted work.[57]

2. The original work was an unpublished manuscript, a point Justice Stevens found to be important. The interest of Harper & Row in confidentiality, he wrote, was irrefutable.[58] In publishing from the work, *The Nation* had exploited its right to use quoted material and "excerpted subjective descriptions and portraits of public figures whose power lies in the author's individualized expression."[59]

3. While an insubstantial amount of the book was published by *The Nation,* O'Connor found that the portion used was "essentially the heart of the book."[60]

4. The publication by *The Nation* had a detrimental effect on the marketability of the original work, the Court held. The fact that *Time* magazine canceled its planned serialization of the memoirs and refused to pay Harper & Row an additional $12,500, as agreed upon, is clear-cut evidence of actual damage, Stevens wrote.[61]

Therefore, O'Connor concluded, *The Nation*'s publication did not meet the requirements of fair use.[62]

Brennan disagreed. Copyright, he wrote, allows protection for a method or style of expression, not restrictions on the use of facts or ideas. The "profound national committment" to wide-open and robust debate, he wrote, "leaves no room for a statutory monopoly over information and ideas."[63] *The Nation* had usurped information and ideas, rather than literary style, from the memoirs. Brennan found the Court's analysis of the case flawed in several respects:

• The Court improperly considered economic harm when it considered the nature of the work. The interest in confidentiality was totally economic, he wrote, and was unrelated to the nature of the work.[64]

• The finding that *The Nation* usurped "the heart of the work" was a result of the Court's failure to distinguish between information and literary form. The Court was evaluating the totality of the information, which is irrelevant, rather than the words or style.[65] Even though *The Nation* "appropriated some literary form of substantial quality," the appropriation was not excessive or inappropriate for news reporting.[66]

• The effect on the market analysis was badly skewed by the focus on the use of information and ideas rather than style. It was the publication of information, Brennan argued, not the publication of a few quotes that caused *Time* magazine to renege on its agreement.[67]

By its "exceedingly narrow approach to fair use," Brennan concluded, the Court allowed Harper & Row to monopolize information, and impose liability on *The Nation* simply because the magazine was first to provide certain information to the public.[68] Therefore, Brennan wrote, the Court may have advanced the ability of a historian or former public official to capture the full economic value of information, but did so "only by risking the robust debate of public issues that is the 'essence of self-government.' "[69]

COMMERCIAL SPEECH

Commercial speech, not unlike pornography, holds a special place under the First Amendment: It is granted protection, but the protection is limited.[70] Commercial speech is considered different from other forms of protected speech because advertisers are particularly well-suited to evaluate "the accuracy of their messages and the lawfulness of the underlying activity," and because "commercial speech, the offspring of economic self-interest, is a hardy breed of expression that is not 'particularly susceptible to being crushed by overbroad regulation.' "[71] Because of the differences, the Court has allowed a more permissive approach to regulation of commercial speech to protect consumers from deception or coercion.[72]

Speech does not lose its First Amendment protection because money is spent to project it, because it is carried in a form that is sold for profit, or because it may involve a solicitation to purchase or contribute. It does lose its protection, however, if it deceives or has a tendency to deceive. "If there is a kind of commercial speech that lacks all First Amendment protection," the Court wrote in *Virginia Pharmacy Board v. Virginia Consumer Council,* "it must be distinguished by its content."[73]

Under this approach, therefore, the Court overruled bans on advertising drug prices[74] and contraceptives.[75] It struck down regulations denying power companies the right to encourage the use of electricity[76] or the right to include inserts in bills discussing controversial issues of public policy.[77] And power companies could not be forced to include messages in billing envelopes with which the companies disagreed.[78] In addition, although some restrictions on advertising by attorneys may be allowed,[79] bans on such advertising are not allowed.[80]

But the Court upheld a Texas law denying the practice of optometry under a trade name on grounds that trade names could be used to mislead the public.[81] The use of a trade name is "a form of commercial speech and nothing more," the Court held.[82] It conveys no information and can be used to manipulate the public.[83] The Court also allowed a ban on advertising gambling casinos in Puerto Rico, even though the casinos were permitted.[84] And the Court allowed a ban on commercial activity in a university residence hall, although the ban was not the least restrictive method of meeting the governmental interest in limiting commercial activity.[85]

The Court, in *Central Hudson Gas & Electric Corp. v. Public Service Commission of New York*,[86] established a four-part test for determining when regulations on commercial speech were permissible. Under the test the Court must first determine whether the expression is protected by the First Amendment. For commercial speech to be protected, it cannot be misleading and it must concern lawful activity. Second, the Court must determine whether the interest asserted by the government to justify the regulation is substantial. If the expression is protected and the governmental interest is substantial, the Court must determine whether the regulation directly advances the asserted governmental interest. Finally, the Court must determine whether the regulation is more extensive than necessary to serve that interest.[87]

Brennan had no complaints with the formula.[88] He did have complaints, however, with how the formula was sometimes applied. The most obvious example was *Posadas de Puerto Rico Associates v. Tourism Council of Puerto Rico*,[89] in which the Court ruled that a state may restrict all true advertising about a legal activity. Justice William H. Rehnquist, for five members of the Court, applied the four-part *Central Hudson* test. He found the speech to be protected,[90] but also found Puerto Rico's interest in the welfare of its citizens to be a substantial governmental interest directly advanced by a restriction,[91] which was no more extensive than necessary.[92]

Brennan, however, charged in a biting dissent that the Court was allowing Puerto Rico to suppress speech "merely to keep its residents ignorant,"[93] a motive not allowed under the First Amendment. When the government attempts to suppress the dissemination of truthful commercial speech related to legal activities, Brennan argued, the regulation should be subject to strict judicial scrutiny instead of the "relaxed standards normally used to test government regulation of commercial speech."[94] In *Posadas,* he wrote, the Court merely tipped its hat to the *Central Hudson* test and ignored the fact that commercial speech "is entitled to substantial First Amendment protection."[95]

He attacked the Court's findings one by one. First, he wrote, there was no evidence that the Puerto Rican legislature believed casino gambling would cause serious harm to its residents. Indeed, since the legislature legalized gambling casinos and permitted its residents to patronize them, the evidence is just the opposite.[96] Second, there was no showing that a ban on advertising would directly advance Puerto Rico's claimed interest in controlling the "serious harmful effects" the Court associates with casino gambling.[97] Finally, there was no showing that the harmful effects associated with casino gambling could not be protected by a more limited regulation. The Court, Brennan wrote, failed to acknowledge a wide range of alternatives less intrusive on expression.[98]

One other case deserves special mention. In *First National Bank of Boston v. Bellotti,*[99] the Court overruled a restriction that did not allow corporations to advocate positions on public issues unless the matters under dispute directly related to the corporations. The Court held that the restriction violated the First Amendment rights of corporations.

Brennan joined Justice Byron White's dissent, a dissent based on the First Amendment rights of the company's shareholders. White argued that to allow corporations to take positions on issues not directly related to the business violated the First Amendment rights of the shareholders by requiring them to support issues with which they might disagree.[100]

Some twelve years later, the Court would adopt White's position in a case involving attorneys. In *Keeler v. California State Bar,*[101] the Court ruled that a state bar association may not use funds collected from mandatory dues of its members to promote political and ideological activities with which the dues-payers may disagree.

BROADCASTING

The underpinning of the Supreme Court's adjudication of cases involving free speech over the airwaves has consistently been the principle that the airwaves belong to the public and that broadcasters are merely acting as trustees who are allowed temporary use of that natural resource.[102] Even though broadcasters retain some editorial control over the material they broadcast,[103] and even though government funding to public broadcast stations is insufficient justification for banning editorial commentary on those stations,[104] using the trusteeship rationale, the Court has ruled that broadcasters

- must air all sides of a public issue, and must allow a person attacked on the air to rebut the charges[105];
- may be restricted from using language the FCC determines to be offensive[106]; and,

• must broadcast advertisements from candidates for federal elective offices.[107]

Brennan agreed with the trusteeship rationale, but often had deep philosophical differences with his colleagues on how the trusteeship model should be applied. Brennan reiterated much of the Court's rationale in the 1984 case, *FCC v. League of Women Voters of California,*[108] in which the Court struck down an FCC prohibition on editorializing by public broadcast stations. It was Brennan's only majority opinion in a broadcasting case, and the opinion was very nearly assigned to Thurgood Marshall by Chief Justice Warren Burger. Only after Marshall responded that he was "tentative—not at rest" did Burger assign the opinion to Brennan.[109]

Broadcasting is technologically different from other forms of mass media, Brennan wrote, because broadcasters must use the airwaves to disseminate their messages.[110] The airwaves belong to the public, and Congress has the well-established right to regulate the airwaves as a "scarce and valuable national resource."[111] Congress, therefore, can ensure that persons licensed to use the airwaves satisfy the requirement to operate in the "public interest, convenience, and necessity,"[112] and that there is "a balanced presentation of information on issues of public importance."[113]

Those principles, of course, had been established by the Court in *Red Lion Broadcasting v. FCC,*[114] but *League of Women Voters* is an important case because Brennan did not stop with the reiteration of the Court's stance on the issue of broadcast regulation; he went further and expanded upon principles he had stated in his dissents in two cases: *Columbia Broadcasting System, Inc. v. Democratic National Committee*[115] and *FCC v. Pacifica Foundation.*[116] The three opinions establish Brennan's philosophy on broadcast regulation in particular and much of his philosophy on the First Amendment freedoms in general. That philosophy is grounded deeply in the concept of the free marketplace of ideas.

League of Women Voters involved a section of the Public Broadcasting Act of 1967 that prohibited editorial commentary by noncommercial, educational broadcast stations that received funds from Corporation for Public Broadcasting.

The question in the case was not whether broadcasting could be regulated; that question had been settled. The question was whether the regulatory scheme allowed a ban on editorializing by educational broadcasting stations that received federal funds. Section 399 of the Public Broadcasting Act prohibited noncommercial educational broadcasting stations from engaging in editorial commentary. The FCC advanced two arguments in support of the ban: first, that it was necessary to protect public broadcast stations from being coerced, as a result of federal funding, into becoming vehicles for government propagandizing; and, second, that it was necessary to keep stations from becoming convenient targets for capture by private interest groups wishing to express their own partisan view-points.[117]

Before addressing the merits of the case, Brennan established that the appropriate standard for reviewing a restriction on broadcasting was whether the restriction was "narrowly tailored to further a substantial governmental interest, such as ensuring adequate and balanced coverage of public issues,"[118] a standard used by the Court in previous cases. In addition, he noted, the thrust of all broadcast regulation had been to secure the public's First Amendment interest in receiving a balanced presentation of views on matters of public concern.[119] Regulation to ensure balance, however, does not necessarily permit controlling content: "If the public's interest is to be fully served, we must necessarily rely in large part upon the editorial initiative and judgment of the broadcasters who bear the public trust."[120] The ban was *contra* to that concept.

The heart of the opinion turned on Congress's restriction—through the FCC—on the free marketplace of ideas.[121] Brennan wrote that the type of speech prohibited by the restriction—editorial opinion—"lies at the heart of First Amendment protection"[122]; it is "precisely that form of speech which the Framers of the Bill of Rights were most anxious to protect."[123] He quoted from *Thornhill v. Alabama* to buoy his point:

> The freedom of speech and of the press guaranteed by the Constitution embraces at the least the liberty to discuss publicly and truthfully all matters of public concern without previous restraint or fear of subsequent punishment. . . . Freedom of discussion, if it would fulfill its historic function in this nation, must embrace all issues about which information is needed or appropriate to enable the members of society to cope with the exigencies of their period.[124]

A second problem with the ban, Brennan wrote, was that it was defined solely on the basis of content: It affected only editorial opinions expressed by operators of public broadcast stations.[125] The prohibition would even prevent a broadcaster from speaking out on public issues in a balanced and fair manner.[126]

Next, Brennan turned to the government's arguments in support of the ban, neither of which met the test of being narrowly tailored to fulfill a significant government interest. First, while concerns about governmental pressure were legitimate, Brennan wrote, the Public Broadcasting Act had built-in safeguards to protect against such pressure.[127] Even if those safeguards were insufficient, suppressing a particular category of speech was not likely to reduce the risk of governmental pressure,[128] particularly considering the character of the public broadcasting system, a system consisting of hundreds of stations in communities throughout the country. "It seems reasonable to infer," Brennan wrote, "that the editorial voices of these stations will prove to be as distinctive, varied, and idiosyncratic as the various communities they represent."[129] The ban, therefore, exceeded the boundaries necessary to protect the government interest without infringing upon protected speech.[130]

Second, even if the government's second concern—that stations not become mouthpieces for private interest groups—is legitimate, Brennan wrote, the ban failed to address that concern. Section 399 prohibited the management of public broadcast stations from expressing partisan views; it did not prohibit stations from presenting the partisan views of others, including private interest groups.[131] In addition, "the public's interest in preventing public broadcasting stations from becoming forums for lopsided presentations of narrow partisan positions is already secured by a variety of other regulatory means that intrude far less drastically upon the 'journalistic freedom' of noncommercial broadcasters."[132]

Brennan's opinion in *League of Women Voters* was very nearly a dissenting rather than a majority opinion. Brennan circulated his first draft May 20, 1984, four months after he was assigned the opinion by Burger.[133] By the end of May, Justices Thurgood Marshall and Lewis Powell had joined Brennan's opinion, William Rehnquist had announced he would write a dissent, and Byron R. White, John Paul Stevens, and Warren Burger had announced they would await Rehnquist's dissent before deciding how to vote.[134] The three of them would eventually join Rehnquist or write their own dissents.

Brennan needed the votes of both Harry Blackmun and Sandra Day O'Connor, therefore, to win a majority. Blackmun was apparently ready to join in early June,[135] but on June 6 O'Connor wrote Brennan that she was having trouble deciding how to vote because of the "long-range ramifications in various areas."[136] Brennan responded the same day: "If there's anything at all you would like me to consider, of course, I would be very happy to do so."[137]

O'Connor, in a memorandum two days later, expressed three primary concerns. First, she was troubled by language in Brennan's opinion indicating the test of whether a regulation was constitutional was whether the regulation "enhanced rather than abridged" freedom of expression or "preserved room for the exercise of editorial discretion and initiative by the broadcaster." She believed the appropriate test to be whether the regulation is narrowly tailored to serve a substantial governmental interest. "I am reluctant to graft on additional requirements to the basic test," she wrote. Second, she expressed concern that Brennan's opinion did not fully address the government's interest that public broadcasting audiences would believe editorials reflected the official views of the government. "I think this is a sufficiently substantial governmental interest to support the statutory restriction," she wrote. Finally, she suggested that the Court not address the constitutional issues at all, but instead to construe the statute in question as allowing each public broadcasting station to "establish 'affiliate' organizations which could then editorialize with non-federal funds."[138]

It took Brennan three days to respond to O'Connor's concerns. First, he suggested that he change the language suggesting a regulation be required to enhance freedom of speech to language indicating that a regulation would be upheld when it "is narrowly tailored to further a substantial governmental interest."[139] Second, he suggested that he add language indicating that the government has a substantial interest in ensuring that audiences not be led to believe that editorials reflect the views of the government and suggesting that a less restrictive alternative would be a requirement that editorials be accompanied by disclaimers stating that the views of the editorials are those of the station and not those of the federal government.[140]

Brennan disagreed with O'Connor on the final point, however. Her suggestion that affiliate editorialists be established, he wrote, could not be reconciled with the language and legislative history of the statute. He offered, however, to add a section to the opinion suggesting that Congress could adopt a revised version of the statute in question allowing educational broadcasting stations to establish "affiliate" organizations to use the station's facilities to editorialize with nonfederal funds.[141]

The changes satisfied O'Connor, who notified Brennan the same day that she would join his revised opinion.[142]

Although Brennan couched his *League of Women Voters* opinion in terms from the marketplace of ideas philosophy, his position in the opinion was somewhat softer than the stance he took in his dissents to *Columbia Broadcasting* and *Pacifica*. In those dissents, however, he was joined only by Marshall, and, therefore, was not required to soften his language in order to win vital votes needed for a majority. The dissents, therefore, may be more representative of the justice's strong views on free expression over the airwaves. They also may better address the apparent contradiction between Brennan's willingness to allow the government to regulate broadcast speech, when he will not allow similar regulation over some other forms of expression.

In *Columbia Broadcasting System Inc. v. Democratic National Committee* Brennan disagreed with the Court's ruling that broadcasters can refuse to accept paid editorial advertisements. The opinion, written by Burger, was based on the argument that Congress had consistently rejected efforts to impose on broadcasters a common-carrier right of access for all persons and that the public interest standard of the Communications Act would not be better served by required access.[143]

Burger also wrote, in a portion of the opinion that did not gain a Court, that a broadcast licensee retains certain journalistic discretion in deciding how to meet its obligation of balanced presentation of matters of public interest and was protected under the First Amendment from being required to accept all paid editorial advertising.[144]

The opinion, therefore, was one that Brennan might be expected to join. His dissent, however, was also based on a First Amendment argument. Brennan had balanced the rights of the broadcaster against those of the audience and against those of persons seeking to express their views over the airwaves. He determined that the rights of the broadcaster should give way. The principle at stake in the case was one of "fundamental importance," he wrote, because it concerned the right to engage in and hear vigorous public debate. The ruling of the Court, he wrote, would "serve only to inhibit, rather than to further, our 'profound national commitment to the principle that debate on public issues should be uninhibited, robust, and wide-open.' "[145]

Brennan's argument was based on the premise that broadcasters use a natural resource, the ownership and control of which remains "vested in the people of the United States."[146] Since the government, through its involvement in broadcast policy, has become responsible for the effects of broadcast policy, Brennan wrote, any absolute refusal to sell advertising on issues of public importance is tantamount to governmental action and "must be subjected to the restraints of the First Amendment."[147]

Brennan began his argument by addressing the First Amendment rights of the audience. The listening and viewing public, he wrote, because of the limited number of broadcast frequencies, retains an interest in free speech over the airwaves. The dominant theme in the application of First Amendment rights is the free trade in ideas in a competitive marketplace,[148] Brennan wrote, and, in the context of radio and television broadcasting, that means the First Amendment protects the right of the public to receive messages.[149] The Fairness Doctrine operates to require adequate coverage of issues of public importance and dissemination of competing opinions,[150] Brennan wrote, but broadcasters "retain almost exclusive control over the selection of ideas and viewpoints to be covered, the manner of presentation, and, perhaps most important, who shall speak."[151] This

> supervised and ordained discussion is directly contrary to the underlying purposes of the First Amendment for that Amendment 'presupposes that right conclusions are more likely to be gathered out of a multitude of tongues, than through any kind of authoritative selection."[152]

In addition, the Fairness Doctrine only calls for broadcasters to present representative community views and voices on controversial issues. Therefore, it is possible for some unrepresentative views and voices to be eliminated from the marketplace of ideas.[153] The Fairness Doctrine, therefore, is insufficient to provide the type of "exchange of views to which the public is constitutionally entitled."[154] Brennan concluded:

> Thus, if the public is to be honestly and forthrightly apprised of opposing views on controversial issues, it is imperative that citizens be permitted at least some opportunity to speak directly for themselves as genuine advocates on issues that concern them.[155]

Next, Brennan focused on the rights of groups and individuals to expression over the airwaves. Speech concerning public affairs," Brennan noted, is the essence of self-government, and citizens are likely to have the need to express their views "directly to the public, rather than through a governmentally appointed surrogate."[156] The broadcast industry, Brennan wrote, with the help of the federal government, has become "potentially the most efficient and effective 'marketplace of ideas' ever devised."[157] It is the public's prime source of information,[158] making "the soapbox orator and the leafleteer virtually obsolete."[159] Therefore, he wrote, "any policy that absolutely denies citizens access to the airwaves necessarily renders even the concept of 'full and free discussion' practically meaningless."[160]

This does not mean, however, that broadcasters have no First Amendment interest in exercising journalistic supervision over the use of their facilities. *Columbia Broadcasting,* Brennan noted, dealt only with advertising time, not with news or entertainment. Thus, Brennan wrote:

> We are concerned here, not with the speech of broadcasters themselves, but, rather, with their "right" to decide which *other* individuals will be given an opportunity to speak in a forum that has already been opened to the public.
>
> Viewed in this context, the *absolute* ban on editorial advertising seems particularly offensive because, although broadcasters refuse to sell any air time whatever to groups or individuals wishing to speak out on controversial issues of public importance, they make such air time readily available to those "commercial" advertisers who seek to peddle their goods and services to the public. Thus, as the system now operates, any person wishing to market a particular brand of beer, soap, toothpaste, or deodorant has direct, personal, and instantaneous access to the electronic media. He can present his own message, in his own words, in any format he selects, and at a time of his own choosing. Yet a similar individual seeking to discuss war, peace, pollution, or the suffering of the poor is denied this right to speak. Instead, he is compelled to rely on the beneficence of a corporate "trustee" appointed by the Government to argue his case for him.[161]

Brennan continued his marketplace of ideas argument in his 1978 dissent to *FCC v. Pacifica.* In *Pacifica* the Court ruled that the FCC could regulate speech that was indecent but not obscene.[162] The speech involved was a monologue by comedian George Carlin aired at about 2 P.M. by a Pacifica-owned radio station in New York. In the monologue, titled "Filthy Words," Carlin repeatedly used seven words he said could never be broadcast. The monologue was part of a program about contemporary society's attitude toward the language and had been preceded by a warning that language offensive to some would be aired.[163]

Brennan was incensed by the ruling. He joined Justice Potter Stewart's dissent—arguing that the monologue could not be prohibited unless it was obscene—but also wrote his own dissent, because, he wrote, "I find the Court's misapplication of fundamental First Amendment principles so patent, and its attempt to impose *its* notions of propriety on the whole of the American people so misguided, that I am unable to remain silent."[164]

As in *Columbia Broadcasting,* the case turned on the right of the listener to receive and the right of the broadcaster to send messages:

> I would place the responsibility and the right to weed worthless and offensive communications from the public airways where it belongs and where, until today, it resided: in a public free to choose those communications worthy of its attention from a marketplace unsullied by the censor's hand.[165]

Brennan sliced away at the arguments the Court used to support the restriction:

- While privacy interests are important, and while there should be concern about what messages reach children,[166] parents, not the government, should make those decisions, and some parents might have wanted their children to hear the way Carlin defused the taboo surrounding words.[167]

- It is "transparently fallacious" to believe that the ruling would have "its primary effect on the form, rather than the content, of serious communication." Content and form, Brennan wrote, cannot always be divorced.[168]

- The notion that persons wanting to hear Carlin's message could do so by buying a copy to play on a phonograph displays "a sad insensitivity" to the fact that many may not be able to afford that alternative and "a naive innocence of the reality that in many cases, the medium may well be the message."[169]

Finally, Brennan found "the Court's attempt to unstitch the warp and woof of First Amendment law in an effort to reshape its fabric to cover the patently wrong result" to be "dangerous as well as lamentable."[170] He found it equally disturbing that the Court had not the ability "to appreciate that in our land of cultural pluralism, there are many who think, act, and talk differently from the Members of this Court, and who do not share their fragile sensibilities."[171] The Court's decision, he wrote, is "another of the dominant culture's inevitable efforts to force those groups who do not share its mores to conform to its way of thinking, acting, and speaking."[172] Indeed, the Court confirmed "Carlin's prescience as a social commentator."[173]

CONCLUSIONS

Brennan recognized that few forms of expression remain unencumbered by some type of regulation. Indeed, he agreed that regulation was necessary. Copyright protects the rights of authors; commercial speech may be regulated because of its economic self-interest; and broadcasting may be regulated to ensure that broadcasters, as public trustees, operate in the public interest, convenience, and necessity.

Regulations on expression, however, must come under strict scrutiny to ensure that protected speech is not encumbered by improper infringements. The regulations, for example, cannot turn on the government's approval or disapproval of a speaker or his message.[174] They cannot improperly restrict legitimate forums for disseminating messages.[175] And they may not be overbroad.

Indeed, regulations on expression, particularly when they are based upon the content of expression, must be narrowly tailored to advance a significant government interest, and the incidental limitation on expression may be no broader than necessary for that government interest, and the incidental limitation on expression may be no broader than necessary for that government interest. The rule was first enunciated in *U.S. v. O'Brien*.[176]

Brennan found regulations to be most obnoxious when they infringed upon open debate in the marketplace of ideas. Indeed, he found that the dominant theme in the application of the First Amendment is the "free trade in ideas in a competitive marketplace."[177] The amendment, he wrote, "presupposes that right conclusions are more likely to be gathered out of a multitude of tongues, than through any kind of authoritative selection."[178] Regulations, therefore, may not infringe upon the dissemination or discussion of ideas, since the "robust debate of public issues" is "the essence of self-government."[179] Thus magazines may be liable for infringing upon the style of a copyrighted work, but not for first publishing the information contained within that work.[180] And broadcasters retain editorial discretion over the ideas and information they want to disseminate. They also have the freedom to air their opinions on matters of public concern, even if they receive federal funding.[181] After all, Brennan wrote, editorial commentary is precisely the type of speech the framers of the First Amendment were most anxious to protect.[182]

Broadcasters, however, do not have the freedom to refuse advertising on matters of public concern. The First Amendment's protection of the marketplace of ideas ensures a right to receive information on such matters, Brennan wrote.[183] Broadcasters, therefore, do not have complete freedom to supervise and ordain who shall take part in a discussion of public issues over the public airwaves, but must give way to the rights of listeners and others who want to speak, because there is a fundamental right to hear and engage in vigorous public debate.[184] Indeed, Brennan found that the public is "constitutionally entitled" to engage in and listen to an exchange of views.[185]

The basis for Brennan's theory of broadcast regulation, as indicated, is that the airwaves belong to the public and broadcasters are merely trustees. The theory may be more important today than when it was first espoused. With the help of the government, Brennan wrote, the broadcasting industry has become "potentially the most efficient and effective marketplace of ideas ever." Any policy, therefore, that absolutely denies citizens access to that marketplace "renders the concept of full and free discussion meaningless."[186]

And to Brennan, the concept of full and free discussion is the primary purpose of the First Amendment.

NOTES

1. San Francisco Arts & Athletics v. U.S. Olympic Committee, 483 U.S. 522, 548 (1987), Justice Brennan dissenting.
2. Harper & Row Publishers v. Nation, 571 U.S. 539, 579 (1985), Justice Brennan dissenting.
3. U.S. Postal Service v. Greenburgh Civic Associations, 453 U.S. 114 (1981).
4. Metromedia, Inc. v. San Diego, 453 U.S. 490 (1981).
5. City Council of Los Angeles v. Taxpayers for Vincent, 466 U.S. 789 (1984).
6. Ward v. Rock Against Racism, 109 S.Ct. 2746 (1989).
7. Uphaus v. Wyman, 306 U.S. 72, 82 (1959), Justice Brennan dissenting.
8. *Id.* at 82–83, Justice Brennan dissenting.
9. *Id.* at 84, Justice Brennan dissenting.
10. Kleindienst v. Mandel, 408 U.S. 753 (1972).
11. *Id.* at 775, Justice Marshall dissenting (joined by Justice Brennan).
12. Metromedia, Inc. v. San Diego, 453 U.S. 490 (1981). The plurality opinion was written by Justice Byron White and joined by Justices Potter Stewart, Thurgood Marshall, and Lewis Powell.
13. *Id.* at 524, Justice Brennan concurring in judgment.
14. *Id.* at 525, Justice Brennan concurring in judgment.
15. *Id.* at 527, Justice Brennan concurring in judgment.
16. *Id.* at 528, Justice Brennan concurring in judgment.
17. City Council of Los Angeles v. Taxpayers for Vincent, 466 U.S. at 819, Justice Brennan dissenting.
18. *Id.* at 819–20, Justice Brennan dissenting.
19. *Id.* at 829, Justice Brennan dissenting.
20. Ward v. Rock Against Racism, 109 S.Ct. at 2760, Justice Marshall dissenting (joined by Justice Brennan).
21. *Id.* at 2763, Justice Marshall dissenting (joined by Justice Brennan).

22. *Id.*, Justice Marshall dissenting (joined by Justice Brennan).
23. U.S. Postal Service v. Greenburgh Civic Association, 453 U.S. 114 (1981).
24. *Id.* at 134, Justice Brennan concurring in the judgment. *See also* Metromedia, Inc. v. San Diego, 453 U.S. 490 (1981), and Regan v. Time, Inc. 468 U.S. 641 (1984).
25. *Id.* at 138, Justice Brennan concurring in judgment.
26. *Id.*, Justice Brennan concurring in judgment.
27. City Council v. Taxpayers, 466 U.S. at 818, Justice Brennan dissenting.
28. U.S. Const., art. I, sec. 8.
29. The Court resolved eight other copyright cases during the period, including Sony Corp. v. Universal Studios, 464 U.S. 417 (1984), and Community for Creative Non-Violence v. Reid, 109 S.Ct. 2166 (1989).
30. 483 U.S. 522 (1981).
31. 471 U.S. 539 (1985).
32. 36 U.S.C., sec. 380.
33. 483 U.S. at 525–27.
34. *Id.* at 528–29.
35. *Id.* at 531–32.
36. *Id.* at 534.
37. *Id.*
38. *Id.* at 534–35.
39. *Id.* at 535.
40. *Id.* at 536–37.
41. *Id.* at 537.
42. *Id.* at 539–41.
43. *Id.* at 541.
44. *Id.* at 542.
45. *Id.* at 547.
46. *Id.* at 548–60, Justice Brennan dissenting.
47. *Id.* at 560, Justice Brennan dissenting.
48. *Id.* at 573, Justice Brennan dissenting.
49. *Id.* at 564, Justice Brennan dissenting.
50. *Id.* at 565–66, Justice Brennan dissenting.
51. *Id.* at 569, Justice Brennan dissenting.
52. *Id.*, Justice Brennan dissenting.
53. *Id.* at 569–70, Justice Brennan dissenting.
54. *Id.* at 570, Justice Brennan dissenting.
55. *Id.* at 570–71, Justice Brennan dissenting.
56. 471 U.S. 539, 562 (1985).
57. *Id.* at 561.
58. *Id.* at 564.
59. *Id.* at 563.
60. *Id.* at 564–65.
61. *Id.* at 566.
62. *Id.* at 569.
63. *Id.* at 582, Justice Brennan dissenting.
64. *Id.* at 598, Justice Brennan dissenting.
65. *Id.* at 600, Justice Brennan dissenting.

66. *Id.* at 601, Justice Brennan dissenting.

67. *Id.* at 602, Justice Brennan dissenting.

68. *Id.* at 605, Justice Brennan dissenting.

69. *Id.*, Justice Brennan dissenting.

70. Virginia Pharmacy Board v. Virginia Citizens Consumer Council, 425 U.S. 748 (1976).

71. Central Hudson Gas & Electric Corp. v. Public Service Commission of New York, 447 U.S. 557, 564, n. 6 (1980).

72. *Id.* at 578.

73. 425 U.S. 748, 761 (1976).

74. *Id.*

75. Bolger v. Youngs Drug Products Corp., 463 U.S. 60 (1983).

76. Central Hudson Gas & Electric Corp. v. Public Service Commission of New York, 447 U.S. 557 (1980).

77. Consolidated Edison Company of New York v. Public Service Commission of New York, 447 U.S. 530 (1980).

78. Pacific Gas & Electric Co. v. Public Utilities Commission of California, 475 US. 1 (1986).

79. In re RMJ, 455 U.S. 191 (1982); Zauderer v. Office of Disciplinary Counsel of Supreme Court of Ohio, 471 U.S. 626 (1985).

80. Bates v. State Bar of Arizona, 433 U.S. 350 (1977); Shapero v. Kentucky Bar Association, 486 U.S. 466 (1988); Peel v. Illinois Attorney Registration & Disciplinary Commission, 110 S.Ct. 2281 (1990).

81. Friedman v. Rogers, 440 U.S. 1 (1979).

82. *Id.* at 11.

83. *Id.* at 13.

84. Posadas de Puerto Rico Associates v. Tourism Company of Puerto Rico, 478 U.S. 328 (1986).

85. Board of Trustees, State University of New York v. Fox, 109 S.Ct. 3028 (1989).

86. 447 U.S. 556 (1980).

87. *Id.*

88. *Id.* at 572, Justice Brennan concurring in the judgment.

89. 478 U.S. 328 (1986).

90. *Id.* at 340.

91. *Id.* at 341.

92. *Id.* at 343.

93. *Id.* at 358, Justice Brennan dissenting.

94. *Id.* at 351, Justice Brennan dissenting.

95. *Id.* at 352, Justice Brennan dissenting.

96. *Id.* at 352–53, Justice Brennan dissenting.

97. *Id.* at 356, Justice Brennan dissenting.

98. *Id.* at 356–57, Justice Brennan dissenting.

99. 435 U.S. 765 (1978).

100. *Id.* at 801, Justice White dissenting (joined by Justice Brennan).

101. 110 S.Ct. 2288 (1990).

102. *See, generally* Red Lion Broadcasting Co. v. FCC, 395 U.S. 367 (1969).

103. Columbia Broadcasting System, Inc. v. Democratic National Committee, 412 U.S. 94 (1973).

104. FCC v. League of Women Voters, 468 U.S. 364 (1984).

105. Red Lion Broadcasting Co. v. FCC 395 U.S. 367 (1969).

106. FCC v. Pacifica Foundation, 438 U.S. 726 (1978).

107. CBS, Inc. v. FCC, 453 U.S. 364 (1984).

108. 468 U.S. 364 (1984).

109. Brennan Papers, Box 649, memorandum of Chief Justice Burger, January 21, 1984.

110. 468 U.S. at 377.

111. *Id.* at 376.

112. *Id.*

113. *Id.* at 377.

114. 395 U.S. at 386–92.

115. 412 U.S. 94, 170 (1973), Justice Brennan dissenting.

116. 438 U.S. 726, 762 (1978), Justice Brennan dissenting.

117. 468 U.S. at 384–85.

118. *Id.* at 380.

119. *Id.*

120. *Id.* at 378.

121. *Id.* at 377.

122. *Id.* at 381.

123. *Id.* at 383.

124. *Id.* at 381–82, quoting Thornhill v. Alabama, 310 U.S. 88 (1949).

125. *Id.* at 383.

126. *Id.* at 385.

127. *Id.* at 388–89.

128. *Id.* at 390.

129. *Id.* at 391.

130. *Id.* at 395.

131. *Id.* at 396–97.

132. *Id.* at 397–98.

133. Brennan Papers, Box 649, memorandum of Chief Justice Burger, January 21, 1984; and memorandum of Justice Brennan, January 23, 1984.

134. *Id.*, memoranda of May 21, 1984; May 22, 1984; May 29, 1984.

135. *Id.* There are no memoranda in the case file relating to Justice Blackmun's position before his June 18, 1984, note joining the opinion.

136. *Id.*, memorandum of Justice O'Connor, June 6, 1984.

137. *Id.*, memorandum of Justice Brennan, June 6, 1984.

138. *Id.*, memorandum of Justice O'Connor, June 8, 1984.

139. *Id.*, memorandum of Justice Brennan, June 11, 1984. The language became part of the opinion; *see* 468 U.S. at 380, and discussion accompanying *supra* note 118.

140. *Id.* The language became part of the opinion; *see* 468 U.S. at 395.

141. *Id.* Part IV was added to the opinion; see 468 U.S. at 399–401.

142. *Id.*, memorandum of Justice O'Connor, June 11, 1984.

143. 412 U.S. at 103–14.

144. *Id.* at 114–21.

145. *Id.* at 172, Justice Brennan dissenting.
146. *Id.* at 173–74, Justice Brennan dissenting.
147. *Id.* at 181, note 12, Justice Brennan dissenting.
148. *Id.* at 183, Justice Brennan dissenting.
149. *Id.* at 184, Justice Brennan dissenting.
150. *Id.* at 185, Justice Brennan dissenting.
151. *Id.* at 187, Justice Brennan dissenting.
152. *Id.* at 191–92, Justice Brennan dissenting.
153. *Id.* at 190, Justice Brennan dissenting.
154. *Id.*, Justice Brennan dissenting.
155. *Id.* at 189–90, Justice Brennan dissenting.
156. *Id.* at 193, Justice Brennan dissenting.
157. *Id.* at 195, Justice Brennan dissenting.
158. *Id.*, Justice Brennan dissenting.
159. *Id.* at 196, Justice Brennan dissenting.
160. *Id.*, Justice Brennan dissenting.
161. *Id.* at 200, Justice Brennan dissenting.
162. 438 U.S. at 738–41.
163. *Id.* at 729–30.
164. *Id.* at 762, Justice Brennan dissenting.
165. *Id.* at 773, Justice Brennan dissenting.
166. *Id.* at 764, Justice Brennan dissenting.
167. *Id.* at 770, Justice Brennan dissenting.
168. *Id.* at 773, Justice Brennan dissenting.
169. *Id.* at 774, Justice Brennan dissenting.
170. *Id.* at 775, Justice Brennan dissenting.
171. *Id.*, Justice Brennan dissenting.
172. *Id.* at 777, Justice Brennan dissenting.
173. *Id.*, Justice Brennan dissenting.
174. Uphaus v. Wyman, 306 U.S. 72, 82 (1959), Justice Brennan dissenting; Kleindienst v. Mandel, 408 U.S. 754, (1972), Justice Marshall dissenting (joined by Justice Brennan).
175. *Metromedia*, 453 U.S. at 523, Justice Brennan concurring in judgment; *City Council of Los Angeles*, 466 U.S. at 818, Justice Brennan dissenting; *Ward*, 109 S.Ct. at 2760, Justice Marshall dissenting (joined by Justice Brennan); *U.S. Postal Service*, 453 U.S. at 134, Justice Brennan concurring in judgment.
176. 391 U.S. 367 (1968).
177. *Columbia Broadcasting System*, 412 U.S. at 183, Justice Brennan dissenting.
178. *Id.* at 190–92, Justice Brennan dissenting.
179. *Harper & Row*, 471 U.S. at 605, Justice Brennan dissenting.
180. *Id.* at 605, Justice Brennan dissenting.
181. FCC v. League of Women Voters of California, 468 U.S. 364 (1984).
182. *Id.* at 383.
183. FCC v. League of Women Voters of California, 468 U.S. at 380.
184. *Columbia Broadcasting System*, 412 U.S. at 172, Justice Brennan dissenting.
185. *Id.* at 190, Justice Brennan dissenting.
186. *Id.* at 196, Justice Brennan dissenting.

8

"*Valuable Public Debate . . .*
Must Be Informed"

The Supreme Court has often expressed high praise for the role of the press in society. The press has been identified as performing a function that is at the core of First Amendment guarantees.[1] It has been "a mighty catalyst in awakening public interest in governmental affairs, exposing corruption among public officers and employees and generally informing the citizenry of public events and occurrences."[2] And it has been recognized as holding a special position under the Constitution:

> The Constitution specifically selected the press . . . to play an important role in the discussion of public affairs. Thus the press serves and was designed to serve as a powerful antidote to any abuses of power by governmental officials and as a constitutionally chosen means for keeping officials elected by the people responsible to all the people whom they were selected to serve. Suppression of the right of the press to praise or criticize governmental agents and to clamor and contend for or against change . . . muzzles one of the very agencies the Framers of the Constitution thoughtfully and deliberately selected to improve our society and keep it free.[3]

Despite the praise, however, the Court has never held that the special constitutional position also grants the institution of the press special protection. Indeed, the Court has repeatedly said that the Constitution grants the press no special guarantees; the position of the institution or its representatives under the First Amendment is no different from the position of any individual.[4] Under such a constitutional theory, therefore, the Court has ruled that journalists have no constitutional right to keep news sources confidential,[5] no constitutional right to interview prison or jail inmates,[6] and no constitutional right of access to public places.[7]

Justice Brennan, however, supported his belief that the press has an important position in society—and under the Constitution—with his votes as well as his words. For Brennan, a key purpose of the First Amendment was to facilitate self-government,[8] so the rights it guaranteed were primarily individual rights. He recognized, however, that society also benefits from a free press.

That concept guided the development of Brennan's theory on freedom of the press, a theory expressed in the 1970s in a handful of cases written, for the most part, by justices other than Brennan and, for the most part, in dissents. In *Branzburg v. Hayes*,[9] *Houchins v. KQED, Inc.*,[10] *Miami Herald v. Tornillo*,[11] and three cases discussed in Chapter 4—*Pell v. Procunier*,[12] *Saxbe v. Washington Post*,[13] and *Nebraska Press Association v. Stuart*[14]—Brennan advanced the theme that the process of informing the public is "the core purpose of the constitutional guarantee of free speech and a free press,"[15] so the free press fulfills an essential role in society. Therefore, to the press attaches the special status of being representatives of the public. The theme was expressed in opinions written by Justices Potter Stewart, John Paul Stevens, Warren Burger, and William O. Douglas, all of whom Brennan joined. In the six cases, Brennan wrote a substantive opinion only in *Nebraska Press Association*.[16]

Brennan contributed an additional gloss to free-press theory, however, in a series of cases involving press coverage of the judiciary. In those cases, he advanced the theory that the press deserved special protection under the "structural model" of First Amendment protections.

SPECIAL STATUS UNDER LAW

The opinion in *Branzburg* turned almost entirely on the Court's willingness—or lack thereof—to recognize a special role of the press in society. Justice Byron White, writing for the majority, paid lip service to the role of the press, but found a rationale for limiting its protection. He wrote that news-gathering might qualify for First Amendment protection, for "without some protection for seeking out the news, freedom of the press could be eviscerated."[17] But, he added, the narrow issue before the Court was whether reporters could refuse to respond to grand jury subpoenas "as other citizens do and to answer questions relevant to an investigation into the commission of crime."[18] They cannot, White wrote.

Branzburg involved three journalists who had refused to identify sources of news reports they had prepared. Two of the journalists had answered grand jury subpoenas but had refused to answer questions; the third refused to appear before the grand jury at all.

White found that the press has neither special immunity from the application of general laws[19] nor special privileges under the law.[20] In addition, he found that the public interest in law enforcement outweighed the uncertain burden on news gathering that would result from the ruling.[21] Journalists, therefore, must respond to questions before the grand jury, even if this means revealing the identities of confidential sources.

Stewart, whose dissent Brennan joined, did not see the case so narrowly. He began his dissent in this way: "The court's crabbed view of the First Amendment reflects a disturbing insensitivity to the critical role of an independent press."[22] By encouraging law-enforcement authorities "to annex the journalistic profession as an investigative arm of government," the Court was ultimately causing more harm than good to the administration of justice.[23]

The purpose of the Constitution's protection of a free press, Stewart wrote, was to protect the "societal interest in a full and free flow of information to the public."[24] The protection, then, is not so much for the benefit of the press as it is for the benefit of society.[25] Wrote Stewart:

> Enlightened choice by an informed citizenry is the basic ideal upon which an open society is premised, and a free press is thus indispensable to a free society. Not only does the press enhance personal self-fulfillment by providing the people with the widest possible range of fact and opinion, but it also is an incontestable pre-condition of self-government.[26]

Since there is a right to publish, Stewart contended, there must be a right to gather news. The right to gather news, in turn, implies a right to confidential sources,[27] otherwise the press would be reduced to merely printing public statements and publishing prepared handouts.[28]

The societal interest of the First Amendment—that is, protection for the press because it benefits society—was also the rationale for three other dissents Brennan joined: Lewis Powell's dissent in *Saxbe,* William Douglas's dissent in *Pell,* and John Paul Stevens's dissent in *Houchins.* In *Saxbe* and *Pell* the Court ruled that the press had no constitutional right to interview prisoners even though the prisoners requested the interviews.[29]

In his dissent, Powell agreed with the majority that neither news organizations nor reporters have constitutional rights superior to those of other citizens.[30] He suggested, however, that the question did not turn on superior or inferior rights. It turned, rather, on "the societal function of the First Amendment in preserving free public discussion of governmental affairs."[31] Powell continued:

> No aspect of that constitutional guarantee is more rightly treasured than its protection of the ability of our people through free and open debate to consider and resolve their own destiny. It embodies our Nation's commitment to popular self-determination and our abiding faith that the surest course for developing sound national policy lies in a free exchange of views on public issues. And public debate must not only be unfettered; it must also be informed.[32]

That was the reasoning, Powell wrote, behind the Court's recognition in *Branzburg* that news gathering deserves First Amendment protection. "An informed public depends on accurate and effective reporting by the news media," he wrote. "By enabling the public to assert meaningful control over the political process, the press performs a crucial function in effecting the societal purpose of the First Amendment."[33]

Citing *Mills,* Powell wrote that the "constitutionally established" role of the press was being infringed by the absolute ban on interviews with prisoners. Unrestrained public access to the prisons was obviously infeasible, he wrote, making the press's right to access even more important. The ban negated the ability of the press to discharge its role: "The underlying right is the right of the public generally. The press is the necessary representative of the public's interest in this context and the instrumentality which effects the public's right."[34]

Douglas made a similar argument in his dissent in *Pell.* Douglas did not debate the Court's contention that the press does not deserve superior constitutional rights. Instead he attacked the notion that a ban on interviews with prisoners was constitutional because it applied equally to nonjournalists.[35] The benefits of a free press, Douglas wrote, are not enjoyed only by the media. "The right of the people, the true sovereigns under our constitutional scheme, to govern in an informed manner" is at stake, he wrote.[36]

The facts of *Houchins v. KQED,* decided four years later, in 1978, were similar to those of *Saxbe* and *Pell.* In the earlier cases, the government had not allowed members of the press to interview prisoners. In *Houchins,* television station KQED sought to film portions of the Alameda County Jail in Santa Rita, California, as part of its continuing coverage on prison conditions.

While noting that the conditions in jails and prisons "are clearly matters 'of great public importance,' " the Court refused to grant the station access to the jail.[37] The government, Burger wrote for the majority, cannot be compelled to provide access on demand.[38]

Stevens dissented, joined by Brennan and Powell, distinguishing *Houchins* from *Pell* and *Saxbe.* Those cases, he wrote, do not mean a state can hide prison conditions from the press by hiding them from the public.[39]

Stevens's primary point, however, was that the First Amendment serves an essential societal function. "Our system of self-government," he wrote, "assumes the existence of an informed citizenry."[40] A "core objective" of the First Amendment, Stevens wrote, has been "the preservation of a full and free flow of information."[41] That means more than protecting the channels of communication from governmental restraint. It also means protection for the acquisition of information about public institutions. Without such protection, "the process of self-government contemplated by the Framers would be stripped of its substance."[42] Therefore, Stevens wrote, there must be some constitutional protection for news gathering. Even that protection, however, is not for the private benefit of representatives of the press, but rather to ensure that citizens "are fully informed regarding matters of public interest and importance."[43]

Stevens's opinion was originally written as an opinion "of the Court." He first circulated it to the conference March 16, 1978.[44] Brennan and Powell joined; Burger reported that he would probably be writing as well.[45] Marshall and Blackmun announced that they would not participate in the case,[46] and the three-to-three split lasted for a month until Stewart announced that he could not join Stevens and would be preparing his own opinion.[47]

Finally, in *Nebraska Press Association*, Brennan noted that "commentary and reporting on the criminal justice system is at the core of First Amendment values," because the press provides information about a system that is of crucial importance to citizens concerned with the administration of government.[48] He rejected Burger's formula that would allow censorship of information about some criminal trials,[49] therefore, and wrote that prior restraint of such information is never permissible, "no matter how shabby the means by which the information is obtained."[50]

And, in *Miami Herald*, Brennan joined Burger's opinion overturning a state law that required equal access to opponents of political candidates endorsed by the press. Burger gave heed to the argument that increased media chains have a detrimental affect on the marketplace of ideas and the media have a responsibility to provide access,[51] but found the law unconstitutional because it controlled the content of newspapers.[52]

THE PRESS AND THE JUDICIARY

Brennan wrote only three opinions in cases involving conflicts between the press and the judiciary during his term on the Court: one for the majority, one in dissent, and one concurring in judgment. In two of those three opinions, however, he enlarged the "societal model" of the First Amendment. Stewart had referred to the "societal model" in *Branzburg*, and the model had been the basis for the dissents in the *Saxbe, Pell, Houchins* line of cases. Brennan, in his concurring opinion to *Richmond Newspapers v. Virginia*,[53] identified a "structural model" of the First Amendment, which was very similar to the "societal model" of the earlier cases. Two years later the "structural model" was incorporated into case law when Brennan used it as the rationale for his majority opinion in *Globe Newspaper Co. v. Superior Court*.[54]

Discussion of this area of the law, of course, must begin sixteen years before *Globe Newspapers* with *Sheppard v. Maxwell*.[55] Although three cases were decided earlier,[56] *Sheppard* is the landmark in free-press-fair-trial case law. In that case the Court held that Dr. Sam Sheppard did not receive a fair trial because of pervasive and biased press coverage and because of "the carnival atmosphere at trial."[57] The Court, however, placed the blame on the trial judge for not controlling the courtroom. The judge should have adopted stricter rules governing the use of the courtroom by newsmen, should have insulated the witnesses, and should have controlled the release of information, the Court held.[58] Although Justice Tom Clark, who wrote the majority opinion, was obviously not endorsing the actions of the press, he noted that had the judge taken control of the trial, "the news media would have soon learned to be content with the task of reporting the case as it unfolded in the courtroom—not pieced together from extrajudicial statements."[59]

Indeed, Clark recognized early in his opinion the importance of the press. He wrote:

> The principle that justice cannot survive behind walls of silence has long been reflected in the "Anglo-American distrust for secret trials. . . ." A responsible press has always been regarded as the handmaiden of effective judicial administration, especially in the criminal field. Its function in this regard is documented by an impressive record of service over several centuries. The press does not simply publish information about trials but guards against the miscarriage of justice by subjecting the police, prosecutors, and judicial processes to extensive public scrutiny.[60]

The Court faced its next major free-press-fair-trial case thirteen years later. In *Gannett v. DePasquale*[61] the Court ruled that members of the public have no independent right to seek access when the defendant in a case has waived his right to a public trial. The right to a speedy and public trial under the Sixth Amendment, the Court ruled, was a right of the accused, and a public trial could not be compelled by a third party.[62]

Brennan joined Justice Harry Blackmun's opinion concurring and dissenting. Blackmun, while noting that the Sixth Amendment "by its literal terms . . . secures the right to a public trial only to 'the accused,'[63] wrote that the Court had previously recognized that the amendment "may implicate interests beyond those of the accused."[64] In addition, the practice of conducting trials in public was well-established in England and in the colonies.[65] Blackmun wrote that he could find no evidence that the defendant's right to waive his right to a public trial compelled a private trial.[66]

Until a month before *Gannett* was delivered, Blackmun's was the opinion of the Court. On May 31, 1979, however, Powell switched his vote, giving Stewart, rather than Blackmun, five votes. A day later, Burger assigned the majority opinion in the case to Stewart.[67] Powell wrote that he originally saw the case as one involving the First Amendment, but "had become persuaded that my views as to the Sixth Amendment coincide substantially with those expressed by Potter, but that I would not rest the

case on that Amendment alone." Stewart, in his most recent draft, recognized the relevance of the First Amendment claim but did not settle that
claim in the case. Powell, therefore, decided to join Stewart's opinion.
Powell wrote Blackmun:

> I know that you have devoted a great deal of time and thought to your
> scholarly opinion, and I am sorry to end up the "swing vote." At Confer-
> ence I voted to reverse. But upon a more careful examination of the facts, I
> have concluded that the trial court substantially did what in my view the
> First Amendment requires.[68]

Gannett brought a storm of protest, and one year later—to the day—the
Court delivered its decision in *Richmond Newspapers,* ruling that access to
trials is guaranteed to the public by the First Amendment. Finding that
the presumption of openness in the English court system passed to the
judicial systems in colonial America,[69] Burger, writing for three members
of the Court, held that "the right to attend criminal trials is implicit in the
guarantees of the First Amendment."[70]

Brennan wrote one of three concurring opinions, the only one that had
a joiner.[71] In his opinion, Brennan noted that, while the First Amendment
had not been viewed as providing uncategorical access to all governmental
information,[72] the Court had not categorically ruled out access in all circumstances; the nature of information sought and countervailing interests
were to be evaluated when access is sought under the First Amendment.[73]

Usually, Brennan wrote, the First Amendment acts to protect communication between speaker and listener.[74] That is not the only purpose of
the First Amendment, however. Wrote Brennan:

> The First Amendment embodies more than a commitment to free expression
> and communicative interchange for their own sakes; it has a *structural* role to
> play in securing and fostering our republican system of self-government.
> . . . Implicit in this structural role is not only "the principle that debate on
> public issues should be uninhibited, robust, and wide-open," . . . but also
> the antecedent assumption that valuable public debate—as well as other civic
> behavior—must be informed.[75]

In making the point, Brennan cited that portion of Powell's dissent in
Saxbe in which Powell referred to the "societal function" of the First
Amendment. The societal function, Powell wrote, protects " 'the ability
of our people through free and open debate to consider and resolve their
own destiny.' " And that public debate—to which the nation is committed—must be informed as well as free.[76] Brennan continued:

> The structural model links the First Amendment to that process of com-
> munication necessary for a democracy to survive, and thus entails solicitude

not only for communication itself, but also for the indispensable conditions
of meaningful communication.[77]

Since the stretch of protection for access to information is theoretically
endless, however, Brennan wrote that "it must be invoked with discrimination and temperance . . . considering the information sought and the
opposing interests invaded."[78] Two principles may be invoked to determine whether the public has a constitutional right of access to information. One is the historical tradition, since "the Constitution carries the
gloss of history." The second is the value of the access. Brennan explained: "Analysis is not advanced by rhetorical statements that all information bears upon public issues; what is crucial in individual cases is whether
access to a particular government process is important in terms of that
very process."[79]

First, Brennan found, trials have been historically open. The English
tradition was inherited by the American colonists.[80] In addition, the Court
"has persistently defended the public character of the trial process."[81] The
Court has recognized that a major purpose of the First Amendment is
discussion of governmental affairs, and public scrutiny of government is
necessary for such discussion.[82]

Second, Brennan found that publicity serves to advance several purposes
of the judicial process. Openness helps assure that the defendant receives a
fair trial, that the appearance of justice is satisfied, and that procedural
rights are respected.[83] In addition, Brennan wrote that trials are matters of
public interest and that publicizing them aids in accurate fact-finding.[84]

Therefore, Brennan wrote, the weight of the historical practice and an
"assessment of the specific structural value of public access," combined
with "our ingrained tradition of public trials and the importance of public
access to the broader purposes of the trial process, tip the balance strongly
toward the rule that trials be open."[85]

Brennan's first reference to the "structural model" of the First Amendment, however, did not come in his *Richmond Newspapers* opinion. Five
months before *Richmond Newspapers* was argued, Brennan referred to the
structural model in a speech dedicating the S. I. Newhouse Center for Law
and Justice at Rutgers University in Newark.[86] Since "the First Amendment protects the structure of communications necessary for the existence
of our democracy," Brennan said, the structural model would provide
additional protection to the press.[87] Under the traditional "speech model"
of press protection, the press is protected only because it has a First
Amendment right to speak.[88] Under the structural model, however, the
press is also protected "when it performs all the myriad tasks necessary
for it to gather and disseminate the news."[89]

Brennan's structural model was the rationale for the Court's ruling two
years later in *Globe Newspaper Co. v. Superior Court*. Although Brennan

did not use that specific language in his majority opinion, he cited his own opinion in *Richmond Newspapers,* in which this language was used.[90] In *Globe Newspaper Co.*, the Court struck down a Massachusetts law that automatically closed a trial involving the victim of a sex crime who was a minor. Brennan recognized that the state had compelling interests for closing such trials, but wrote that the interests did not justify a mandatory closure; closure should be determined on a case-by-case basis.[91]

In making the ruling, Brennan summarized the two justifications for open trials he made in his concurring opinion to *Richmond Newspapers:* Trials have historically been open, and openness plays a significant role in the functioning of the judicial process.[92]

Brennan prefaced that argument, however, by returning to his "structural model" of the First Amendment. Although access to trials is not mentioned in the First Amendment, he wrote, the Court has long eschewed a narrow, literal conception of the Amendment's terms:

> for the Framers were concerned with broad principles, and wrote against a background of shared values and practices. The First Amendment is thus broad enough to encompass those rights that, while not unambiguously enumerated in the very terms of the Amendment, are nonetheless necessary to the enjoyment of other First Amendment rights.[93]

The common understanding of the First Amendment, he continued, is that it had as a major purpose protection of the free discussion of governmental affairs. So, "by offering such protection, the First Amendment serves to ensure that the individual citizen can effectively participate in and contribute to our republican system of self-government."[94] The First Amendment embraces the concept that discussion of public affairs must be informed. The Amendment, therefore, ensures informed discussion of the judicial system by allowing access to trials.[95]

Originally, Brennan's discussion of the unenumerated rights under the First Amendment was even stronger. In an early draft of his opinion, the final sentence of the section quoted above read this way:

> The First Amendment is thus broad enough to encompass those rights that, while not unambiguously enumerated in the very terms of the Amendment, are nonetheless necessary to the enjoyment of other First Amendment rights or are implicit in the very structure of self-government established by the Constitution.[96]

White objected to the language, however, and threatened to write separately if it remained in the opinion.[97] Blackmun also asked that the language be removed.[98] Brennan complied.

CONCLUSIONS

Brennan believed in a "structural model" of the First Amendment. Such a model would help ensure that debate about matters of public concern would be not only robust but also informed. The press, as an essential element in robust and informed debate, therefore, deserved additional First Amendment protection to act as the representatives of the public in gathering information.

The structural model was based on a simple syllogism: A core purpose of the First Amendment is to ensure to citizens the ability to govern themselves; essential to self-government is the freedom to examine and debate matters of public concern; information is essential to the freedom to debate since one must be informed in order to participate in meaningful debate; therefore, the First Amendment protects information-gathering, particularly by the press, which, as a representative of the public, is society's chief information-gatherer and is thus essential to the structure of communication in a free society. Even though access to trials and other functions of government is not specifically mentioned in the First Amendment, therefore, access is guaranteed because the amendment's framers, concerned with broad principles, wrote an amendment "broad enough to encompass those rights that, while not unambiguously enumerated in the very terms of the Amendment, are nonetheless necessary to the enjoyment of other First Amendment rights."[99]

The "structural model" of press freedom was related to the "societal role" of the First Amendment alluded to by Stewart in his dissenting opinion to *Branzburg*. The significance of the full and free flow of information to the public, Stewart wrote, means that protection of a free press is not so much for the benefit of the press as it is for the benefit of society.[100]

The theme was carried through the opinions of Powell in *Saxbe*, Douglas in *Pell*, and Stevens in *Houchins*. All three opinions, which were joined by Brennan, focused on "the societal function of the First Amendment in preserving free public discussion of governmental affairs."[101]

Brennan used the term "structural model" in carrying the theme from the *Saxbe, Pell, Houchins* line of cases to cases involving access to trials. In *Richmond Newspapers* he wrote that the "structural role" of the First Amendment secured and fostered the republican system of self-government, which assumed that "valuable public debate . . . must be informed."[102] And, in *Globe Newspaper, Co.*, he wrote that by providing access to trials and other government functions, the First Amendment ensured that citizens can "participate in and contribute to our republican system of self-government."[103]

NOTES

1. *See, for example,* FCC v. League of Women Voters of California, 468 U.S. 364, 381 (1984).

2. Estes v. Texas, 381 U.S. 532, 539 (1965).

3. Mills v. Alabama, 384 U.S. 214, 218–19 (1966).

4. *See, e.g.,* Branzburg v. Hayes, 408 U.S. 665 (1969); Pell v. Procunier, 417 U.S. 817 (1974); Saxbe v. Washington Post Co., 417 U.S. 843 (1974).

5. Branzburg v. Hayes, 408 U.S. 665 (1969).

6. Pell v. Procunier, 417 U.S. 817 (1974); Saxbe v. Washington Post Co., 417 U.S. 843 (1974).

7. Houchins v. KQED, Inc., 438 U.S. 1 (1978).

8. *See, for example,* New York Times Co. v. Sullivan, 376 U.S. 254 (1964).

9. 408 U.S. 665 (1969).

10. 438 U.S. 1 (1978).

11. 418 U.S. 241 (1974).

12. 417 U.S. 817 (1974).

13. 417 U.S. 843 (1974).

14. 427 U.S. 539 (1976).

15. *Branzburg,* 408 U.S. at 726, notes 1 and 2, Justice Stewart dissenting. *See also, Houchins,* 438 U.S. at 30 (1978), Justice Stevens dissenting.

16. 427 U.S. at 572, Justice Brennan concurring in judgment. In *Miami Herald* Justice Brennan wrote a one-paragraph concurrence noting that the majority opinion addressed only right-of-reply statutes and not retraction statutes, 418 U.S. at 258.

17. 408 U.S. at 681.

18. *Id.* at 682.

19. *Id.* at 683.

20. *Id.* at 684.

21. *Id.* at 690–91.

22. *Id.* at 725, Justice Stewart dissenting.

23. *Id.,* Justice Stewart dissenting.

24. *Id.,* Justice Stewart dissenting.

25. *Id.* at 726, Justice Stewart dissenting.

26. *Id.* at 726–27, Justice Stewart dissenting.

27. *Id.* at 727–28, Justice Stewart dissenting.

28. *Id.* at 729, Justice Stewart dissenting.

29. *See* text accompanying *supra* notes 70–77, Chapter 4.

30. 417 U.S. at 847, Justice Powell dissenting.

31. *Id.* at 862, Justice Powell dissenting.

32. *Id.* at 862–63, Justice Powell dissenting.

33. *Id.* at 863, Justice Powell dissenting.

34. *Id.* at 864, Justice Powell dissenting.

35. 417 U.S. at 838–39, Justice Douglas dissenting.

36. *Id.* at 839–40, Justice Douglas dissenting.

37. 438 U.S. at 8.

38. *Id.* at 9.

39. *Id.* at 29, Justice Stevens dissenting.

40. *Id.* at 31, Justice Stevens dissenting.

41. *Id.* at 31–32, Justice Stevens dissenting.

42. *Id.* at 32, Justice Stevens dissenting.

43. *Id.*

44. Brennan Papers, Box 472, circulation of Justice Stevens, March 10, 1978.

45. *Id.*, memorandum of Justice Brennan, March 16, 1978; memorandum of Justice Powell, March 23, 1978; memorandum of Chief Justice Burger, March 28, 1978.

46. *Id.*, memoranda of Justices Marshall and Blackmun, June 13, 1978.

47. *Id.*, memorandum of Justice Stewart, April 24, 1978.

48. 427 U.S. at 587, Justice Brennan concurring in the judgment.

49. *Id.* at 572, Justice Brennan concurring in judgment. *See also* discussion accompanying *supra* notes 52–54, Chapter 4.

50. *Id.* at 588.

51. *Miami Herald,* 418 U.S. at 245–54.

52. *Id.* at 256–58.

53. 448 U.S. 555 (1980).

54. 457 U.S. 596 (1982).

55. 384 U.S. 333 (1966).

56. In all three cases the Court held that defendants were denied fair trials due to prejudicial publicity, Irwin v. Dowd, 366 U.S. 717 (1961); Rideau v. Louisiana, 373 U.S. 723 (1963); Estes v. Texas, 381 U.S. 532 (1965). In *Rideau* the prejudice was caused by a television station's broadcast of Wilbert Rideau's confession to a murder. Justice Stewart, for the Court, wrote: "For anyone who has ever watched television the conclusion cannot be avoided that this spectacle, to the tens of thousands of people who saw and heard it, *was* Rideau's trial—at which he pleaded guilty to murder," 373 U.S. at 726. In *Estes* the court held that the defendant did not receive a fair trial because the trial was broadcast. Justice Brennan dissented and noted that the decision is not a blanket constitutional prohibition of the broadcast of trials, 381 U.S. at 617, Justice Brennan dissenting.

57. 384 U.S. at 358.

58. *Id.* at 358–60.

59. *Id.* at 362.

60. *Id.* at 350.

61. 443 U.S. 369 (1979).

62. *Id.* at 384.

63. *Id.* at 415, Justice Blackmun concurring and dissenting.

64. *Id.*, Justice Blackmun concurring and dissenting.

65. *Id.* at 419–21, Justice Blackmun concurring and dissenting.

66. *Id.* at 427, Justice Blackmun concurring and dissenting.

67. Brennan Papers, Box 499, memorandum of Chief Justice Burger to the Conference, June 1, 1979.

68. *Id.*, memorandum of Justice Powell to Justice Blackmun, May 31, 1979.

69. 448 U.S. at 567, opinion of Chief Justice Burger.

70. *Id.* at 580, opinion of Chief Justice Burger.

71. Justice Marshall joined. Only Justice Rehnquist dissented; Justice Powell did not participate.

72. 448 U.S. at 585, Justice Brennan concurring in judgment.

73. *Id.* at 586, Justice Brennan concurring in judgment.

74. *Id.*, Justice Brennan concurring in judgment.

75. *Id.* at 587, Justice Brennan concurring in judgment. Emphasis in the original.

76. *Id.* at note 3, Justice Brennan concurring in judgment. Justice Powell, who did not participate in the case, sent a handwritten note to Justice Brennan thanking him for the cite. "You are a scholar and a gentleman—and a generous one!" Powell wrote. Brennan Papers, Box 535, memorandum of Justice Powell, June 6, 1980.

77. *Id.* at 587–88, Justice Brennan concurring in judgment.

78. *Id.* at 589, Justice Brennan concurring in judgment.

79. *Id.*, Justice Brennan concurring in judgment.

80. *Id.* at 590, Justice Brennan concurring in judgment.

81. *Id.* at 591, Justice Brennan concurring in judgment.

82. *Id.* at 592, Justice Brennan concurring in judgment.

83. *Id.* at 593–95, Justice Brennan concurring in judgment.

84. *Id.* at 596, Justice Brennan concurring in judgment.

85. *Id.* at 598, Justice Brennan concurring in judgment.

86. Brennan, Address, 30 Rutgers L. Rev. 173 (1979).

87. *Id.* at 176–77.

88. *Id.* at 176.

89. *Id.* at 177.

90. 457 U.S. at 604, citing 448 U.S. at 587–88, Justice Brennan concurring in judgment.

91. *Id.* at 607–8.

92. *Id.* at 605–6.

93. *Id.* at 604.

94. *Id.*

95. *Id.* at 604–5.

96. Brennan Papers, Box 600. May 24, 1982, circulation of Justice Brennan.

97. *Id.*, memorandum of Justice White, May 25, 1983.

98. *Id.*, memorandum of Justice Blackmun, June 17, 1982.

99. *Richmond Newspapers,* 448 U.S. at 604, Justice Brennan concurring in judgment.

100. 408 U.S. at 726, Justice Stewart dissenting.

101. *Saxbe,* 417 U.S. at 862, Justice Powell dissenting.

102. 448 U.S. at 587, Justice Brennan concurring in judgment.

103. *Id.* at 604.

9

. . . And Freedom of Expression

Freedom of expression may be the most cherished of the guarantees enumerated in the Bill of Rights. The right to express an opinion, to engage in debate, and to criticize those in power is characteristic of a free society. Indeed, a democratic government is built on the premise that the individual, rather than the society, is superior.[1] Under such a premise, freedom of expression and democracy may be synonymous—each essential to the welfare of the other. Sometimes, however, freedom of expression is not seen as an essential partner to democracy; it is seen as a privilege resulting from democracy.[2]

While it cannot be disputed that free expression is a benefit enjoyed by those who live in a democratic society, Supreme Court Justice William J. Brennan, Jr., spent thirty-four years developing a reverse hypothesis: Free expression is the benefactor in the relationship. One theme running throughout Brennan's writings on free expression is that the marketplace of ideas is more than an esoteric metaphor, it is a functioning model that, allowed to operate properly, will ensure the proper operation of government. Indeed, under the paradigm developed by Brennan, free expression is essential to democracy. Thomas Jefferson, if given the choice between a government and newspapers, might have chosen the latter,[3] but Brennan would argue that government—a democratic government at any rate—cannot exist without a free press.

Brennan's commitment to the premise that free expression is essential to democracy dominated his writings and votes in expression cases. It was that commitment that prompted him to write that citizens have a duty to criticize their governors,[4] and that some falsity must be endured to ensure the debate on public matters, which is essential to a free society.[5] That commitment was at the heart of Brennan's finding that any ideas with the slightest redeeming value are protected by the First Amendment.[6] Speech may be offensive, tawdry, silly, or repugnant; it may hamper government operations, espouse unpopular or immoral ideas, or embarrass. Because free speech is essential to democratic society, however, in only rare cases may it be restricted. Wrote Brennan:

> The First Amendment mandates that we presume that speakers not the government know best what they want to say and how to say it. . . . To this end, the government, even with the purest of motives, may not substitute its judgment as to how best to speak for that of speakers and listeners; free and robust debate cannot thrive if directed by the government.[7]

Brennan's free-expression theory, therefore, can be summed up in this way: Self-government is the primary purpose of the First Amendment; therefore, matters related to self-government—matters of public concern—are at the core of First Amendment protection; to ensure robust, uninhibited, and wide-open debate about such matters, the marketplace of ideas must be protected; indeed, the dominant theme of the First Amendment is the free trade in ideas in the competitive market. In addition, because this free trade of ideas is essential to a properly functioning government, and because members of society must be informed in order to participate fully in self-government, each individual has an inherent right to receive information; the right is not explicitly stated in the Constitution, but is essential to the enjoyment of other First Amendment guarantees, so it is part of a package of fundamental rights.

Underlying this paradigm, as indicated, is the premise that the "marketplace of ideas" metaphor is a functional model that works to the benefit of the individual and society, and, therefore, to that of government as well.

Brennan's seminal writing in this area, of course, was *New York Times Co. v. Sullivan.*[8] The case, certainly, was not the first utterance on free expression for either Brennan or the Court. Brennan, as a matter of fact, had hinted at some of the themes developed in *Times v. Sullivan* in his earlier opinions. Seven years earlier, for example, in the first free-expression opinion he wrote for the Court, Brennan recognized the importance to a free society of the discussion of matters of pubic concern[9] and the dangers to a free society of inhibiting unorthodox, controversial, or hateful ideas.[10] And, a year later, in *Speiser v. Randall,*[11] Brennan expressed concern that judicially required justifications for speech might prompt self-censorship.[12]

In *Times v. Sullivan,* however, Brennan delineated for the first time the First Amendment theory that would guide much of his writings for the next twenty-six years. Citizen participation in government was one of the keys to the determination of the case. In a democracy, Brennan wrote, absolute sovereignty lay with the people.[13] The discussion of government, governors, and other public business, therefore, is fundamental to the operation of a democracy,[14] and a duty of citizenship.[15]

The general themes outlined in *Times v. Sullivan* became the foundation for Brennan's free-expression theory.

SELF-GOVERNMENT AND SPEECH THAT MATTERS

No theme is expressed more strongly in Brennan's free-expression opinions than that of the necessity of the First Amendment rights of free speech and press in self-government.[16] A free press, he wrote, "assures the maintenance of our political system and an open society."[17] He called speech on matters of public concern "the essence of self-government."[18] The free-speech and free-press guarantees, he believed, "constituted the cornerstone of a government 'of the people, by the people, and for the people' "[19]; democracy only perseveres because of a "profound national commitment to the principle that debate on public issues should be uninhibited, robust, and wide-open."[20] As indicated, Brennan went so far as to adopt portions of what has been called the "social responsibility" theory of the press,[21] writing that discussion of matters of public concern is a public duty[22] that includes the responsibility of criticizing those in government.[23]

Brennan defined matters of public concern as "information on the basis of which members of our society may make reasoned decisions about the government,"[24] including, "discussions of candidates, structures and forms of government, the manner in which government is operated or should be operated, and all such matters relating to political processes."[25] Political speech and activity, therefore, constituted, "core conduct protected by the First Amendment,"[26] even if it is virulent and inflammatory,[27] advocates violence as a means of social change,[28] or might hamper governmental operations.[29] "The protection given speech and press," Brennan wrote, "was fashioned to assure unfettered interchange of ideas for the bringing about of political and social changes desired by the people."[30]

Brennan's definition of matters of public concern extended beyond that of purely political speech, however. The ability of an individual or group to proselytze and hand out religious literature, for example, constituted "core First Amendment rights,"[31] as did commentary and reporting on the criminal justice system.[32] In addition, Brennan found all forms of art to constitute speech involving matters of public concern,[33] as he did commentary on and discussion of sexual matters.[34] Brennan's definition of matters of pubic concern would match Alexander Meiklejohn's definition of matters of self-governing importance, which included the arts and education as well as politics.[35]

SELF-GOVERNMENT AND
THE MARKETPLACE OF IDEAS

Just as expression is essential to a democratic society, the marketplace of ideas is essential to expression. Only when a multitude of voices is free to debate in the marketplace can truth become recognizable and drive the democratic system, which, Brennan believed, "thrives on the uninterrupted interchange of ideas."[36] In fact, Brennan found the dominant theme in the application of the amendment to be the "free trade in ideas in a competitive marketplace,"[37] which "presupposes that right conclusions are more likely to be gathered out of a multitude of tongues, than through any kind of authoritative selection."[38]

The marketplace model, therefore, as Brennan sees it, has several implications for expression. First, the First Amendment protects the structure of communication as well as the act of communicating. This means, essentially, that the government may not simply allow freedom of expression, the government must promote freedom of expression.[39] Second, the First Amendment guarantees the right to receive information just as it protects the right to speak.

Brennan admitted that neither of these rights is expressly granted in the Constitution. But, he wrote in *Globe Newspaper Co. v. Superior Court:*

> The Framers were concerned with broad principles, and wrote against a background of shared values and practices. The First Amendment is thus broad enough to encompass those rights that, while not unambiguously enumerated in the very terms of the Amendment, are nonetheless necessary to the enjoyment of other First Amendment rights.[40]

One of those unenumerated rights, Brennan believed, is the right to receive information,[41] a right ensured only when the marketplace of ideas is protected.[42] Individuals are "constitutionally entitled" to engage in and listen to an exchange of views, Brennan found.[43] "The free speech guarantee," he wrote, "gives each citizen an equal right to self-expression and to participation in self-government. This guarantee also protects the rights of listeners to 'the widest possible dissemination of information from diverse and antagonistic sources.' "[44] Indeed, Justice William O. Douglas, quoting from Brennan's opinion in *Times v. Sullivan* emphasized that interference with the right to receive information was at odds "with the 'uninhibited, robust, and wide-open' debate and discussion that are contemplated by the First Amendment."[45]

The added protection Brennan would grant to the press was directly due to this constitutional right to receive information.[46] Debate on matters of public concern, Brennan believed, should not only be robust, it should also be informed. The press performs an important function in society by helping inform the citizenry. Since the system of self-government assumes the existence of an informed citizenry, a "core objective" of the First Amendment has been "the preservation of a full and free flow of information."[47] Without protection for the press, therefore, "the process of self-government contemplated by the Framers would be stripped of its substance."[48] The press is protected when it clamors and contends for change[49] because editorial opinion lies at the heart of First Amendment protection—it was precisely what the framers of the amendment were most anxious to protect.[50] And the press is "one of the very agencies the Framers of our constitution thoughtfully and deliberately selected to improve our society and keep it free."[51] So protection for the press does not simply benefit the press; it benefits society.[52]

In addition, the press often acts as an agent, or necessary representative, of the public.[53] The press, then, is more than a voice seeking to enter the marketplace of ideas. The free press acts as both a representative and a messenger for society. The "structural model" of the First Amendment that Brennan advocated, therefore, would do more than protect the press in its free-speech rights; it would protect the press "when it performs all the myriad tasks necessary for it to gather and disseminate the news."[54]

The Brennan paradigm does not mean that individuals receive less First Amendment protection than the press. The rights of the institutional media, Brennan wrote, are neither lesser nor greater than those of individuals.[55] Indeed, Brennan found that the press was protected, at least in part, because of the importance of free speech to individual participation in government. He wrote:

> Freedom of speech is itself an end because the human community is in large measure defined through speech; freedom of speech is therefore intrinsic to individual dignity. This is particularly so in a democracy like our own, in which the autonomy of each individual is accorded equal and incommensurate respect.[56]

The press is protected, Brennan wrote, "to ensure the vitality of First Amendment guarantees." But, he noted, "this solicitude implies no endorsement of the principle that speakers other than the press deserve less First Amendment protection. . . . The free speech guarantee gives each citizen an equal right."[57] The added protection for the press under Brennan's model is not added protection for communicating; it is added protection for the structure of communication—that is, for the activities directly related to speaking.

RESTRICTING THE MARKETPLACE

Brennan was committed to the principal that the marketplace of ideas is more than a philosophical metaphor; it is a functioning model that is mandated by the First Amendment. That is, Brennan believed that the "marketplace of ideas" model genuinely worked for the betterment of society. Expression, therefore, should be regulated by the marketplace, not by government: It is the responsibility of the marketplace, rather than government, to weed out worthless communications[58]; it is the people, not the government, who hold censorial power.[59]

This is not to say, however, that the marketplace is absolutely free from government regulation. Like Alexander Meiklejohn,[60] Brennan believed that speech concerning matters of public concern deserved sturdy protection. He would fall short of granting absolute protection, however. For example, while he believed a military base could not ban picketing and similar expressive conduct within its boundaries, even though such speech might hamper base operations,[61] Brennan would allow speech that caused an inevitable, direct, and immediate breach of national security to be censored,[62] even if that speech involved matters of public concern.

The chief purpose of the First Amendment, Brennan found, is to prohibit prior restraint.[63] Any system of prior restraint, therefore, comes to the Court "bearing a heavy presumption against its constitutional validity."[64] Prior restraint is allowed only in exceptional cases and only when procedural safeguards are in place that assure an almost immediate judicial determination of its validity.[65] In addition, the governmental regulations must be narrowly tailored to advance a significant government interest, and the incidental limitation on expression may be no broader than necessary for that government interest.[66] Methods for identifying proscribed speech "must be subjected to close analysis and critical judgment,"[67] the regulations may not be vague,[68] they cannot improperly restrict the dissemination of information through legitimate forums,[69] and they may not turn on the government's approval or disapproval of the speaker or the speaker's message.[70] "If there is a bedrock principle underlying the First Amendment," Brennan wrote, "it is that the Government may not prohibit the expression of an idea simply because society finds the idea itself offensive or disagreeable."[71]

Ultimately, then, Brennan's marketplace paradigm requires balancing. It would allow restrictions on the press only when the government had a specific interest to promote that was unrelated to restricting expression and that only incidentally restricted expression. Legitimate time, place, and manner restrictions are allowable, therefore, even for political speech.[72] Speech can be restricted to ensure order in a school,[73] to protect the welfare of children,[74] and to protect national security.[75] And the model also allows greater restrictions on commercial speech, a particularly hardy type of speech because of its economic self-interest.[76]

In addition, some restrictions are allowed that benefit the operation of the marketplace of ideas. When the Court, in *Columbia Broadcasting System v. National Democratic Party*,[77] upheld the right of broadcasters to refuse to accept political editorial advertisements, for example, Brennan dissented, arguing that the Court was allowing broadcasters too much control over the marketplace. Brennan's argument was based on the Court's long-time view of broadcasters as trustees over a national resource[78] that had achieved immense power. The broadcasting industry, Brennan wrote, with the government's help, has become "potentially the most efficient and effective marketplace of ideas ever." Any policy that absolutely denies citizens access to that marketplace, therefore, "renders the concept of full and free discussion meaningless."[79] Brennan found it significant that the case did not concern what broadcasters could or could not say over the air, but concerned the right of broadcasters to decide what others could say through editorial advertisements.[80]

Brennan found, however, that most restrictions on speech do not benefit the marketplace of ideas. He almost always found such restrictions to be unconstitutional. Embarrassing material,[81] unorthodox on unconventional ideas,[82] offensive conduct,[83] even the advocacy of illegal action[84] or possible threats to national security are protected under the First Amendment.[85] Brennan would not allow restrictions that halted governmental employees from participating in political campaigns,[86] banned access by the press to prisons or prisoners,[87] or restricted students from publishing unpopular or controversial material in high school newspapers.[88]

Many of these legal precepts, and much of Brennan's First Amendment theory, have been accepted by the Court. Often, however, Brennan and his colleagues have disagreed on the interpretation or application of the precepts. Brennan believed the First Amendment to be essential to a democratic society. The criteria for restricting expression in the Brennan paradigm, therefore, were more difficult to meet than those of some other members of the Court. When lines were to be drawn, Brennan almost always drew them to grant broad free-expression rights; his tendency was to err on the side of free expression. "Even minor intrusions" on First Amendment rights, he wrote, are not allowed under the Constitution.[89] Since "the line between ideological and nonideological speech is impossible to draw with accuracy," the line should be drawn to allow freedom to nearly all speech that might be ideological.[90]

Brennan, for example, found public forums in places foreign to other members of the Court. Mailboxes are public forums, because the mail is a vital national medium of expression[91]; a state fair is "truly a marketplace of ideas and a political forum in the communication of ideas and information"[92]; and military bases are public forums—at least for the military personnel at those bases—because of the unique nature of the bases and of the military.[93] Since the military is susceptible to politicization, Brennan wrote, to isolate military personnel from ideas is dangerous to the concept of a politically neutral military.[94] The military base, therefore, must necessarily be the place for the free communication of thoughts.[95]

In addition, Brennan would not allow overbroad restrictions on bill-boards because he found them to be a well-established medium of communication,[96] and he would not allow cities to ban the posting of signs on public property on the basis of content.[97] The posting of signs, Brennan wrote, is a time-honored and cheap means of communicating "a broad range of ideas and information."[98] While time, place, and manner restrictions are allowed under the Constitution, once a city has opened a forum for communication, it may not regulate that forum on the basis of content.[99]

Few of Brennan's colleagues on the Court were willing to allow such protection. While the Court accepted Brennan's theory that the First Amendment was designed to encourage robust debate about matters of self-government, and that the marketplace of ideas must be protected, a majority never consistently applied that theory with the broad sweep of Brennan. A majority accepted Brennan's contention that obscenity lay outside First Amendment protection because it was without value,[100] for example, but when the justice, after a tortuous journey, decided that obscenity could not be regulated because it could not be sufficiently identified, for example, the majority left him. The Court continues to hold to the *Roth* doctrine, using the test for obscenity established in *Miller v. California*.[101]

Brennan also believes that obscene material—material without any redeeming social value—is not protected by the Constitution and may be proscribed. Early in the Court's dealings with obscenity, however, he recognized that protected speech could easily get caught in the web of tests that entangled obscenity. Due care was needed, therefore, to ensure that obscenity tests not be overbroad, and that methods of restricting obscenity remain within constitutional bounds. In 1962 he wrote, "We risk erosion of First Amendment liberties unless we train our vigilance upon the methods whereby obscenity is condemned no less than upon the standards whereby it is judged."[102] Brennan decided that no methods were acceptable; after sixteen years of attempting to identify obscene material, he decided that the task was very nearly impossible and that most tests of obscenity are not sufficiently precise to avoid restricting protected speech.[103] Therefore, he determined that criminal sanctions for the production or dissemination of sexually explicit material were unconstitutional. It is more important under the Brennan paradigm for some obscene material to exist in the marketplace of ideas—absent a showing of actual harm—than it is for some protected speech to be proscribed. Constitutional guarantees are too precious, Brennan believed, to sacrifice in the name of controlling obscene material, and material with even the "slightest redeeming social importance" is protected. Brennan's theory remains intact in pornography law, but Brennan and a majority of the Court have parted ways on the application of the theory.

Similarly, Brennan often found that laws restricting or punishing abusive speech were unconstitutional because of the danger of catching protected speech in the net of restrictions. Under his marketplace theory, even virulent or abusive language was protected because it might contribute to self-government. Intimations that the president should be assassinated are protected, for example, because the speech relates to matters of public concern[104]; strong language cannot be proscribed because form and ideas cannot always be divorced[105]; and abusive language aimed at police officers cannot be punished because "freedom to verbally oppose police action without fear of imprisonment is basic to a free nation."[106]

In libel law, where Brennan's majority opinion in *New York Times v. Sullivan* became the touchstone in much of the Court's First Amendment cases, the Court has been willing to accept Brennan's theory, but not willing to extend First Amendment protection to the degree Brennan believed was demanded by the marketplace model. The Court backed away from the model in *Gertz v. Robert Welch, Inc.,*[107] for example, when it ruled that discussion of matters of public concern was insufficient to invoke extra protection for libel defendants.

In addition, a majority never fully accepted Brennan's structural model of the First Amendment, which would grant protection to news gathering as well as to expression and, to Brennan's way of thinking at any rate, was justified because of its benefit to society. The Court gave lip service to the model, noting that news–gathering deserved some degree of protection, but never granted that protection to the structure of communication.[108]

All this demonstrates one of the problems with the Brennan paradigm: It is driven by subjective rather than objective tests. That is, it is based upon subjective interpretations of judges and justices for its workability, thereby allowing a judge to accept Brennan's theory, but apply that theory in a manner that would not grant the sturdy degree of protection Brennan would apply.

In the final analysis, however, the justice was successful in establishing a theory of expression that would grant sturdy protection to speech that advanced the marketplace of ideas. He believed strongly in the workability of that metaphor and was able to apply the theory consistently to expand free speech and press rights. Brennan believed the First Amendment to be "explicit and indispensable" in the attempt to "secure the Blessings of Liberty to ourselves and our Posterity."[109] It is a noble proposition and rarely in judicial history has it been expressed more nobly, powerfully, and consistently than by Mr. Justice Brennan.

NOTES

1. *See, generally,* F. Siebert, T. Peterson, W. Schramm, Four Theories of the Press (1972).

2. *Id. See also* F. Siebert, Freedom of the Press in England, 1476–1776 (1965).

3. *See* F. Mott, Jefferson and the Press (1943).

4. New York Times Co. v. Sullivan, 376 U.S. 254, 383 (1964).

5. *Id.* at 271–72.

6. Roth v. U.S., 354 U.S. 476, 484 (1957).

7. Riley v. National Federation of the Blind of North Carolina, Inc., 108 S.Ct. 2667, 2674 (1988).

8. 376 U.S. 254 (1964).

9. *Roth,* 354 U.S. at 487–88.

10. *Id.* at 484.

11. 357 U.S. 513 (1958).

12. *Id.* at 521–26. Compare to 376 U.S. at 278–80.

13. 376 U.S. at 274–75.

14. *Id.* at 275.

15. *Id.* at 270.

16. *Id.* at 275.

17. Time, Inc. v. Hill, 385 U.S. 374, 389 (1967).

18. Garrison v. Louisiana, 379 U.S. 64, 74–75 (1964).

19. Brennan Papers, Box 234, draft opinion of Rosenbloom v. Metromedia, Inc., circulated February 17, 1971.

20. Gertz v. Robert Welch, Inc., 418 U.S. 323, 361–62 (1974), Justice Brennan dissenting.

21. Siebert et al., *supra* note 1.

22. 376 U.S. at 270.

23. *Id.* at 282.

24. Connick v. Myers, 461 U.S. 138, 161 (1983), Justice Brennan dissenting.

25. *Id.*, Justice Brennan dissenting, quoting Mills v. Alabama, 384 U.S. 214, 218–19 (1966).

26. Hynes v. Mayor of Oradell, 425 U.S. 610, 626 (1976). *See also,* Brown v. Hartlage, 456 U.S. 45, 52–53 (1982).

27. Carroll v. Princess Anne, 393 U.S. 175 (1968).

28. Brandenburg v. Ohio, 395 U.S. 444 (1969).

29. Haig v. Agee, 453 U.S. 280, 310 (1981), Justice Brennan dissenting.

30. *Roth,* 354 U.S. at 484.

31. Heffron v. International Society for Krishna Consciousness, 425 U.S. 640, 662 (1981), Justice Brennan concurring and dissenting.

32. Nebraska Press Association v. Stuart, 427 U.S. 539 (1976). *See also* Time, Inc. v. Firestone, 424 U.S. 448 (1976).

33. Brennan Papers, Box 101, Obscenity Memorandum at 36–40.

34. *Roth,* 354 U.S. at 487.

35. Meiklejohn, The First Amendment Is an Absolute, 1961 Sup. Ct. Rev. 245, 255.

36. Procunier v. Martinez, 416 U.S. 396, 427 (1974), Justice Marshall concurring (joined by Justice Brennan).

37. Columbia Broadcasting System v. Democratic National Committee, 412 U.S. 94, 183 (1973), Justice Brennan dissenting.

38. *Id.* at 191–92, Justice Brennan dissenting.

39. *See, e.g.,* Rosenbloom v. Metromedia, Inc., 403 U.S. 29, 41–43 (1971).

40. Globe Newspaper Co. v. Superior Court, 457 U.S. 596, 604 (1982). *See also*

Griswold v. Connecticut, 381 U.S. 479, 492 (1965), Justice Goldberg concurring (joined by Justice Brennan).

41. Lamont v. Postmaster General, 381 U.S. 301, 308 (1965), Justice Brennan concurring.

42. FCC v. League of Women Voters, 468 U.S. 364, 380 (1984).

43. *Columbia Broadcasting System,* 412 U.S. at 172, Justice Brennan dissenting.

44. Dun & Bradstreet v. Greenmoss Builders, 472 U.S. 749, 783 (1984), Justice Brennan dissenting, citing Associated Press v. U.S., 326 U.S. 1, 20 (1945).

45. *Id.* at 307, quoting *Times v. Sullivan,* 376 U.S. at 270.

46. Pell v. Procunier, 417 U.S. 817, 837–41, Justice Douglas dissenting (joined by Justice Brennan).

47. Houchins v. KQED, 438 U.S. 1, 31–32 (1978), Justice Stevens dissenting (joined by Justice Brennan).

48. *Id.* at 32, Justice Stevens dissenting (joined by Justice Brennan).

49. Mills v. Alabama, 384 U.S. 214, 219 (1966).

50. FCC v. League of Women Voters, 468 U.S. 364, 381 (1984).

51. *Mills,* 384 U.S. at 219.

52. Branzburg v. Hayes, 408 U.S. 665 (1972), Justice Stewart dissenting (joined by Justice Brennan).

53. Saxbe v. Washington Post Co., 417 U.S. 843 at 864 (1974), Justice Douglas dissenting (joined by Justice Brennan). *See also,* Herbert v. Lando, 441 U.S. 153, 181–94 (1979), Justice Brennan dissenting.

54. Brennan, Address, 30 Rutgers L. Rev. 173, 177 (1979).

55. *Dun & Bradstreet,* 472 U.S. at 784, Justice Brennan dissenting.

56. Herbert v. Lando, 441 U.S. at 183–84, note 1, Justice Brennan dissenting in part.

57. *Dun & Bradstreet,* 472 U.S. 749 (1984).

58. FCC v. Pacifica Foundation, 438 U.S. 726, 772 (1978), Justice Brennan dissenting.

59. *Times v. Sullivan,* 376 U.S. at 275, 282.

60. *Supra* note 35.

61. *See, for example,* Greer v. Spock, 424 U.S. 828 (1976); and Brown v. Glines, 444 U.S. 348 (1980).

62. *See, for example,* New York Times Co. v. U.S., 403 U.S. 713, 726–27 (1971), Justice Brennan concurring.

63. *Nebraska Press Association,* 427 U.S. at 588- 89, Justice Brennan concurring.

64. Bantam Books v. Sullivan, 372 U.S. 58, 70 (1963).

65. *Id. See also,* Freedman v. Maryland, 380 U.S. 51, 58 (1965).

66. U.S. v. O'Brien, 391 U.S. 367 (1968).

67. Speiser v. Randall, 357 U.S. 513, 520 (1958).

68. *See, for example,* Interstate Circuit, Inc. v. Dallas, 390 U.S. 676 (1968); Broadrick v. Oklahoma, 413 U.S. 601, 621 (1973), Justice Brennan dissenting.

69. Metromedia, Inc. v. San Diego, 453 U.S. 490, 523 (1981), Justice Brennan concurring in the judgment.

70. Uphaus v. Wyman, 306 U.S. 72, 82 (1959), Justice Brennan dissenting.

71. Texas v. Johnson, 109 S.Ct. 2533, 2542–43 (1989).

72. Lehman v. Shaker Heights, 418 U.S. 298, 311 (1974), Justice Brennan dissenting.

73. Bethel School District No. 403 v. Fraser, 478 U.S. 675, 687 (1986), Justice Brennan concurring.

74. *See, for example,* Ginzburg v. U.S., 383 U.S. 463 (1966); and New York v. Ferber, 485 U.S. 747 (1982).

75. New York Times Co. v. U.S., 403 U.S. 713 (1971).

76. Central Hudson Gas & Electric Corp. v. Public Service Commission of New York, 447 U.S. 557 (1980); Virginia State Board of Pharmacy v. Virginia Citizens Consumer Council, 425 U.S. 748 (1976).

77. 412 U.S. 94 (1973).

78. Red Lion Broadcasting Co. v. FCC, 395 U.S. 267 (1969); FCC v. Pacifica Foundation, 438 U.S. 726 (1978).

79. 412 U.S. at 196, Justice Brennan dissenting.

80. *Id.* at 200, Justice Brennan dissenting.

81. Carey v. Population Services International, 431 U.S. 678 (1977).

82. Kingsley International Picture Corp. v. Regents of New York University, 360 U.S. 684 (1959).

83. Cohen v. California, 403 U.S. 15 (1971); Texas v. Johnson, 109 S.Ct. 2533 (1989).

84. Carroll v. Princess Anne, 393 U.S. 175 (1968); Brandenburg v. Ohio, 395 U.S. 444 (1969).

85. Haig v. Agee, 453 U.S. 280, 319 (1981), Justice Brennan dissenting.

86. Broadrick v. Oklahoma, 413 U.S. 601, 621 (1973), Justice Brennan dissenting.

87. Pell v. Procunier, 417 U.S. 817, 837 (1974), Justice Douglas dissenting (joined by Justice Brennan); Saxbe v. Washington Post Co., 417 U.S. 843, 850 (1974), Justice Powell dissenting (joined by Justice Brennan); Houchins v. KQED, 438 U.S. 1, 19 (1978), Justice Stevens dissenting (joined by Justice Brennan).

88. Hazelwood School District v. Kuhlmeier, 484 U.S. 260, 280 (1988), Justice Brennan dissenting.

89. Lamont v. Postmaster General, 381 U.S. 301, 309 (1965), Justice Brennan concurring.

90. *Lehman,* 418 U.S. at 319, Justice Brennan dissenting.

91. U.S. Postal Service v. Council of Greenburgh Civic Association, 453 U.S. 114, 134 (1981), Justice Brennan concurring.

92. Heffron v. International Society for Krishna Consciousness, Inc., 452 U.S. 640, 656, 658, note 2 (1981), Justice Brennan concurring and dissenting.

93. Greer v. Spock, 424 U.S. 828, 869 (1976), Justice Brennan dissenting.

94. Brown v. Glines, 444 U.S. 348, 372 (1980), Justice Brennan dissenting.

95. *Greer,* 424 U.S. at 852, Justice Brennan dissenting.

96. Metromedia, Inc. v. San Diego, 453 U.S. 490, 524 (1981), Justice Brennan concurring in judgment.

97. City Council of Los Angeles v. Taxpayers for Vincent, 466 U.S. 789, 818 (1984), Justice Brennan dissenting.

98. *Id.* at 819, Justice Brennan dissenting.

99. *Lehman,* 418 U.S. at 310–11.

100. *Roth,* 354 U.S. 467 (1957).

101. 413 U.S. 15 (1973).

102. Manual Enterprises v. Day, 379 U.S. 478, 497 (1962), opinion of Justice Brennan.

103. Paris Adult Theatre I v. Slaton, 413 U.S. 49, 103 (1973), Justice Brennan dissenting.

104. Rankin v. McPherson, 483 U.S. 378 (1987).

105. FCC v. Pacifica Foundation, 483 U.S. 726, 775–76 (1978), Justice Brennan dissenting.

106. Houston v. Hill, 482 U.S. 451, 462–63 (1987).

107. 413 U.S. 323 (1974).

108. *See, for example,* Branzburg v. Hayes, 408 U.S. 665 (1972).

109. *Greer,* 424 U.S. at 852, Justice Brennan dissenting.

Appendix:
The Free-Expression Opinions
of Justice William J. Brennan, Jr.

Anderson v. Liberty Lobby, Inc., 477 U.S. 242 (1986). Dissent. Libel.

Bachellar v. Maryland, 397 U.S. 564 (1970). Opinion of the Court. Picketing.

Bantam Books v. Sullivan, 372 U.S. 58 (1963). Opinion of the Court. Prior restraint.

Barenblatt v. U.S., 360 U.S. 109 (1959). Dissent. Refusal to answer.

Barr v. Matteo, 360 U.S. 564 (1959). Dissent. Libel.

Beckley Newspapers Corp. v. Hanks, 389 U.S. 81 (1967). *Per curiam* opinion.* Libel.

Bethel School District No. 403 v. Fraser, 478 U.S. 675 (1986). Concurrence in judgment. Reprisals for speech.

Blount v. Rizzi, 400 U.S. 410 (1971). Opinion of the Court. Obscenity.

Board of Education, Island Trees v. Pico, 457 U.S. 853 (1982). Plurality, joined by Justices Marshall, Stevens, and Blackmun (in part). Prior restraint.

Board of Regents v. Roth, 408 U.S. 564 (1972). Dissent, joined by Justice Douglas. Reprisals for speech.

Boos v. Barry, 108 S.Ct. 1157 (1988). Concurrence, joined by Justice Marshall. Picketing.

Brandenburg v. Ohio, 395 U.S. 444 (1969). *Per curiam* opinion. Prior restraint.

Broadrick v. Oklahoma, 413 U.S. 601 (1973). Dissent, joined by Justices Marshall and Stewart. Prior restraint.

Brockett v. Spokane Arcades, Inc., 472 U.S. 491 (1985). Dissent, joined by Justice Marshall. Obscenity.

Brown v. Glines, 444 U.S. 348 (1980). Dissent. Picketing.

Brown v. Hartlage, 456 U.S. 45 (1982). Opinion of the Court. Prior restraint.

* *Per curiam* opinions are listed only if authorship by Justice Brennan has been verified by documents in his papers.

Brown v. Louisiana, 383 U.S. 131 (1966). Concurrence in judgment. Expressive conduct.

Brown v. Oklahoma, 408 U.S. 914 (1972). *Per curiam* opinion. Abusive language.

California v. LaRue, 409 U.S. 109 (1972). Dissent. Obscenity.

Cameron v. Johnson, 390 U.S. 611 (1968). Opinion of the Court. Picketing.

Capital Cities Cable v. Crisp, 467 U.S. 691 (1984). Opinion for a unanimous Court. Prior restraint.

Carey v. Brown, 447 U.S. 455 (1980). Opinion of the Court. Picketing.

Carey v. Population Services International, 431 U.S. 678 (1977). Opinion of the Court. Prior restraint.

Central Hudson Gas & Electric Corp. v. Public Service Commission of New York, 447 U.S. 557 (1980). Concurrence in judgment. Corporate speech.

City Council of Los Angeles v. Taxpayers for Vincent, 466 U.S. 789 (1984). Dissent. Restrictions on communications.

Columbia Broadcasting System, Inc. v. Democratic National Committee, 412 U.S. 94 (1973). Dissent, joined by Justice Marshall. Broadcasting.

Communist Party of Indiana v. Whitcomb, 414 U.S. 441 (1974). Opinion of the Court. Oaths.

Connick v. Myers, 461 U.S. 138 (1983). Dissent, joined by Marshall, Blackmun, and Stevens. Reprisals for speech.

Curtis Publishing Co. v. Butts, 388 U.S. 130 (1967). Concurrence and dissent. Libel.

Dombrowski v. Pfister, 380 U.S. 479 (1965). Opinion of the Court. Prior restraint.

Dun & Bradstreet, Inc. v. Greenmoss, 472 U.S. 749 (1984). Dissent, joined by Justices Marshall, White, and Stevens. Libel.

Dyson v. Stein, 401 U.S. 200 (1971). Pornography. Concurrence in result, joined by Justice Marshall.

Eaton v. Tulsa, 415 U.S. 697 (1974). *Per curiam* opinion. Abusive language.

Estes v. Texas, 381 U.S. 532 (1965). Free press/fair trial. Dissent.

FCC v. League of Women Voters of California, 468 U.S. 364 (1984). Opinion of the Court. Broadcasting.

FCC v. Pacifica Foundation, 438 U.S. 726 (1978). Dissent, joined by Justice Marshall. Broadcasting.

FEC v. Massachusetts Citizens for Life, 479 U.S. 238 (1986). Opinion of the Court. Restriction on speech.

First Unitarian Church v. Los Angeles, 357 U.S. 545 (1958). Opinion of the Court. Oaths.

Freedman v. Maryland, 380 U.S. 51 (1965). Opinion of the Court. Prior restraint.

Frisby v. Schultz, 487 U.S. 474 (1988). Dissent, joined by Justice Marshall. Picketing.

FW/PBS, Inc. v. Dallas, 110 S.Ct. 596 (1990). Concurrence in judgment, joined by Justices Marshall and Blackmun. Obscenity.

Garrison v. Louisiana, 379 U.S. 64 (1964). Opinion of the Court. Libel.

Gertz v. Welch, Inc., 418 U.S. 323 (1974). Dissent. Libel.

Ginsberg v. New York, 390 U.S. 629 (1968). Opinion of the Court. Obscenity.

Ginzburg v. U.S., 383 U.S. 463 (1966). Opinion of the Court. Obscenity.

Globe Newspaper Co. v. Superior Court, 457 U.S. 596 (1982). Opinion of the Court. Free press/fair trial.

Gooding v. Wilson, 405 U.S. 518 (1972). Opinion of the Court. Abusive language.

Greer v. Spock, 424 U.S. 828 (1976). Dissent. Picketing.

Haig v. Agee, 453 U.S. 280 (1981). Dissent, joined by Justice Marshall. Prior restraint.

Hamling v. U.S., 418 U.S. 87 (1974). Dissent, joined by Justices Marshall and Stewart. Obscenity.

Harper & Row Publishers v. Nation, 471 U.S. 539 (1985). Dissent, joined by Justices Marshall and White. Copyright.

Hazelwood School District v. Kuhlmeier, 484 U.S. 260 (1988). Dissent, joined by Justices Blackmun and Marshall. Prior restraint.

Heffron v. International Society for Krishna Consciousness, 452 U.S. 640 (1981). Concurrence and dissent. Picketing.

Heller v. New York, 413 U.S. 483 (1973). Dissent, joined by Justices Marshall and Stewart. Obscenity.

Herbert v. Lando, 441 U.S. 153 (1979). Dissent in part. Libel.

Houston v. Hill, 482 U.S. 451 (1987). Opinion of the Court. Expressive conduct.

Hutchinson v. Proxmire, 443 U.S. 111 (1979). Dissent. Libel.

Hynes v. Mayor of Oradell, 425 U.S. 610 (1976). Concurrence in part. Picketing.

In re Anastaplo, 366 U.S. 82 (1961). Dissent, joined by Chief Justice Warren. Refusal to answer.

In re Sawyer, 360 U.S. 622 (1959). Plurality opinion, joined by Justices Warren, Black, and Douglas. Reprisals for speech.

Jacobellis v. Ohio, 378 U.S. 184 (1964). Plurality opinion, joined by Justice Goldberg. Obscenity.

Jenkins v. Georgia, 418 U.S. 153 (1974). Concurrence in the result. Obscenity.

Kaplan v. California, 413 U.S. 115 (1973). Dissent, joined by Justices Marshall and Stewart. Obscenity.

Keeton v. Hustler Magazine, Inc., 465 U.S. 770 (1984). Concurrence in judgment. Libel.

Kelly v. Ohio, 416 U.S. 923 (1974). *Per curiam* opinion. Abusive language.

Keyishian v. Board of Regents of University of State of New York, 385 U.S. 589 (1967). Opinion of the Court. Oaths.

Kingsley Books v. Brown, 354 U.S. 436 (1957). Dissent. Obscenity.

Konigsberg v. State Bar of California, 366 U.S. 36 (1961). Dissent, joined by Chief Justice Warren. Refusal to answer.

Laird v. Tatum, 408 U.S. 1 (1972). Dissent, joined by Justices Stewart and Marshall. Data collection systems.

Lakewood v. Plain Dealer Publishing Co., 486 U.S. 750 (1988). Opinion of the Court. Prior restraint (newsrack licensing).

Lamont v. Postmaster General, 381 U.S. 301 (1965). Concurrence, joined by Justices Goldberg and Harlan. Oaths.

Lee Art Theatre, Inc. v. Virginia, 392 U.S. 636 (1968). *Per curiam* opinion. Obscenity.

Lehman v. Shaker Heights, 418 U.S. 298 (1974). Dissent, joined by Justices Marshall, Powell, and Stewart. Prior restraint.

Lewis v. New Orleans, 415 U.S. 130 (1974). Opinion of the Court. Abusive Language.

Lucas v. Arkansas, 416 U.S. 919 (1974). *Per curiam* opinion. Abusive language.

McDonald v. Smith, 472 U.S. 479 (1985). Concurrence, joined by Justices Marshall and Blackmun. Libel.

McKinney v. Alabama, 424 U.S. 669 (1976). Concurrence in judgment. Obscenity.

Madison v. Wisconsin Employment Relations Commission, 429 U.S. 167 (1976). Concurrence in judgment, joined by Justice Marshall. Prior restraint.

Manual Enterprises v. Day, 370 U.S. 478 (1962). Concurrence in result, joined by Justices Douglas and Warren. Obscenity.

Marcus v. Search Warrants, 367 U.S. 717 (1961). Opinion of the Court. Obscenity.

Marks v. U.S., 430 U.S. 188 (1977). Concurrence and dissent, joined by Justices Marshall and Stewart. Obscenity.

Massachusetts v. Oakes, 109 S.Ct. 2633 (1989). Dissent, joined by Justices Marshall and Stevens. Pornography.

Memoirs v. Massachusetts, 383 U.S. 413 (1966). Plurality opinion, joined by Justices Fortas and Warren. Obscenity.

Metromedia v. San Diego, 453 U.S. 490 (1981). Concurrence in judgment. Restrictions on communications.

Miami Herald v. Tornillo, 418 U.S. 241 (1974). Concurrence, joined by Justice Rehnquist. Restrictions on the press.

Milkovich v. Lorain Journal, 110 S.Ct. 2695 (1990). Dissent, joined by Justice Marshall. Libel.

Miller v. California, 413 U.S. 15 (1973). Dissent, joined by Justices Marshall and Stewart. Obscenity.

Mishkin v. New York, 383 U.S. 502 (1966). Opinion of the Court. Obscenity.

Nebraska Press Association v. Stuart, 427 U.S. 539 (1976). Concurrence in judgment, joined by Justices Marshall and Stewart. Prior restraint.

New York v. Ferber, 458 U.S. 747 (1983). Concurrence in judgment. Obscenity.

New York Liquor Authority v. Dennis Bellancer, 452 U.S. 714 (1981). Dissent. Obscenity.

New York Times Co. v. Sullivan, 376 U.S. 254 (1964). Opinion of the Court. Libel.

New York Times Co. v. U.S., 403 U.S. 713 (1971). *Per curiam* opinion and concurring opinion. Prior restraint.

Osborne v. Ohio, 110 S.Ct 1691 (1990). Dissent, joined by Justices Marshall and Stevens. Pornography.

Paris Adult Theatre I v. Slaton, 413 U.S. 49 (1973). Dissent, joined by Justices Marshall and Stewart. Obscenity.

Perry v. Sindermann, 408 U.S. 593 (1972). Opinion concurring and dissenting, joined by Justice Douglas. Reprisals for speech.

Philadelphia Newspapers v. Hepps, 475 U.S. 767 (1986). Concurrence, joined by Justice Blackmun. Libel.

Pinkus v. U.S., 436 U.S. 293 (1978). Separate opinion. Obscenity.

Pope v. Illinois, 481 U.S. 497 (1987). Dissent. Obscenity.

Posadas de Puerto Rico Associates v. Tourism Co. of Puerto Rico, 478 U.S. 328 (1986). Dissent. Advertising.

Quantity of Copies of Books v. Kansas, 378 U.S. 205 (1964). Plurality opinion, joined by Justices Goldbert, Warren, and White. Obscenity.

Regan v. Time, Inc., 468 U.S. 641 (1984). Opinion concurring and dissenting. Restrictions on the press.

Renton v. Playtime Theatres, 475 U.S. 41 (1986). Dissent, joined by Justice Marshall. Obscenity.

Richmond Newspapers v. Virginia, 448 U.S. 555 (1980). Concurrence in judgment, joined by Justice Marshall. Free press/fair trial.

Riley v. National Federation of the Blind of North Carolina, 108 S.Ct. 2667 (1988). Opinion of the Court. Prior restraint.

Roaden v. Kentucky, 413 U.S. 496 (1973). Concurrence in judgment, joined by Justices Marshall and Stewart. Obscenity.

Rosen v. California, 416 U.S. 924 (1974). *Per curiam* opinion. Abusive language.

Rosenblatt v. Baer, 383 U.S. 75 (1966). Opinion of the Court. Libel.

Rosenbloom v. Metromedia, Inc., 403 U.S. 29 (1971). Plurality opinion joined by Justices Burger and Blackmun. Libel.

Rosenfeld v. New Jersey, 408 U.S. 901 (1972). *Per curiam* opinion. Abusive language.

Roth v. U.S., 354 U.S. 476 (1957). Opinion of the Court. Obscenity.

Rowan v. U.S. Post Office Department, 397 U.S. 728 (1970). Concurrence, joined by Justice Douglas. Prior restraint.

Sable Communications v. FCC, 109 S.Ct. 2829 (1989). Opinion concurring and dissenting, joined by Justices Marshall and Stevens. Pornography.

San Francisco Arts and Athletics v. U.S. Olympic Committee, 483 U.S. 522 (1987). Dissent, joined by Justice Marshall. Restrictions on communications.

Seattle Times Co. v. Rhinehart, 467 U.S. 20 (1984). Concurrence, joined by Justice Marshall. Prior restraint.

Secretary of the Navy v. Huff, 444 U.S. 453 (1980). Dissent. Petitions.

Shapero v. Kentucky Bar Association, 486 U.S. 466 (1988). Opinion of the Court. Commercial speech.

Smith v. California, 361 U.S. 147 (1959). Opinion of the Court. Obscenity.

Smith v. U.S., 431 U.S. 291 (1977). Dissent, joined by Justices Marshall and Stewart. Obscenity.

Speiser v. Randall, 357 U.S. 513 (1958). Opinion of the Court. Oaths.

Teitel Film Corp. v. Cusack, 390 U.S. 139 (1968). *Per curiam* opinion. Prior restraint.

Texas v. Johnson, 109 S.Ct. 2533 (1989). Opinion of the Court. Expressive conduct.

Texas Monthly v. Bullock, 490 U.S. 1 (1989). Plurality opinion. Restrictions on the press.

Time, Inc. v. Firestone, 424 U.S. 448 (1976). Dissent. Libel.

Time, Inc. v. Hill, 385 U.S. 374 (1967). Opinion of the Court. Invasion of privacy.

Uphaus v. Wyman, 360 U.S. 72 (1959). Dissent, joined by Justices Warren, Black, and Douglas. Restrictions on communications.

U.S. v. Eichman, 110 S.Ct. 2404 (1990). Opinion of the court. Expressive conduct.

U.S. v. Orito, 413 U.S. 139 (1973). Dissent, joined by Justices Marshall and Stewart. Obscenity.

U.S. v. 12 200-Ft. Reels of Film, 413 U.S. 123 (1973). Dissent, joined by Justices Marshall and Stewart. Obscenity.

U.S. Postal Service v. Council of Greenburgh Civic Associates, 453 U.S. 114 (1981). Concurrence in judgment. Restrictions on communications.

Virginia v. American Booksellers Association, 484 U.S. 383 (1988). Opinion of the Court. Obscenity.

Walker v. Birmingham, 388 U.S. 307 (1967). Dissent. Picketing.

Wilkinson v. U.S., 365 U.S. 399 (1961). Dissent, joined by Justice Douglas. Refusal to answer.

Wolston v. Reader's Digest Association, 443 U.S. 157 (1979). Dissent. Libel.

Younger v. Harris, 401 U.S. 37 (1971). Concurrence in result, joined by Justices White and Marshall. Reprisals for speech.

Zauderer v. Office of Disciplinary Counsel of Supreme Court of Ohio, 471 U.S. 626 (1985). Opinion concurring and dissenting. Advertising.

Zwickler v. Koota, 389 U.S. 241 (1967). Opinion of the Court. Picketing.

Bibliography

ARTICLES

"American Defamation Law: From Sullivan, Through Greenmoss, and Beyond."
48 *Ohio State Law Journal* 513 (1987).

Anastaplo, George. "Justice Brennan, Due Process and the Freedom of Speech: A Celebration of Speiser v. Randall." 20 *John Marshall Law Review* 7 (Fall 1986).

Anderson, David. "The Origins of the Press Clause." 30 *U.C.L.A. Law Review* 455 (1983).

Bolick, Clint. "Abandoning Government by Constitution: The Legacy of William Brennan and Thurgood Marshall." 2 *Cognitions on Law and Government* 1 (No. 2, September 1984).

Brennan, William J. "Address." 30 *Rutgers Law Review* 173 (1979).

———. "Address." 6 *University of Hawaii Law Review* 1 (1984).

———. "The Bill of Rights and the States: The Revival of State Constitutions as Guardians of Individual Rights." 61 *New York University Law Review* 535 (October 1988).

———. "Constitution of the United States: Contemporary Ratification." 19 *University of California-Davis Law Review* 2 (Fall 1985).

———. "Constitutional Adjudication." 50 *Notre Dame Lawyer* 559 (No. 6, August 1965).

———. "Guardians of Our Liberties: State Courts No Less than Federal." 15 *Judges Journal* 82 (No. 4, Fall 1976).

———. "How Goes the Supreme Court?" 36 *Mercer Law Review* 781 (Spring 1985).

———. "In Defense of Dissents." 37 *Hastings Law Journal* 427 (January 1986).

———. "My Encounters with the Constitution." 26 *Judges Journal* 6 (Summer 1987).

———. "The Supreme Court and the Meiklejohn Interpretation of the First Amendment." 79 *Harvard Law Review* 1 (1965).

"The Brennan Doctrine." *National Review,* November 15, 1985, p. 20.

"Brennan for the Court." *Washington Post,* October 1, 1956, p. 24.

Collins, E. L., K. Beitler, and J. Osborne. "Miller and Its Progeny: Foreseeing Problems with the Foreseeability Issue." *Communications Yearbook 3,* 1979, p. 295.

"Defamation Law—Libel and Slander—Private Individual Required to Show Actual Malice to Prove Defamation Where Topic of Speech is of Genuine Public Concern." 19 *Rutgers Law Journal* 157 (Fall 1987).

Denvir, John. "Justice Brennan, Justice Rehnquist, and Free Speech." 80 *Northwestern University Law Review* 285 (April 1985).

Goldberg, Arthur. "Mr. Justice Brennan and the First Amendment." 4 *Rutgers-Camden Law Journal* 8 (1972).

Goldman, Ari L. "Brennan Attacks Changes in Court; Sees a 'Disturbing' Decrease in Concern for Rights of Individual Citizens." *New York Times,* May 5, 1985, p. 18.

Gora, Joel M. "William J. Brennan, Jr.: A Justice for All Seasons." 72 *American Bar Association Journal* 18 (June 15, 1986).

Green, Lewis C. "The New York Times Rule: Judicial Overkill." 12 *Villanova Law Review* 730 (1967).

Grunes, Rodney. "Obscenity Law and the Justices: Reversing Policy on the Supreme Court." 9 *Seton Hall Law Review* 403 (No. 3).

Hager, Philip. "Brennan, Near 90, Holds Firm to Court Pact." *Los Angeles Times,* April 19, 1988, p. 1.

Heck, Edward V. "Justice Brennan and Freedom of Expression Doctrine in the Burger Court." 24 *San Diego Law Review* 1153 (September/October 1987).

———. "Justice Brennan and the Heyday of Warren Court Liberalism." 20 *Santa Clara Law Review* 841 (1980).

Hentoff, Nat. "The Constitutionalist." *The New Yorker,* March 12, 1990, p. 45.

———. "Justice Brennan, the 'Radical Egalitarian.' " *Washington Post,* September 27, 1988, A27.

Huston, Luther A. "Senate Confirms 2 for High Court." *New York Times,* March 20, 1957, p. 23.

"An Inside Look at Supreme Court and Its Cases." *New York Times,* June 14, 1988, p. 10.

"The Jaunty Judge." *New York Times,* September 30, 1956, p. 76.

Kamon, Al. "Brennan: Tipping the Scales of Justice at 80—Supreme Court's Most Enduring Figure Celebrates His Longevity in Liberal Fashion." *Washington Post,* April 25, 1986, p. A17.

Kilpatrick, James J. "It Was Bill Brennan's Term." *Washington Post,* July 23, 1987, p. A21.

Langvardt, Arlen W. "Media Defendants, Public Concerns, and Public Plaintiffs: Toward Fashioning Order from Confusion in Defamation Law." 49 *University of Pittsburgh Law Review* 91 (Fall 1987).

Leeds, Jeffrey T. "A Life on the Court." *New York Times Magazine,* October 5, 1986, p. 24.

Meiklejohn, Alexander. "The First Amendment Is an Absolute." 1961 *Supreme Court Review* 245.

"The Mind of William Brennan." *National Review,* December 5, 1986, p. 20.

Mott, Kenneth and Christine Kellett. "Obscenity, Community Standards and the Burger Court: From Deterrence to Disarray." 13 *Suffolk University Law Review* 14.

"The New York Times Rule—The Awakening Giant of First Amendment Protection." 62 *Kentucky Law Journal* 824 (1974).

Pear, Robert. "Aide in Justice Department Holds That Brennan Has 'Radical' Views." *New York Times,* September 13, 1988, p. 1.

Phelps, Glenn A. "Brennan v. Rehnquist: The Politics of Constitutional Jurisprudence." 22 *Conzaga Law Review* 307.

"President Names Jersey Democrat to Supreme Court." *New York Times,* September 30, 1956, p. 1.

Press, Aric. "Intent of the Framers: A Row Over How Courts Should Read the Constitution." *Newsweek,* October 28, 1985, p. 97.

Press, Aric, and Ann McDaniel. "Renaissance of an Octogenarian Liberal." *Newsweek,* July 6, 1987, p. 18.

Ray, Laura K. "Justice Brennan and the Jurisprudence of Dissent." 61 *Temple Law Review* 307 (Summer 1988).

"Reason, Passion, and Justice Brennan: A Symposium." 10 *Cardozo Law Review,* nos. 1–2 (October/November 1988).

"The Revival of Involuntary Limited-Purpose Public Figures." 1987 *Brigham Young University Law Review* 313.

Robins, William M. "Bibliography of Associate Justice William J. Brennan, Jr." 12 *Seton Hall Law Review* 430 (1982).

Rostow, Eugene V. "Unsolicited Counsel to Justice Brennan." 3 *Yale Law Report* 11 (Fall 1957).

"Senate Unit Votes 11 to 0 for High Court." *New York Times,* March 29, 1957, p. 38.

Shannon, William V. "Common Sense of Mr. Justice Brennan." 11 *Catholic University of America Law Review* 3 (January 1962).

Sherrill, Michael S. "The Power of William Brennan; How a Canny Liberal Became the Court's Master Strategist." *Time,* July 22, 1985, p. 92.

Stewart, David O. "Justice Brennan at 80." 73 *American Bar Association Journal* 61 (January 1987).

"The Supreme Court." *New York Times,* October 1, 1956, p. 26.

Taylor, Stuart, Jr. "Brennan: 30 Years and the Thrill is Not Gone." *New York Times,* April 18, 1988, p. 19.

———. "The Court and the Constitution." *New Republic,* January 6 & 13, 1986, p. 45.

———. "The Court and the Constitution: Meese v. Brennan." *Current,* September 1986, p. 30.

———. "Court Curbing Libel Suits Against Press." *New York Times,* June 28, 1988, p. 8.

———. "Meese v. Brennan: Who's Right About the Constitution?" *New Republic,* January 6, 1986, p. 17.

"Tribute to Justice Brennan." 15 *Harvard Civil Rights—Civil Liberties Law Review* 279 (1980).

Weiner, Max. "Brennan, Son of Irish Immigrants, Is Known as Moderate Liberal." *Washington Post,* September 30, 1956.

Wermeil, Stephen. "Four Justices Seem Prepared to Assent to a Full-Time Role Focusing on Dissent." *Wall Street Journal,* October 18, 1989, p. 8.

Winfield, Richard N. "The Sound of Libel in the Key of B(ose) Goes Flat." *Communications Lawyer,* Fall 1984, 1.

Yoder, Edwin. "A Court Divided?" *U.S. News & World Report,* January 13, 1986, p. 14.

BOOKS

Bayley, Edwin R. *Joe McCarthy and the Press.* New York: Pantheon, 1981.

Friedman, Leon, and Fred L. Israel. *The Justices of the Supreme Court.* New York: Chelsea House, 1969.

Friedman, Stephen J. *William J. Brennan, Jr.—An Affair With Freedom.* New York: Antheum, 1967.

Haiman, Franklyn S. *Speech and Law in a Free Society.* Chicago: University of Chicago Press, 1981.

Hopkins, W. Wat. *Actual Malice Twenty-Five Years after Times v. Sullivan.* New York: Praeger, 1989.

Levy, Leonard. *Emergence of a Free Press.* New York: Oxford University Press, 1985.

Malmuth, Neil M., and Edward Donnerstein. *Pornography and Sexual Aggression.* Orlando, Fla.: Academic Press, 1984.

Milton, John. *Complete Poems and Major Prose.* Ed. Merritt Y. Hughes. New York: Odyssey, 1957.

Mott, Frank L. *Jefferson and the Press.* Baton Rouge: Louisiana State University Press, 1943.

Prosser, William. *The Law of Torts,* 3d ed. Mineola, N.Y.: Foundation Press, 1971.

Schwartz, Bernard. *Super Chief: Earl Warren and His Supreme Court—A Judicial Biography.* New York: New York University Press, 1983.

Siebert, Fredrick S. *Freedom of the Press in England, 1476–1776.* Urbana, Il.: University of Illinois Press, 1965.

Siebert, Fredrick S., Theodore Peterson, and Wilbur Schramm. *Four Theories of the Press.* Urbana, Il.: University of Illinois Press, 1956.

Talese, Gay *Thy Neighbor's Wife.* New York: Doubleday, 1980.

White, Edward. *Earl Warren: A Public Life.* New York: Oxford University Press, 1982.

MISCELLANEOUS

Blackstone, William. *Commentaries.* South Hackensack, N.J.: Rothman Reprints, 1969.

Brennan, William J. Interview with Nina Totenberg, All Things Considered, National Public Radio, 1987.

———. Papers. Manuscript Division, Library of Congress, Washington, D.C.

Del Guidice, R. "Justice Brennan and Freedom of Expression." Unpublished Ph.D. dissertation, University of Massachusetts, 1975.

MacNeil–Lehrer Newshour, PBS, July 23, 1990.

Nomination of William Joseph Brennan, Jr., to the United States Supreme Court, Hearings Before the Senate Judiciary Committee, 85th Congress, 1st Session, February 26 & 27, 1957.

Case Index

Subject Index

ABOUT THE AUTHOR

W. WAT HOPKINS is Assistant Professor of Communication Studies at Virginia Polytechnic Institute and State University. He is the author of *Actual Malice: Twenty-Five Years After Times v. Sullivan* (Praeger, 1989) and a number of articles on communications law topics.